The Great Remobilization

The Great Remobilization

Strategies and Designs for a Smarter Global Future

Olaf Groth, Mark Esposito, and Terence Tse

The MIT Press
Cambridge, Massachusetts
London, England

The MIT Press would like to thank the anonymous peer reviewers who provided comments on drafts of this book. The generous work of academic experts is essential for establishing the authority and quality of our publications. We acknowledge with gratitude the contributions of these otherwise uncredited readers.

This book was set in ITC Stone Serif Std and ITC Stone Sans Std by New Best-set Typesetters Ltd. Printed and bound in the United States of America.

Library of Congress Cataloging-in-Publication Data

Names: Groth, Olaf, author. | Esposito, Mark, author. | Tse, Terence C. M., author.
Title: The great remobilization : strategies and designs for a smarter global future / Olaf Groth, Mark Esposito, and Terence Tse.
Description: Cambridge, Massachusetts : The MIT Press, [2023] | Includes bibliographical references and index.
Identifiers: LCCN 2022061666 (print) | LCCN 2022061667 (ebook) | ISBN 9780262047937 (hardcover) | ISBN 9780262373807 (epub) | ISBN 9780262373791 (pdf)
Subjects: LCSH: Globalization. | Climatic changes. | Technological innovations—Economic aspects. | Sustainable development.
Classification: LCC JZ1318 .G797 2023 (print) | LCC JZ1318 (ebook) | DDC 303.48/30286—dc23/eng/20230503
LC record available at https://lccn.loc.gov/2022061666
LC ebook record available at https://lccn.loc.gov/2022061667

10 9 8 7 6 5 4 3 2 1

To the young leaders in every corner of the world, including our own kids, with whom we hope to build the operating system of the cognitive economy that will run a more resilient, dignified, and equitable world.

Contents

Introduction

The sheer speed stunned medical experts. In March 2020, global health-care systems struggled to cope with a novel coronavirus that no one could fully explain, other than realizing it moved fast and took lives. Demand for personal protective equipment overwhelmed suppliers, and other manu-facturers quickly retrofitted their lines to produce masks and other gear. Medical treatments sometimes worked, sometimes didn't. The constant stress of permanent uncertainty still caused plenty of problems nearly three years later, but nothing could compare to the mayhem at the outset of the pandemic. Within the first three months, investigational treatments for COVID-19 accounted for 60 percent of all the drug shortages reported in the United States.[1]

Fortunately, 83 percent of those shortages could be addressed with alter-native treatments that could fill the gap, and the pharmaceutical industry had shifted into high gear. The scientists at BioNTech, Moderna, and Pfizer went to work, developing mRNA treatments that showed promise against this new virus. They stood on the shoulders of brilliant researchers who had developed the genetic science and sequencing tools that laid the foun-dation for this emerging class of drugs—a network of research with roots in US Defense agencies, labs in Europe, and factories across Asia. Mean-while, Sinovac and Johnson & Johnson developed other effective vaccines based on variants of the virus itself. Within nine months of the outbreak and those early drug shortages—on December 2, 2020—the mRNA vaccine developed by Pfizer and BioNTech received emergency-use approval from UK regulators. The previous record for fastest vaccine development, for mumps in the 1960s, took *four years* from viral sampling to approval.

Despite plenty of progress in the decades since mumps, the fact that multiple pharmaceutical companies would develop and distribute a vaccine within a year "was far from a foregone conclusion," said Tom Frieden, former head of the Centers for Disease Control (CDC) and the founder and CEO of Resolve to Save Lives, a global health organization working to combat heart disease and improve pandemic preparedness. He recalled his days at the CDC, when he and his colleagues advised the makers of the 2011 movie *Contagion*. The film starred Matt Damon as a father who loses his wife and son to a virulent disease, while he remains in quarantine and immune to its effects. The story follows the panicked public reactions and the mad dash by the CDC to learn about the virus and develop a remedy. The movie didn't get great reviews, but Frieden said it at least portrayed the CDC pretty accurately. The one point he remembered as outlandish at the time was the idea that the movie scientists found a cure within four months. "Now that we have mRNA platforms," he told us in 2021, "it's no longer as implausible as it was when the movie came out."

The speedy development of COVID vaccines might portend great things for tackling new pandemics and existing maladies, but Frieden expressed something less than confidence about the efficacy of our overall response. He lamented the inequitable distribution of vaccines around the world, as well as global preparedness to react to subsequent health crises that will inevitably arise. And he bristled at Moderna's refusal to allow third parties to manufacture and distribute the company's vaccine, arguing that it limited distribution and broke a trust by accepting public resources but hoarding profit in the name of intellectual property protections. "I hope there will be collaboration" with China, he said. "Even at the height of the Cold War, the US and the then Soviet Union collaborated on the global eradication of smallpox. And we really are connected by the air we breathe, the food we eat, the water we drink, the microbes we're exposed to."

On the Razor's Edge

All three of us had an epiphany during the worst of the pandemic. When Olaf cut short a family road trip because so many people were going unmasked at a time when infection numbers were swelling, he realized that the biological, ecological, social, financial, digital, and cognitive forces of the world had intertwined in ways that would alter our reality from the inside out, turning a virus into a geotechnological, geopolitical, and geoeconomic issue all at once. It was when Mark realized, after police in Spain briefly detained his father during a walk to the pharmacy, that our democratic governments no longer preserved the crucial balance of individual freedom and collective responsibility with agility. And it was when Terence realized, after seeing panicked investors abandon a host of return-generating financial assets in the singular pursuit of the US dollar, that the global economic and financial systems were facing unprecedented uncertainties and radical change.

Yet each of us also realized the pandemic only revealed these insights—these forces, logics, phenomena, and impacts were already deeply ingrained elements of our faltering global systems. COVID might not be the bug that takes the whole system down, but it showed just how tenuous a time we live in. Even if competing geopolitical actors decide to collaborate on future global health responses, the pandemic laid bare the fragility of the systems that dictate much of our economies, societies, businesses, and communities. We don't yet know how dramatically our lives will change, but the lockdowns and disruptions have underscored one immutable fact—our existing global systems cannot accommodate the future toward which we're hurtling. Combined with the fraying of our Globalization 1.0 systems over the past twenty years, the pandemic has revealed a reality where any number of isolated disruptions could ripple through and rupture our supply chains, foment digitally fueled social unrest, or even spark armed conflict between global powers. Our societal, political, and economic systems have exhausted themselves, and we need to understand why before we can repair them.

Consider, for example, the underlying pattern that ran through the global financial crises of recent decades. We have gone through these wild swings so often that we have come to accept them as an inherent part of a global economy. Yet, as University of California, Berkeley, economics professor Christina Romer notes, business cycles are not an immutable law of the economic universe. Even a cursory understanding of the linkages between one crisis and the next reveals how we injected the pathologies, particularly the addition of cheap capital, that spur economic volatility. Yet with each new financial crisis, the pressure on the system ratcheted higher—to the point where the global economy no longer has places where all that capital can easily flow and continue our endless game of trillion-dollar whack-a-mole. Because we tend to think of recessions on a one-off, country-by-country, or regional basis, we have failed to remedy the broader contagion. So, by late 2021, we had already begun to see eerily familiar signs of asset inflation in real estate and equities in China. The system now has so much pressure, with a global network of economies so intertwined, that there are few places for the money to go next. The existing interventions that regulate the flash-flows of capital might not prove effective enough to avoid a deep and lasting economic downturn.

Atop this overpressurized global financial system, we have piled compounding layers of complexity and increased the divergence across and between our governance, cultures, and societies. It's not too far a leap to imagine that this combination of financial pressure cooker and growing tribalization and politicization could spark more serious breakdowns—critical inequality, food insecurity, waves of migration, armed conflicts, cyber-cataclysms, and the attendant health and welfare costs that attend each of these. In a system less free, open, and cooperative than in previous decades, pressure can no longer self-balance in the ways we once assumed. What if, in the next big crisis, the system truly fractures for an extended period of time? What happens when the monetary and financial tools that fixed the past recessions fail or, even worse, accelerate the fall? The global system of finance involves far more than mere flows of capital when a person with an unknown virus can travel to another country and shut down an entire marketplace. The margins are gone, so our responses will require a far more holistic and multidisciplinary set of remedies. We need to develop systems that facilitate more wisdom and antifragility.

Fortunately, current and former policymakers are starting to see this, thanks largely to the confluence of the pandemic, Russia's war in Ukraine, and the growing chain of climate disasters. In August 2022, when central bankers from around the world gathered for their annual meeting in Jackson Hole, Wyoming, a consensus emerged that the current methods for managing through business cycles (i.e., the ups and downs in national, regional, and global economies) are woefully insufficient for managing today's current economic and societal crises. "We have the energy crisis, we have the food crisis, we have the supply chain crisis and we have the war, all of which has profound implications for the economic performance of the world, for the nature in which the world is interconnected and most importantly, for the relative prices of many, many things," Jacob Frenkel, the former governor of the Bank of Israel and chair of the Group of 30, an independent consortium of ex-policymakers, told the *Financial Times*.[2] But given the limited ability of central bankers and their government peers to address large supply chain shocks, environmental crises, migration- and identity-related upheaval, and sustained wars, the need for unorthodox new approaches and innovative design thinking in both academic and policy fields has become all too apparent.

The business cycle as we knew it, manufactured by narrow fiscal and monetary policies, made sense when the global financial system had fewer interlocking nonfinancial systems. The inability to accommodate far more complex overlaps of global systems risks sinking incomes, growing inequality, and rising social tensions that could lead "not only to a fractured society but a fractured world," Ian Goldin, professor of globalization and development at Oxford University's Martin School of Business and former vice president at the World Bank, told the *New York Times*.[3] "We haven't faced anything like this since the 1970s, and it's not ending soon." Yet this fragmentation has been underway for the past twenty years as systems grew faster, more intertwined, and increasingly complex, all adding greater levels of entropy and pressure. Our integrated governance didn't evolve, confined instead in vertical stovepipes as volatility spread horizontally. While the horizontal shifts and ruptures have been coming for a while, we now can see the dramatic cracks that spread across the economic, ecological, sociological, biological, and infrastructural dimensions of our societies.

Our financial crises are no longer centered on paper money sloshing around the world. Those problems we could address with expansionary or restrictive monetary policy and the signals that central bankers' decisions would send into the financial markets. Relief was just a matter of turning the spigot one way or the other. No such spigot exists to regulate the economic and social effects of greenhouse gas emissions, viruses, violent protests, DNA alterations, and energy supply chains.

The stakes are higher than ever before. "I think we're living through the biggest development disaster in history, with more people being pushed more quickly into dire poverty than has ever happened before," Goldin said. "It's a particularly perilous time for the world economy." The facts bear this out. In the past decade alone, we lived through the deepest global recession in memory (−5.4 percent GDP per capita) and the broadest since the 1870s (more than 90 percent of all countries in recession). According to the United Nations, the pandemic led to the first increases in extreme poverty and food insecurity in 20 years, with as many as 811 million people facing hunger worldwide in 2020.[4] We need to move our world from the great volatility of the early 2020s to a Great Remobilization for the late 2020s and beyond.

And to do that, we need to design nothing less audacious than a smarter world.

Design Activism

We cannot look back at this crucial moment in our history and regret a missed opportunity to collectively redesign and reshape the global systems that govern our societies, economies, businesses, and lives. Efforts to merely update Globalization 1.0 will not fix the inequality, environmental damage, fragmentation, and volatility we struggle to address today. In past attempts to reconceive globalization, we lacked the will to tear down so we can build anew, choosing instead to tinker with fundamentally flawed structures and leaving the dysfunction to perpetuate itself. We cannot wait any longer to deconstruct our decaying global systems and build for the better.

Doing so will require a rethink of these existing systems, but also an accommodation for the pressures that new technologies put on everything from global trade to individual decision-making. The rise of identity-shaping technologies will continue to redefine our social fabric, our political convictions, and our consumption needs. The confluence of the new digital realms—AI, data science, compute power, Web3, and the Internet of Everything—with revolutionary new biological techniques such as genomics, synthetic biosciences, neuroscience, and brain-computer interfaces will pry open the gates to the inner sanctum, connecting our genetic code and the hundred billion neurons in our brains to the 340 trillion trillion trillion IP addresses available under new internet standards.[5] We are on the threshold of having our identities reshaped not just by the outside-in digital technologies but by inside-out biological technologies, as well.

It's not hard to envision how solutions created within our existing systems will bend toward extractive and inequitable ends, as large companies and governments seek to hoard the avalanche of data produced by this confluence of digital and biological spheres. As of 2021, the technology research firm IDC estimated that the global datasphere would expand to more than 180 zettabytes by 2025—and that doesn't even include the commercialization of quantum computing, neuromorphic computing, and other domains expected to achieve some degree of maturity by 2030. The entities that place themselves at the intersection of inside-out and outside-in data flows will hold massive economic and political power for years to come. An educated, creative technorati class in charge of cognitive platforms might lead us into data colonialism, as we've seen with Google, Meta, and the other digital barons already. Or we can actively work to design new governance structures and other tools that redefine the incentives and foster more equitable, resilient, and sustainable growth.

We have no time to lose. Our existing systems are crumbling, and these new forces are rearranging the pieces in novel ways. The actors best placed to establish the new frameworks and models for the future might not have all stakeholders' interests at heart. So, all of us who claim the moniker of "leader," whether accomplished or in the making, need to help rebuild this rickety machine—to exercise our voices and our agency so we can help design the future in which we want to live. We need to become design activists who are willing to tear down what's not working, gather the pieces that do work, and rebuild global systems for a better world. It's not a choice but a critical responsibility.

FLP-IT Forward

We cannot expect a Great Remobilization to materialize if we don't have a vision and strategic framework to guide us. We need a model that would help government, business, and community leaders flip their gaze forward, away from what we lost and toward what we might gain from this unprecedented moment. After two decades of reflection on a globalization model that has finally exhausted itself, the three of us crafted a new framework—based on the scenario-planning ideas established by the likes of Herman Kahn, Pierre Wack, Peter Schwartz, and others—that leaders at all levels of society can use to reconstruct the atrophied systems that inhibit our progress on a local, industrial, or global scale.

The FLP-IT model we created charts a path of analysis and decision-making for these unprecedented times: Assess the dominant tectonic *forces* that will have high impact and high uncertainty on your domain. Identify the new dominant *logic* that emerges as these forces collide. Recognize the *phenomena* that arise from that logic. Diagnose the *impact* of all those on your stakeholder system and value chain. And then *triage* your resources and programs to address those impacts and how they might evolve across plausible future scenarios. Together, these steps form a holistic strategy that helps people address the challenges they face anytime they're confronted with shocks that create the types of tectonic shifts we are currently experiencing.

The framework is neither prescriptive nor exhaustive, but it guides users through a flexible and evolving series of reflections that start at a macro level—an assessment of major shocks and how they change the nature of our businesses and lives—and then drill down to the specific actions we can take to recognize opportunities and drive toward them. Ultimately, the FLP-IT framework empowers an informed triage process that leaders can use to prioritize, communicate, and lead others through the actions they and their organizations or constituencies can take to chart an innovative path forward in times of economic and societal convulsion.

We wrote this book to present a vision for how we might design smarter systems for a new kind of global order—a Great Remobilization toward a better future. It's not intended to be a step-by-step "how to" guide to the FLP-IT process. However, we organized the book in a way that guides you through the framework, beginning with a deeper explanation of it in chapter 1. In part II, we cascade through what we call the five tectonic forces—China, COVID and pandemic response, climate change, cybersecurity, and cognitive technologies. Like the earth's tectonic plates, the collisions between these forces are radically reshaping the macro (global, geopolitical), meso (industrial, organizational), and micro (individual, personal) facets of our world. Needless to say, there are many other forces at work at this pivotal moment, but we believe these will fundamentally shape others, such as identity and inequality. In part III, we then dive into the logics and phenomena that are coalescing in our lives and economies, including considerations of trust and identity; the paradox of a world that's connected but not convergent; and the tension between centralization and decentralization expressed in the ongoing "flight forward" toward the crypto ecosystem, Web3, and the metaverse. Finally, in part IV, we discuss impacts and triage, sketching out plausible scenarios that hint at the possible impacts that await us in the decade-plus ahead, and then closing with triage and redesign proposals that address the most crucial tectonic shifts disrupting the world today.

Throughout, we discuss ways in which different types of leaders might apply FLP-IT to redesign systems both small and large: Central bankers and governments might use it to better understand the intertwined complexity of today's global systems and rebalance monetary, fiscal, and other regulatory policy across previously narrow and stovepiped mandates. The CEO of a startup might employ it to generate more insight into an ongoing series of market disruptions, and then decide where to cut spending and where to reinvest. Parents might use it to identify the shifts in educational practices, curricula, and the college admissions process to rebalance their savings for their children's futures. The core focus of this book, however, is on how FLP-IT can facilitate the global systems redesigns necessary to address the most disruptive forces buffeting the world today. Until we solve these structural global issues, we cannot create a healthier and more equitable world.

Tectonic Shifts

Ultimately, we will need to enhance trust in our systems and designs if we hope to dictate beneficial outcomes in the decades ahead. Because our current global "operating system" created the turbulence and uncertainty we presently face, a mere update cannot restore the widespread faith and acceptance necessary for true progress. We need a re-architected OS for the globe, one that solves the problems that undermine the core of the current version and steers us away from the cliff toward which we're headed. We cannot predict every exact detail of the new operating system—much will have to be designed on the fly, as new circumstances emerge—but we can use FLP-IT to lay out some cornerstones, design imperatives, and recommendations upon which we can act immediately. Most of them emerge from five extraordinary forces—tectonic shifts—that have radically altered our lives: COVID and pandemic management, the cognitive economy, cybersecurity, climate change, and China. We call these the *Five Cs*, and we discuss them often throughout the book, because we believe these extraordinary forces will dictate the future no matter how we react to our current crises.

At the core, though, we believe these tectonic shifts will require that we steer toward a new cognitive economy, in which scientific and technological leadership becomes fully integrated with geopolitical and cultural power. While the gravity of different global and regional powers will rise and fall over time, the US and China will lead the cognitive economy in the decades to come. Europe's "third way" and, to a lesser extent, India will take a backseat to those powers, although they both will remain important stalwarts of digital identity and agency, as well as massive markets with the ability to safeguard the flows of people, capital, data, energy, and other resources necessary to secure national or regional prosperity.

Although the relative power asymmetry of the US and Chinese economies vis-à-vis others will continue unabated in the coming decades, economic size will no longer be the only critical factor in international power. The absolute value of GDP mattered when post–World War economics surged, but a more diverse set of capabilities and attributes will rise in this new cognitive economy. Countries now can multiply their economic and geopolitical reach through innovation and cognitive technologies, opening new roads for smaller economies to take leadership roles in global systems. Those digital and cognitive tech-force multipliers helped California ascend from the fifth- to the fourth-largest economy in the world, overtaking Germany as we wrote this, with a still-massive economic, regulatory, and cultural influence on the globe.[6]

However, a country like India doesn't need to reach the pinnacle of innovation across multiple sectors and industries to expand its power. It might instead use the nation's considerable technological resources and expertise in specific cognitive-tech domains to extend its reach beyond its limiting factors, much like China has done. Of course, India's industrial structure is very different from China's, and reaching similar levels of success and influence will take decades. But today, India and other emerging economies across the Global South can accelerate their journeys by augmenting existing physical and digital resources in their manufacturing and service industries with cognitive resources they can access and adapt from globally distributed networks. India, for example, could leverage its rare-earth minerals for battery and computer technologies—already an indispensable resource for the cognitive economy and one that advanced, postindustrial economies desperately need. This way, the country could use incoming capital and expertise to enhance productive capacity in health, transportation, education, and governance areas where it has both the greatest need and some proven success stories. Given its sheer mass, this injection of resources could generate economies of scale and exportable services and solutions.

In fact, India's existing digital assets and institutes of technology have already put it in a good position to take advantage of the opportunities the cognitive economy provides. And its slow turn toward a more liberal foreign direct investment regime is making it even more attractive, allowing it to play a role in and learn from the supply chains of the world's best-in-class manufacturers and service providers—in particular, through its $10 billion incentive package to entice leading global chipmakers to build new semiconductor factories there. These potential investors, such as the International Semiconductor Consortium and GlobalFoundries, will need to find and train generations of qualified, high-skilled workers in India, and they will demand assurances of a transparent rule of law in a notoriously complex and fractious cultural and legal environment. But if India can reliably provide those fundamental requirements, it will become an increasingly formidable partner and voice among the global powers.

However, India also has significant barriers to overcome before it ascends to a place among the world's "great powers" and superpowers—the countries with the influence to both propose and push through designs for a new model of globalization. India has yet to reach the "middle-income trap," the development threshold at which a nation's prosperity makes continued rapid economic growth harder to maintain and a dominant voice on the global economic and military stage harder to attain. The country's population growth is also a dual-edged sword: while it will soon surpass China as the most populous country in the world, more and more people will amplify the country's existing structural problems. That will only increase the fragility of its domestic systems and the systems it shares with its neighbors.

The increasing weight of India and the Global South, combined with their scant influence on how to fix fragmented global systems, makes it all the more urgent that we nurture a new set of more inclusive mechanisms to foster trust and open up the global pinch points that inhibit flows of talent, IP, data, capital, genetic code, and other natural and cognitive resources. These new governance mechanisms will need to be as multifaceted as the flows they're designed to encourage. And they will need to be smart enough to manage the complexity of how all these flows intertwine and interplay with one another. Hence, we need to bolt a cognitive layer to the infrastructural, ecological, biological, and psychological layers of our systems. Otherwise, we end up with a detachment of the nervous system from the muscles and bones of the global economy and society.

To strike the right balance in this hybrid model, we need to overhaul existing governance institutions and create new ones, even if this means that we significantly rework and transform the Bretton Woods institutional model that defined globalization as it exists today. Rather than monolithic organizations, the cognitive economy will require interlocking and highly flexible networks of virtual and physical actors who bring a diverse expertise and an innate ability to toggle between the analog world and the anonymity of the emerging decentralized paradigms. Institutions will need to develop the reconnaissance tools to keep up or even stay ahead of these evolving constructs, but they will also need to walk a fine line between surveillance to achieve situational awareness and surveillance for political or economic control. The smartest institutions will furnish safe spaces for hybrid experimentation, glean promising ideas, promulgate successful designs as best practices, and then integrate them into national political systems, ideally retaining interoperability across borders.

In a world that fuses the ecological and physical with the digital and cognitive, split-second actions can take down entire systems and wreck human and political health, so governance systems must embody automated vigilance and response mechanisms that can quickly report and counterbalance disruptions. Within one institution or country, particularly those with more centralized power, integrating these types of automated surveillance and response systems is difficult enough. Yet, in an interconnected cognitive economy, these mechanisms will need to establish hyper-agile communications to quickly facilitate broad equilibria between countries and regions, while also remaining flexible enough to work both on the global scale and on the local level where flash changes among financial systems, population groups, food and energy stockpiles, DNA, and data movements are the most fungible and least physically visible. Framing the rules for this cognitive economy will require entirely new bodies of law, such as a law of the metaverse and a global accord for cybersecurity for all on-offensive, nonmilitary assets.

All of these efforts will be terribly complicated, but already we have seen early indications that these types of institutions and regulations are possible. Indeed, our belief that we can build these governance systems is rooted in a transformation that's already underway, though largely unexpressed. But we cannot stress enough that these ideas will only come together if we actively design incentives using modern cognitive tools. Otherwise, we will continue to deploy systems that may or may not prove beneficial, but either way will rely on a static and deliberate architecture that cannot adapt to the speed of global transformation and will eventually break down. We cannot turn back the clock. We cannot wish away flash crashes, flash mobs, or flash pandemics. Instead, we can and must shape new cognitive tools that process and react to the sparks that fly out of the intersection of the physical, biological, and digital. In a cognitive economy, this is how we augment our humanity and improve the welfare of our societies.

To get this balance right, we have to understand the tangible health, security, and economic benefits these systems can provide. At a minimum, we will have to dissolve concentrations of power that lead to monopolies on decisions and resources, whether political or economic. Again, this will require the kind of diffused, multi-stakeholder mode of governance that reconsiders everything from political parties and election processes to the regulation of financial systems and corporate entities. We have already seen the emergence of tools that can, once mature, power this transformation, such as new digital forms of organization and governance facilitated by blockchain technologies. As we wrote this in 2022, the hype around crypto, Web3, and metaverse ecosystems felt similar to the run-up to the dot-com bubble. Yet, as happened when that bubble burst, the current frenzy of activity in these new fields is creating pillars that will outlast the chaos and support new digital governance structures that distribute control away from oligopolies.

We should note that we do not advocate a complete rejection of our current Westphalian system of nation-states. In fact, states are one critical form of "clubs" in a new system. However, like economic and industrial supply chains that face ever greater pressurization, these systems need to become smarter to enable more agile reconfiguration and renegotiation. We can already see the efficiency challenges that economies and industries need to master—from basic physical blockages like freighters stuck in canals to the massive disruption to production and distribution wreaked by an unseen and unexpected virus. The smarter designs we employ to move us forward will inevitably require enhanced security and transparency to foster much-needed trust and accountability in these radically new systems—especially in critical food, energy, and health care supply chains. We cannot build trust and create value unless we center cyber-security as a primary geopolitical, geotechnological, and geo-economic concern. Now that our systems have gone virtual and, thanks to AI and related technologies, increasingly cognitive, we need a collective and transparent reconnaissance and surveillance scheme for all the nodes in our digital communities, much like we do with neighborhood watches in our physical communities.

Similar empowerment of and feedback from stakeholders on the ground can help recalibrate trust and action on the greatest existential crisis our planet faces: climate change. There is no substitute for the "ground truths" experienced by people living real lives, and top-level technocrats need more access to them. We need to amplify the voice of community, city, and small-business stakeholders—the backbones of our economies—in the generation of "best foot forward" solutions at global emissions negotiations, and then integrate new ideas with pricing incentives for carbon and other critical natural resources. This doesn't happen at Davos and it doesn't happen enough in COP-style climate accord negotiations.

Of course, an array of national carbon-mitigation efforts, such as those enacted with the 2022 Inflation Reduction Act in the US and embodied within China's 14th Five-Year Plan, have already made progress toward much-needed emission reductions. While this patchwork of regulations does not go far enough, it has channeled billions of dollars into green energy technologies, incentives for consumers, and, importantly, the promise of new jobs and greenfields for investment. But because this money could create new bubbles, we need real-time reconnaissance for where and how it is spent and whether it results in real productivity and innovation rather than more hot air. Any future system needs to marry these economic incentives, jobs, and investment opportunities to the new "ground truth" stakeholders in cities, small towns, and rural villages in countries worldwide.

That wide diversity of ideas can generate the innovation to drive a much-needed pivot on carbon. In recent years framed as a toxic substance because of its polluting effects in the form of CO_2 and other greenhouse gases, carbon remains the core building block of life. New technologies to effectively and efficiently capture, sequester, and reinject carbon into natural and industrial processes can underscore its role as a valuable resource to curate and tightly control, regulate, and trade. Such technologies have not yet reached the levels of maturity needed for commercial scalability, but a global moonshot-type program that drives carbon-technology innovation, such as a scaled-up and multilateral version of the $100 million Carbon

Removal XPrize, could get us there, especially if the US, Europe, China, and India collaborate.

It will not work without China. In fact, the "Chinaization" of the global economy, as problematic as it can be, makes the Middle Kingdom an indispensable partner for any global systems redesign. China is big, increasingly innovative, and influential. It remains a system competitor to Western democracy, but that does not make it exceptional or an inherent enemy of Western nations. Productive vigilance and the art of the well-designed deal with safeguards can establish an ongoing modus operandi that allows us to address climate and carbon, COVID-like pandemics, crypto governance and even cybersecurity. We may never agree on domestic political governance, and human rights will remain a crucial point of contention. But mutually agreeable solutions on the treatment of Taiwan can be found, as can rules of the road for engagement in both allied and competitive countries—if we get the right governing principles in place. Fragility of countries, the breeding of extremism, mass starvation, or unmanaged mass migration will help no one in Beijing, Washington, Brussels, or Delhi. So why not embrace an overlapping Venn diagram of global governance?

Building a foundation for partnership on contentious issues can begin with collaboration on shared concerns, particularly scientific and technological development for climate, carbon, clean energy, health, education, migration, infrastructure, and transportation. We might even turn Taiwan into one of a number of incubation spaces for joint solutions. Either way, given the sheer size of its economy and its influence on the geopolitical stage, no global system redesign will work without China eventually at the table.

A Global Rite of Passage

We often identify rites of passage with the vital ceremonies of our lives—graduation from high school, our wedding day, or a baptism or bat mitzvah. Yet, when Arnold van Gennep first defined the concept in his 1909 book *The Rites of Passage*, he saw the rites as just one part of a far more significant transition, often framing them in terms of social regeneration. Van Gennep took interest not just in the rituals themselves but in the ways that people moved throughout time and space. Through youth, marriage, and death, what came before and after that singular event mattered as much as the transition itself. He postulated three phases of that journey: (1) the separation, when people leave the point at which they were; (2) the liminal, a transitional period of uncertainty and change; and (3) the reincorporation, when they move into a new stable existence.

During the coronavirus pandemic, amid all the masks, Zoom calls, and lockdowns, cultural anthropologist Genevieve Bell began to reflect on van Gennep and what his century-old theories might tell us about this moment of upheaval. Bell spent years immersed in Silicon Valley innovation and culture, and now directs the School of Cybernetics at the Australian National University, and she remains a vice president and a senior fellow in the advanced research and development labs at Intel Corp. The idea of our pandemic environment as a rite of passage sent her back to her freshman-year anthropology classes: "I had this moment of thinking, 'Actually, I know exactly what this is,'" she said. "This is liminality."

This liminality was shaping our work and lives in profound ways, Bell explained when we spoke in 2021. Our sense of space, mobility, and the balance of physical and virtual warped into social distancing, home offices, and Zoom calls. Perceptions of time became distorted, slowing down, speeding up, and flattening out. Intermediation blurred as we grappled with new definitions of boundaries and interactions, including relationships broken and reconnected across global supply chains. Even our personal and societal conceptions twisted into new, uncomfortable, and constraining questions about identity and sense of self. "In any rite of passage, whether it was through time or space, secular or profane, there's the first bit where you have to be basically separated from the world you've been in before," Bell explained. "You have a moment in the middle where you are liminal, where all bets are off and you are not fully of the place you've been or of the place you're going, and it's a time when things feel unfamiliar, disorienting, destabilized, where rules about dressing and eating and behaving are all a bit weird."

The rites and rituals of reincorporation, then, will need to satisfy two crucial requirements, Bell said. First, they will need to stabilize most of the elements that the pandemic destabilized. This doesn't mean a return to the state from which we departed; who you are when you emerge from a liminal phase is inevitably different from who you were when you entered. Second, reincorporation will require a clear moment of transition, where we establish ourselves and our identities as something new in the world that we've entered. So the rite of passage means we arrive at a new place through a moment of clear transition.

For most of human history, the powered elites governed these rites of passage. The church and/or state established the requirements and the rituals for marriage. The university governed the transition from student, through graduation, and then out into the working world, equally dominated by ever larger, more globally connected enterprises or government organizations. No doubt governments, businesses, churches, and other kinds of powerful social institutions will govern much of our reincorporation into the Cognitive Era. But even top-down governance extends from the bottom-up legitimacy provided by the people—whether at the US ballot box or through a collective belief in China's one-party government. And increasingly, technologies based on decentralization of control could challenge the legitimacy of models based on full central authority. So, in this connected and cognitive world, a much broader array of leaders, activists, and thinkers can influence structural, social, commercial, and regulatory reforms. We can all take part in a conscious reconsideration of values and aspirations, and we can all help shape the global reincorporation of the Cognitive Era.

This is our book's ultimate ambition: to help individuals and leaders actively design those new regimes in ways that promote agency, equity, sustainability, resilience, and the greater welfare of the earth and its people. While neither Bell nor we expect governments, businesses, and other seats of power to give equal voice to all the people, we remain optimistic about the role of smaller societal institutions and social movements. We believe that our leaders and our neighbors, when called on to undertake this crucial twenty-first-century rite of passage, will become the design activist leaders (DALs) needed to shape a new narrative (see figure 0.1).

Redesigning a Smarter World

We have little interest in incremental fixes, so what follows, particularly in the closing chapter, focuses on step-change redesigns of our global frameworks. For many, including the three of us, the pandemic triggered a realization that our prior efforts at reform and reconstruction were futile. We cannot keep trying to fix the unfixable. Our current road maps don't lay out any clear paths to a full and healthy recovery (a term that, in itself,

The Design Activist Leader (DAL)

1) **Zeroth-Principles Discovery:** Assumes that nothing is impossible. Not limited by the constraints of the current systems.

2) **Systems Foresight:** Thinks in terms of societal systems instead of industries, territorial boundaries, or narrow market segments. Foresees the second- and third-order effects of decisions and actions.

3) **Cross-Tribal Empathy:** Empathizes with the perspectives and needs of others, appeals to tribes, builds bridges, and incorporates diverse elements into solution models.

4) **Hybrid Venture Building:** Achieves scale across geospatial nodes in physical and virtual worlds, Web2 and Web3 platforms, and global institutions and tribes.

Figure 0.1

suggests a return to some previous state). Those twentieth-century frameworks will not work in our new age. We need to build a new operating system. We need a new approach to governance that respects and accommodates the deep interconnections between the global (macro), industrial and commercial (meso), and local community or individual (micro) stakeholders in global systems.

It sounds like the proverbial "bridge too far," but humans have always been natural toolmakers and builders. Our evolutionary path led to increasingly sophisticated ideas and technologies that lifted billions of people out of poverty, significantly reduced child mortality rates, cured wickedly complex diseases, created the internet, and forged relatively stable if divergent political constructs in three of the world's largest economic systems—North America, the European Union, and China, which collectively contain almost a third of the global population. We design quantum computers, Mars rockets, and fusion energy. We decode the genome and have started to decode the brain itself—perhaps the most complex system of all. Surely we have the capacity to create a new architecture for a more thoughtful, smart, and balanced fabric for our global systems.

Because we believe that humanity remains an incurably optimistic species and will continue to yearn for discovery and new frontiers, we have taken pains to avoid pessimism in this book wherever possible. Yes, we have deep concerns about the trajectory of many global trends, but we can remain upbeat largely because of our conversations with the people trying to redesign global systems, develop new technologies, and craft better ways of life.

We remain fascinated by the possibilities that could emerge from the confluence of advanced technology fields, such artificial intelligence, biosciences, social sciences, quantum computing, and brain-computer interfaces. Despite the constant threat of cyberattacks and theft of our digital and biological identities, we envision, create, and implement new designs for cybersecurity and data autonomy that return power and value to the individual company or person while also effectively governing for the collective. Carbon emissions continue to threaten our environment, yet incredible innovations will arise to reduce our reliance on fossil fuels and capture and repurpose the carbon that we do emit into the atmosphere—if we choose to implement them effectively.

All these changes are playing out against an increasingly complex environment of global dynamics. While growing more connected, the world has become increasingly tribalized in ways that ostracize rather than coalesce. Whether through the rise of competing political and governance regimes or social media's algorithmic narrowing of our perspectives, tribalism has become the primary obstacle to our passage to reincorporation. We cannot design new global systems that foster worldwide prosperity and well-being without a dedicated effort to discover and develop spaces for collaboration that bridge our fractured islands of thought and belief. But this cuts against the grain of global trends. Reconstituting the bonds frayed by growing fragmentation and tribalism will take more than an analysis of the Five Cs, a little money, and a global summit. It will take a collective recommitment, led by leaders who embrace design activism, to build upon shared values and collaborate on efforts to promote equity and sustainability. It will require systems redesigns that integrate new measures of prosperity.

Most importantly, though, this Great Remobilization will require a foundation of trust, the most valuable global currency on both individual and institutional levels. Today, though, trust is compromised, carelessly wasted, and relegated to ring-fenced groups. We can't apply the same rules from the old analog world—the firm handshake and a look in the eye—in this cognitive economy. Now, trust is also built upon concepts such as digitally intermediated identity, authenticity, and veracity. As business school professors at international institutions, we see subtle versions of these identity conflicts, as multiple cultures blend to create a community with uncertain norms in a high-pressure environment. Where does the trust that underlies freedom, prosperity, and security take root in that environment?

Understanding the loss of trust and flipping that into ideas for rebuilding it will require a tremendous group of experts, leaders, and students who come at global challenges from different perspectives. In bringing this multitude of voices together, for instance, we relied heavily on the help of our friend and colleague Dan Zehr, whose craft as a journalist includes an uncanny ability to make complexity accessible without becoming reductionist.

Ultimately, the systems we collectively design to enhance trust will dictate the outcomes we experience in the decades ahead. We need leaders to become design activists to build a smarter world. And every leader needs a strategic framework to help them identify, analyze, and plan for the tectonic shifts that transform our world—the COVID-like biological threats, the cognitive economy, cybersecurity, climate change, and China. We need to identify the forces at play, understand the logic and phenomena those forces create, recognize the emerging impacts they have on our domains, and then triage our resources accordingly. We need to FLP-IT forward.

I

1 From Crises to Opportunities: FLP-IT Forward

The earth and its environment are always wobbling, constantly buffeted by a deluge of forces from the cosmic to the microscopic. Yet somehow it finds a tenuous balance that preserves the vitality and health of the planet and the humanity that calls it home. We feel the same in our own lives, in our ongoing struggle to understand and adapt to the small and large forces that cause our lives, businesses, nations, and economies to teeter. In recent years, we experienced an unprecedented combination of extraordinary forces—the pandemic, the rise of cognitive computing, digital threats to our well-being, extreme natural disasters due to climate change, and a major reshuffling of our global political and economic order. Most of us lived at the mercy of the unknowns, fretting about our individual and collective health, income, inequality, and fragmentation. Already simmering tensions rose to a boil—science and politics at odds with each other, blurring distinctions between despots and democracies, the US and the West in turmoil while China and Asia flexed new geopolitical muscle. The haves, such as the large technology platforms and their founders and executives, amassed trillions of dollars. The have-nots struggled to make it through with their health and some sort of financial stability intact.

Despite the anxiety roiling the world at the start of this decade, the three of us remained hopeful. We began to see opportunities to remobilize our resources and our energy. And since we each have one foot in academia and one in entrepreneurial or advisory practice, we naturally gravitated toward strategy frameworks to get some sort of clarity. The problem was that none of the existing models seemed to fit the extraordinary circumstances we faced. Some offered visionary ways to motivate and drive confidence in times of volatility but didn't provide the pragmatic decision-making tools needed when the foundations below us start to shift. Others

The FLP-IT Framework

FLP-IT is a holistic strategy that helps leaders address the future challenges caused by major disruptions, shocks, and tectonic shifts in their domains.

Forces	**L**ogic	**P**henomena	**I**mpact	**T**riage
Assess the dominant forces that have high impact and high uncertainty.	Identify the new dominant logic and principles that arise as these forces collide.	Recognize the phenomena that emerge from the logic and forces at play.	Diagnose the impacts these FLPs will have on your stakeholders and value chain.	Identify and seize opportunities to triage resources across plausible future scenarios.

Figure 1.1

excelled at those practical and analytical steps but didn't embody the imaginative leadership skills that could drive both empathetic and empirical decisions in times when people struggled with fundamental questions about their physical and mental well-being. So, we started piecing together our own model, one that could inform the "hard" and "soft" leadership decisions that are vital anytime but were especially critical during times of massive disruption.

What resulted was FLP-IT, a strategic leadership framework designed to help government, business, and community leaders make sound and forward-looking decisions in even the most chaotic of times (see figure 1.1). The first three concepts in the acronym—forces, logic, and phenomena— help formulate an understanding that leaders can apply to almost any form of shock. We begin with a recognition of the critical *forces* that generate the major changes in our reality or our perception of it. Because these forces typically originate from the source or nature of the shock itself, we want to identify the ones that change our fundamental perception of normalcy and our access to everyday activities, such as work, education, and health care. As we developed the FLP-IT framework, we first identified a series of critical forces that we expected to play out—some related directly to COVID, including the mortality rate of the virus and the time it would take to produce and scale an effective vaccine. Other forces were those that would play out in the economy and industry, such as changes in entrepreneurial startup rates and the financial impact of lockdowns. And we considered geopolitical and global factors, including the degree of coordination between countries and societal institutions, as well as the size and effect of government stimulus packages.

The collisions of all those forces created liminal circumstances that would inevitably spawn their own *logic*, which we thought of as the new rules that guide our daily operations (i.e., our "operating logic"). We can see trends begin to emerge—the new normal(s) that rise out of the turbulence. These often include new behaviors that will persist after the disruption, such as the wholesale shift to remote work and the reimagined work-life integration that results from combining office and living space. But more fundamentally for the pandemic, our analysis included the guiding logic of the economic and political recovery we might experience. At the time, we envisioned possible recoveries that could be V-shaped, with a straightforward downturn and recovery to new levels of growth around the world; U-shaped, featuring a slower global recovery led by technocracies, particularly in Asia; bathtub-shaped, where we drop into a low level of economic activity and remain stuck there as oligarchies rise in power; and W-shaped, with a perpetual toggling of restraint and relief as waves of the virus keep coming and subsiding. We've seen features of each, but these types of outcomes are not mutually exclusive, and elements of each could have a consequential effect on what happens after the shock.

The *P* in "FLP-IT," then, is the particular *phenomena* that crystallize into discrete, repetitive occurrences, eventually nudging us to create new architectures and business models for societies and organizations alike. These typically cascade down from the macro (global) level to the meso (community or industry) level as businesses craft new behaviors in response to the new normal(s). They then trickle down again to the micro level (an individual person, community, or organization) as we adjust to the new demands placed on our lives. Indeed, we've ordered much of this book to follow that cascade from the macro, to the meso, and to the micro levels of consideration.

Because we tend to initially notice these phenomena at an organizational (meso) or individual (micro) level, we sometimes recognize them before we fully understand the logic that is driving them. Consider the phenomena we analyzed early in the pandemic. We thought a great deal about workplace phenomena, including hybridized online/offline work, and the balance of the local and the virtual. We foresaw a rise in decentralized supply chains, automation, and digital platform power, all of which occurred (and have continued) to varying degrees. They might very well change over time, but getting an initial sense for the emergent patterns is necessary before you assess the potential impacts on your life, business, or society.

The "FLP" side of the acronym illuminates the practical effects of the shock and the thrusts that recast the landscape, providing a powerful lens to view the macro, meso, and micro levels in a way that accommodates the complexity and chaos of interconnected systems of systems. The "IT" part of the acronym drills down into the impacts the FLP will have on the value chain of industries or ecosystems of societal stakeholders, as well as the triage of resources and investments needed to capitalize on the opportunities created.

When considering *impact*, we scrutinize how organizations operated at the time of the shock and how we can expect them to perform under the new, radically different conditions. In the most tactical sense, the impact step analyzes the effects that the forces, logic, and phenomena will have on our lives, businesses, economies, or countries. Put another way, if the forces, logic, and phenomena are *what* comes at you, impact imagines *how* they will affect you, your community, and your stakeholders. For example, consider how one global fashion house had to assess the impact of the pandemic across the different parts and players in its value chain. Restrictions on physical labor hurt supplies of raw materials. Delays in shipping bottlenecked inventories. Brick-and-mortar store sales, responsible for 86 percent of the prior year's revenue, inevitably fell. On the plus side, the company had already accelerated investments in research and development to streamline their design process and, since 80 percent of its manufacturing occurred in Europe, it could avoid the worst of factory disruptions.

Finally, the eliminations and changes we make in response to current or expected impacts comprise the final *triage* phase of the framework. Here, we prioritize the set of choices we need to make about what we will do (or not do anymore) and where we will invest (or stop investing). Strategy is as much about closing old valves as it is about opening new ones. For this, we have to create a "culture of rethink" and of innovation that allows us to pivot to various forms of pilots, experiments, and trials to gather a clearer understanding of the transformed marketplace or life arena and our place in it. Done well, triage should guide organizations toward ways to test and validate ideas within the market or target-space itself, allowing for more and faster feedback about the new expectations and dynamics that customers, partners, and constituents exhibit. And since we are doing so with foresight, we can practice our positioning amid potential future disruptions ahead of time.

The examples of triage are endless because they're specific to individual processes in individual organizations. But for the sake of illustration, imagine how much better positioned we would have been had drug companies opted to stitch together global networks of COVID vaccine manufacturing centers prior to the pandemic, or Japan had preplanned special measures to keep citizens and athletes safe so the Olympics could continue (or at least avoid a yearlong delay for athletes at the peak of their training cycle). Had the UAE launched its significant investments in aeroponics and other domestic food production earlier, it would have established greater food security for the Emirates before supply chain disruptions left some grocery shelves bare. Regardless of the large and small impacts of the micro-level decisions we make in this triage process, use of the FLP-IT model now can help clarify the options that lead to more antifragile and sustainable operations in the future.

Strategic Leadership in the FLP-IT Model

For strategies to work effectively in human organizations and societies, we also need to think in terms of leadership, adding a creative-imaginative element as we synthesize new options, especially in times of significant disruption. As Lloyd Williams, the chief academic officer of Transcontinental University and a longtime friend and mentor to Mark, so eloquently puts it, true leadership requires both cognition and emotion—brain and heart. "If you're too cognitive, you forget about the human condition," Williams says. "If you're too emotional, you forget about the ability to think. So, change occurs because you're able to balance the two to create a pathway for people to move." This might feel obvious at first, but most business and government leaders struggle to strike and maintain the right balance of the two. Every step of the way, we need to understand both the objective measurable elements of a force and the perceived elements of a force. How do we account for the measurable, cognitive stuff *and* the qualitative, emotional side of things? Both are equally important.

Consider, for example, existing attitudes about globalization. The polarized arguments over the benefits and damages of our current global systems too often swing to cognitive or emotional extremes, outside the narrow balance where constructive dialogue, change, and experience can occur. FLP-IT, however, integrates cognitive and emotional processes that, when combined, flip an individual's or organization's gaze toward a better future state while also providing an actionable toolset to move forward. This makes it easier to get over hurdles created by imbalances between cognition and emotion and develop the prototypes and actions necessary to bring a vision to fruition.

FLP-IT provides an excellent process for the analytical and strategic outlook that leaders need to inform their foresight and craft future scenarios, but using it requires more than metrics and data points. It requires a leadership view based on experience and an ability to understand the world, including humanity and identity-centric values within it. It infuses the strategic processes with an understanding and true appreciation for the social and emotional dynamics of markets, organizations, economies, and societies. Some forces and logics will identify quantifiable flows of resources. Others will surface ebbs and flows of emotion and morale.

As leaders examine the F and L in the FLP-IT process, they will realize that some of the softer and less objective emotional dimensions play a crucial role in disruptive times. Nearly every data point suggested the UK would lose out if it left the EU, and the confidence in that data blinded the Tory government to the true sentiment of the majority. As we should all know by now, history isn't always concocted from rational ingredients. The redefinition and reconstruction of truth at this still-liminal phase of recovery means we have no choice but to lead through fear, doubt, and anxiety to get to hope and aspiration.

With that balance maintained, a macro FLP-IT exercise will illuminate the emerging forces that create societal shifts. A meso-level exercise will reveal how those larger forces—from government policies to consumer sentiment—will shape the future direction of industries. A micro review will provide a sense of how employees have responded to a shock and how, from a change management perspective, a leader can guide workers toward a different intent. Because FLP-IT centers humanity and the cognitive-emotional balance necessary for positive change, it can apply to individuals, a small community, a large and growing company, or an entire nation.

Whatever the scale, FLP-IT helps us craft a pathway for action, experimentation, and innovative behavior in times of radical shock.

This kind of combined thinking does not come naturally to most leaders. It's not often taught in MBA programs and executive training workshops. When the emotional side is addressed, it's usually in leadership training focused on sociopsychological or organizational behavior perspectives. Conversely, technology, for all its advantages, has only worsened our obsession with the quantifiable, harder, and structural elements of organizations because it makes people more measurable—or at least makes us believe we can measure the previously unquantifiable. The moment you can start counting how many minutes workers actually work in a shift, you start seeing them as mere biological machines. But machines, no matter how sophisticated, cannot yet understand identity, dreams, mission, or purpose.

We have believed, wrongly, that we could become better humans as a result of abundance, too often prioritizing measurable profit over the uncomfortable fuzziness of values, empathy, and well-being. And when we do, everything becomes a transaction. "What began to occur in the late eighties and early nineties was a shift to money becoming the equivalent of a person, rather than money being a tool," Williams of Transcontinental University said. "So when it became the equivalent of a person, it created greater friction between the people in the society. If you don't have a certain amount of money, you are considered a lesser part of the society." That fragmentation eroded a fuller sense of humanity, creating a lack of care for one another, and weakening the bonds necessary to address the world's shared challenges. "There's no human identity, no personal identity anymore," he says. "There's a money identity, and the money identity says you either have it or you don't."

So how do we go about repurposing and reinvigorating the emotional construct of identity—not just personal identity or individual identity but the construct of a communal identity? From a strategic planning perspective, we need to use FLP-IT or other models that balance cognition and emotion and integrate economic, humanist, and bio-ecological values. Money might force us to revise the time frame for implementation of our plans, but we can no longer make decisions or craft strategies based strictly on financial considerations. We need to question why Jeff Bezos, who made some $205 million per day during the pandemic, would thank his employees when he blasted into orbit on his "best day ever" while Amazon shortchanged new parents, patients dealing with medical crises, and other vulnerable workers on leave.[1] It's easy to shrug off casual comments such as these, but we need to find a better way to measure human growth as driven by purpose, empathy, community, and identity—and then hold ourselves to a clear standard. As those we lead regain trust in our intentions, measured growth and money will follow.

FLP-IT provides a framework to enhance that understanding and trust, allowing leaders to access an opportunity by balancing the cognitive and emotional in ways that seek to add more ideas and insights into the mix. But all this assumes leaders will aim to enhance and expand the idea of augmenting humanity, rather than relegating people to "other" status or downgrading them to biological machines to be measured. Each of the FLP-IT steps provides us an opportunity to develop strategies for a human-centric future.

Forces

Some situations focus the mind like no others. Taking fire or sending soldiers into a battle is one of those. Maybe it's no surprise, then, that Gen. (ret.) George Casey's mind goes back to 9/11 when asked about how he assesses major disruptive forces. The events of that day forever changed global perceptions of the US and its role in the world. With nearly three thousand casualties sustained after an attack on its home soil, America immediately and radically transformed its defense posture. Terrorism at home became real in a way that citizens in other countries had long known. The country's defense preparations shifted from conventional warfare between states to asymmetric warfare against non-state actors often hiding in plain sight. "We moved away from conventional war to learning how to fight irregular war *while we were fighting it*," Casey recalled.

For a superpower primarily geared toward securing domestic and international peace and prosperity abroad, the new paradigm forced leaders to work together more closely to navigate the new reality. "There wasn't an omniscient leader who knew everything, and there never will be," Casey said. "We had to work together to figure it out. And even as you are dealing with current realities, things change—the geopolitical reality twenty years later has returned to near-peer competition in a very conventional way." The threat of terrorism remains, but Russia's invasion of Ukraine and the rise of China has brought back a more traditional sense of warfare, forcing different sides to invest in technologies and capabilities that counter their rivals' strengths while enhancing their own.

The power of major global forces has only amplified in recent years, as the blistering pace of change sparks unprecedented disruptions—including some genuinely existential threats. In particular, Five C tectonic forces have shifted the very foundations of our lives, identities, security, environment, and global order. Much like with geological ones, these technological, political, and economic tectonic forces cannot be stopped. However, they can be shaped, bent, and bundled. In fact, they provide us with a set of variables to help design smarter global systems, but we have not yet evolved our strategies and tools to account for the complex systems of systems through which their ripple effects meet, amplify, or counter one another. So, we can begin by using them as a lens to analyze the pathways that might move our societies forward, as we do throughout the book in the examples of the Five Cs. For instance, future pandemic responses and climate change will require globally coordinated approaches to manage and mitigate harm. Effective cybersecurity will require widely accepted legal and enforcement mechanisms that flow cross borders as seamlessly as data do.

COVID and pandemic management—This C encompasses the confluence of digital and biological sciences and their management to combat the virus. The pandemic expanded our reliance on digital tools and data, speeding up the already evolving trends of an emerging cognitive economy. It permanently altered our relationship with work and drew more attention to concerns about cybersecurity and data privacy. It pushed our understanding of virus genetics and associated genomic and informatic technologies, thanks to some six million SARS-CoV-2 genomes having been sequenced in just two years (compare with a total of sixteen thousand HIV-AIDS genomes to date).[2] And it finalized the world's transition from the Digital Era to a new Cognitive Era, layering the inside-out effects that genetic and molecular science can exert directly on the fundamental building blocks of our lives. The tectonic force of pandemics only hint at what could emerge as the complexity and interconnectedness of our societies, living conditions, dynamism, and global systems collide. But we can take lessons from both their painful disruptions and the promising innovation in everything from biological sciences to infrastructure technologies (and the connections between them).

The cognitive economy—This C refers to the emerging era of digital and biological algorithms and related technologies that cut across infrastructure and environment. These cognitive tools will replace more human decisions and tasks, spinning out ever more data and insights to fuel the thinking and learning machines that will become the engines of our societal and economic processes, contracts, and business models. In the subtitles for our previous books, *Solomon's Code* (2018) and *The AI Republic* (2019), we called this "humanity in a world of thinking machines" and the "nexus between humans and intelligent automation."[3] As noted by our colleague Mark Nitzberg, the executive director of the UC Berkeley Center for Human-Compatible AI, this tectonic force only accelerated with the widespread move to home offices, squeezing years of technological development into months and forcing a scramble to establish the robust and trusted data privacy regimes we need to distribute the benefits of the cognitive economy to everyone. Whether those structures are centralized or decentralized, the cognitive economy will need trusted global data markets and governance mechanisms, so leaders can establish credibility and accountability with consumers, constituents, and employees.

Cybersecurity—Only time will tell whether the inexorable drive into the cognitive economy benefits humanity. Either way, though, our lives and livelihoods will become far more digitized, datafied, codified, cognified, quantified, and metricized, providing us the potential for significant human and economic growth—but also leaving us increasingly vulnerable to the hackers, cyberterrorists and cybercriminals who have gotten significantly better organized, better capitalized, and more globalized. This C takes on even greater urgency when the internet and other digital systems reach more deeply into our lives and bodies, from national infrastructure like power grids to our individual health and genetic records. The more we digitize and cognify our personal, societal, and business existence—including our own genetic codes and brain functions—the more enticing a target we become for cyberattack. In a world of interconnected drones, autonomous cars, factory robots, smart clothing, wirelessly connected tags and even lightbulbs, we constantly need to protect new flanks of deeper vulnerability.

Climate change—This tectonic force represents the single most urgent existential threat to humanity. It will alter pretty much everything we breathe, eat, and do, including our infrastructure, supply chains, migration patterns, systems of geopolitical cooperation, health care, insurance—you name it. We have only started to see some of the ways climate and carbon emissions will ripple across our global systems, but enough evidence has accumulated that only the most committed cynics do not acknowledge the broad economic, social, and health consequences of our warming planet. Yet in our day-to-day existence, many of us fail to recognize climate change as an acute threat. We have yet to develop the real-time impact awareness, the political will, and the cooperation necessary to produce solutions at the global systems level. To get there, we will have to develop combinations of old and new mechanisms and incentives to truly keep this existential threat front and center amid everything we have on our minds each day. Nowhere do we need the design activism of the planet more.

China—No global systems redesign will work without a constructive China at the table. The decisions and actions taken by the Chinese government in the years to come will impact the lives of every single inhabitant of this world. Such moves might be as specific as the Chinese government's 2021 order to halt trading of Didi, the Chinese equivalent of Uber, on a US stock exchange, inflicting losses on many US pension funds and investors, or as striking and large as catastrophic attempts to absorb Taiwan into the PRC. They might also be as far-reaching and enlightened as efforts to reduce global carbon emissions on a scale never before seen, or to get to Mars before anyone else does. But in each case, the balance of competition and cooperation between China and the West will also dictate the outcome of the world's complicated risk-reward scenarios—everything from the science needed to combat the next pandemic to the diplomacy and governance needed to avoid armed conflict with autonomous weapons systems.

Some of our best-laid plans to address these tectonic, Five C forces—let alone a seamless combination of them—will fail. As General Casey said, there are two kinds of plans—those that *might* work and those that *won't* work. Indeed, trying to envision the complexity of these tectonic forces will require imaginative muscles that leaders rarely need to flex. It's the kind of imagination that takes time and continuity, especially in a world moving at the hyperspeed of technological innovation. Yet that type of contemplation also helps leaders develop empathy, which has become an especially critical leadership trait in recent years. Imaginative empathy in the FLP-IT model puts leaders into the shoes of the widest array of people involved in the anthropo-political or techno-commercial forces reshaping the world.

Even when we disagree, we need to have enough empathy to take stock of competing viewpoints in a neutral fashion, and then validate the evolving forces fairly and wholly before rendering judgment. That's a rare skill among executives and leaders who have been trained to act fast, but it opens more and richer possibilities for moving an organization forward. "People who are resisting change are often just resisting uncertainty, because it means potential negative consequences. That's self-preservation," says Richard Lyons, chief innovation and entrepreneurship officer at UC Berkeley and a former chief learning officer at Goldman Sachs. "If you treat them like reasonable skeptics and involve them in imagining a desirable shared vision, you get valuable inputs and they are less threatened." Sometimes you have to think and feel slow to act fast.

Logic

Most business leaders have neither the time nor the inclination to wander through hypotheticals, but contemplating an emerging logic requires that leaders simply be open to the distant possibilities, not dwell on them. Even that can feel like a challenging leap, because understanding a new operating logic forces us to reform or even abandon the logic to which we've grown accustomed. "The most remarkable thing about the pandemic was that no one was able to predict the economic impact," says Christophe Le Caillec, the deputy CFO at American Express. "No one actually saw the flip side. We thought there would be an absolute bloodbath for small businesses, but if you look at the bankruptcy level, it's at a record low. It's the opposite of what every economic theory would have told you."

Granted, the huge amount of money that governments pumped into the economy helped prop up a lot of people and companies that might have failed otherwise, but then few people would have predicted the use of the "Big Bazooka," either. So how can we find logic in such an unpredictable world?

For business leaders, sometimes it's by recalibrating our view of what's important. "Last year [in 2020], people were thinking about death. There was really a moment of two months where, frankly speaking, the world was shaking," said Rémy Baume, CEO of the French luxury brand Zadig&Voltaire. "In this context, people saw [the fashion industry] as nonsense. After all, this industry is selling not-being-naked on the outside."

So Baume and his colleagues shifted their view to see what logic would emerge next for fashion, and they realized their consumers were placing a much higher premium on sustainability, especially as the pandemic shifted the trend toward shopping online, where information on environmental impact was much more accessible. Consumers don't always vote for the environment with their wallets, but the writing was on the wall. "If you want to fight to be one out of ten to be surviving in a shrinking market, sustainability is not optional anymore," he said. "You have to be better than the competition." That's not always easy for an industry that relies on handcrafted products and seeks to source the finest materials from all over the globe, Baume said, often from "super traditional" suppliers who don't welcome automation or transparency. But the demands from customers led Zadig&Voltaire to look at new technologies, including blockchain, to provide more insight into the sustainability and environmental impact of its value chain.

This new operating logic—the rules and axioms that might change across or within an economy, industry, or society—does not always show up in explicit legislation or regulation. However, it will always manifest in the ways a society or economy works, because it generates the substrate off which people feed. The work that leaders do in this phase of the FLP-IT process should mitigate bias and be open to the possibility of radical change. Blue-sky thinking, greenfield building, or zeroth-principle questioning—whatever your favorite colorful phrase for the practice, the logic considered should serve as an amplifier for nearly anything that the sparks of the colliding forces might generate. One might start by asking how the ways they govern, incentivize, transact, and relate will change as thrusts destroy existing systems, upgrade them, or create entirely new ones. Will consumer interest in sustainability sway the market toward transparency? Will a new metaverse platform help industries or companies we wouldn't expect, as leaders in those fields exercise the imagination and vision to tap into new types of multisided Web2 platforms or leverage emerging Web3 protocols? Or will a reputation and social-credit system radically redefine people's status and market access, despite United Nations ethics principles that hope to limit such systems?[4]

Regardless of the degree of disruption, an emerging logic will shift our foundations and the institutions and processes we built upon them. Because these changes will ripple through entire systems, we need to let go of probability thinking, which tends to narrow our view toward a small set of simplified future end states. Instead, we need to embrace the "path-thinking" or "pattern-thinking" that encompasses more facets of what might lie ahead. For example, the metaverse holds any number of possibilities for the accumulation of status, power, and wealth. Already in 2021, companies had invested millions of dollars in metaverse "real estate," with demand apparently deriving from the prospect of access and "proximity" to a virtual landmark as a symbol of status. Rather than thinking in terms of a virtual land grab and falling victim to hype, a path-thinking approach might envision a world in which we're heading toward an attitude of "less is more"—a dematerialized economy that values experiences and metaverse services rather than tangible, physical goods. More and more people are willing to hold non-fungible tokens (NFTs) to "own" something intangible. Will people find more fulfillment from virtual experience than physical things? Will NFTs and decentralized ownership prevent already wealthy individuals or organizations from amassing more power with new kinds of governance mechanisms? Could we be on a very different path? If so, which aspects of it are worth embracing and which are overblown? Whether or not we actually end up far down this path or just borrow some of its elements becomes a secondary question, because we've extracted those innovations that are worth building a future with.

We have been living in a "more is more" paradigm for decades, and our business models reflect that. Even the first hints of a shift toward virtual abundance, where less of the physical might well be more, could generate a widespread reconsideration of business models, marketplaces, and product road maps. A "less is more" paradigm would require redesigns that accommodate the new, more frugal operating logic, says Navi Radjou, a former Gartner analyst and coauthor of the bestseller *Jugaad Innovation* (2012). Companies would need to go lean, human-centric, circular, and creative, Radjou says, and they would have to enlist and share resources with others in the ecosystem. That takes time and brings its own risks, especially when we engineer our technical, logistic, and business systems so tightly that they become fragile.

Seeing a new logic emerge and then converting it into a workable business model—while still operating within the existing logic—will help leaders set aside entrenched interests in their current investments, especially in their business and operating models. It takes skill to understand the new logic that's arising, and a great deal of resolve to redirect the organizational ship into uncharted waters, but the FLP-IT process helps leaders navigate the turbulence. It still takes the courage to buck all the training, incentives, and inertia that permeate business and society today, and to prioritize empathy and imagination over profit. But the leaders who use FLP-IT to envision the emerging operating logic of an uncertain and changing world will build better businesses, better livelihoods, better careers, and a better society.

Phenomena

If forces generate the thrust and power to change the underlying operating logic of our societies and economies, then phenomena refer to the discrete ways this logic expresses itself within a domain. Leaders need to understand phenomena for three reasons. First, the emerging phenomena will have direct implications for the arena, domain, or industry in which leaders are acting. Second, leaders cannot fully understand the implications of change unless they first understand the nuances within the phenomena that emerge. And third, leaders need to decide which phenomena to reincorporate around to provide a degree of stability for their constituents. The US newspaper industry largely overlooked the emergence of digital platforms and their hoarding of digital advertising revenues, a phenomenon that left them with few options to support traditional newsrooms and struggling to develop a workable business model. By not understanding these platforms and the nuances within them, they could not see and react to the full implications of lost advertising revenues. Both the industry and the country are suffering from that oversight today, as unreliable information platforms and their monetization models are wreaking havoc on the social fabric on both the local and national level.

Perhaps without even understanding why, younger digitally native generations of leaders have started to personify how design activist leaders grasp and respond to developing phenomena. Helena Storckenfeldt is one such leader. After studying global economics with Mark and Olaf at Hult, Storckenfeldt was elected to Sweden's Riksdag in 2019, at age twenty-four becoming the youngest parliamentarian in her party at the time. "I don't think that we're really looking for that hero anymore," she said. "We're looking for someone who is real."

Driven largely by a new logic that puts a greater premium on authenticity than perfection, many managers and politicians like Storckenfeldt have adopted different types of leadership. In this mold, an authentic leader will admit when they lack a skill or insight, but they know how to augment their shortcomings. The concept of authentic leadership has been around for decades, of course, but it continues to mature. And with Generations Y and Z, who for much of their lives have seen system collapses that threaten their income potential, it might have a chance to become the dominant leadership model. Leaders cannot so easily win over these younger generations of workers with rational dealmaking or feigned toughness. For many of them, toughness has taken on a different meaning, increasingly referring to the conviction that we can be fine even when everything around us isn't. It means that leaders are not afraid to bring active empathy and authentic emotion to their communication of tough messages, relying on both a pure heart and a focused mind as they navigate through upheaval.

By contrast, in the prevailing paradigm, too many leaders project confidence over competence, refusing to admit they don't have all the answers. In his book *Invisible Leadership*, former US Army ranger Shawn Engbrecht writes that, as a leader, you "can promise everything to the many until you are unable to deliver even a little to the few." He encourages leaders to "embrace the suck" and notes that "failure to tell the truth rapidly erodes trust and confidence in higher command."[5]

True trust and authenticity begins with an acknowledgment of the bad, Storckenfeldt has said, and then builds upon true understanding, empathy, and humility. For all of social media's ills, it provides a valuable conduit for leaders to interact directly with their constituents, if they choose to use it as a transparent channel of communication. With that open and honest interaction established, leaders and their constituents can look for ways to address the situation together. It's a new phenomenon in leadership that Storckenfeldt has seen taking root in Europe and around the world. "I can't do everything; nobody can," she explained. "Acknowledging that and showing that, showing those insecurities that you actually have, can be a very valuable strength in being inspirational going forward."

Her brand of leadership has become increasingly effective in recent years, as workers and constituents grapple with a complex web of unknowns. Indeed, Storckenfeldt has become an increasingly influential voice in her

party, and she now serves on the Riksdag's prestigious Committee on Foreign Affairs. When we spoke again in 2021 for this book, she said most
leaders have yet to adopt more empathetic leadership styles, especially
because in times of crisis "we demand someone who really takes control
and is more of the hard type of leadership." Storckenfeldt admitted she
doesn't know how these emerging leadership phenomena will play out
long term, whether we'll swing toward soft or hard or "just right" situation
by situation. But she recognizes this new phenomenon is already playing
out around the world as managers respond to the new forces and logic that
younger generations are injecting into society.

A deeper exploration of phenomena will become even more critical if
new viral variants make hope for a "new normal" feel more like resignation
to a "never-again normal." The wave peaks will probably disappear over
time, and COVID might become more endemic, like the flu, but even then
we might need to deal with follow-on consequences of an increasingly difficult scope. In that case, global supply chains, for example, will have to
integrate new methods of acquisition and distribution as they are buffeted
by more and different pressures. Indeed, as *The Economist* noted in September 2021, companies didn't abandon their global supply chains during the
pandemic; they began to adapt.[6] Some companies added redundancies in
their value chains, while others pulled sourcing closer to their end customers. To meet the heavy demand for luxury goods in China, suppliers built
automated distribution centers at breakneck speeds, said Wilson Wong,
a global supply chain expert based in China. Recognizing the new phenomena emerging and seeing how they would impact their businesses—
the Ever Given container ship stuck in the Suez Canal became the perfect
metaphor—they improvised and found ways around the snags. Retailers
chartered entire ships for their own freight or retrofitted passenger aircraft
to carry cargo. Add in a layer of emerging cognitive technologies that allow
a company to track not just raw materials and products but the forces that
could potentially disrupt the flow of those goods, and supply chains begin
to decentralize and add layers of resilience.

Clearly, we will see no shortage of new phenomena in the years to
come, and business and government leaders around the world will need
to take a much wider and longer view of the future. But the identification of critical phenomena is not some sort of mystical process. More than

anything, leaders simply need to know where to look and what questions to ask. Indeed, throughout our interviews for this book, many of the most interesting answers we received came in response to the foresight question, *If you had an oracle before you, what question would you ask?* The potential answer set gets far more difficult to ascertain when the scope of that question stretches out to three, five, or ten years from now. We set our sights on 2035, and we asked the network of leaders and experts we interviewed to think in those terms. We encourage you to do the same. Yes, that may be uncomfortable, because we have no data on the future. But when we begin to look almost fifteen years ahead, it forces us to think about new phenomena for which we do not yet have empirical evidence—new employee loyalties, new leadership styles, new work environments, new forms of team dynamics, new geopolitical balances, new supply chain structures, and new ways to assess productivity and reward achievement.

All of this comes back to imagination, empathy, and design activism as increasingly indispensable leadership traits in the cognitive economy. Given the added complexity of multiple, layered crises across global systems of systems, leaders will need to lean on all three skills to effectively assess how new forces, logics, and phenomena will impact their organizations and especially their people. They will need to develop new systems that replace the patterns and phenomena that fractured in recent years. And, ultimately, they'll need to accommodate and adjust to the impacts that these new phenomena will generate for the people they lead.

Impacts

You might be wondering, *So, what does all this mean for my country, my company, and my life?* With an analytical understanding of forces, logic, and phenomena in hand, leaders can assess the impacts they will have on their constituencies, industries, communities, and families at various levels (i.e., macro, meso, and micro). There is no shortage of tools and processes to help home in on the implications of disruption and upheaval. One might use an amended version of Michael Porter's Diamond Model—which helps people understand how certain resources, strategies, and conditions give one nation or group a competitive advantage over others—tailoring it to assess the implications of the FLPs on the unique blend of economic policies, corporate strategies, demand conditions, and labor, land, and infrastructure factors directly relevant to them.[7] Another might work the problem through the lens of product and service value chains or nodal networks, which consider how each unit or productive output of an organization is woven into a much more complex, multidimensional network. Each node builds on, enables, or bypasses these units.[8] Keeping a watchful eye on those nodal dynamics and the health and prosperity of each node on a granular level can amplify the entire network. In the FLP-IT context, an impact analysis could assess how the health of critical productive nodes in an organization has evolved. A leader could even look internally at how the new operating logic might change the value of their own or their company's resources and capabilities, using well-known strategy concepts like the resource-based view of the organization or the dynamic capabilities framework.[9] Will any resources or capabilities become or cease to be strategic? On any of these levels, though, leaders can simply ask who gains and who loses—whether power, value, or position—or contemplate who is leaving their domain, who is entering, and who is exerting pressure on other players to compensate for or react to them. It's not always easy, but sometimes one can see the new physics quickly, identifying new energies at play and the directions in which they're moving—the very core of what basic systems dynamics thinking teaches us.

Regardless of the models that leaders use—even a simple brainstorm exercise to imagine potential outcomes of new projects would be a start—they need to layer new questions atop their frameworks. They need to ask themselves how the new operating logic and prevailing phenomena will change incentives and motivations—and therefore the constellation of actors and flows that shape the organization's business. These impacts are one of the most critical components of the framework, because they allow us to witness how global and macro forces can influence the ways individual people and businesses behave. In essence, they teach us which factors matter more and which matter less.

During the pandemic, supply chain disruptions emerged as a critical phenomenon that affected everything from national economic development to the shelves of neighborhood grocery stores. Leaders must take this recognizable phenomenon and assess the long-term effects that ongoing supply chain bottlenecks will have on their business, employees, and customers. Take, for instance, the vital semiconductor supply chain: On a macro scale, we've seen the US leverage its leadership in semiconductor

technologies against China, while moving to shore up its domestic manufacturing capacity lest it lose control over critical choke points in the chip
supply chain. On a meso level, automakers grappled with long lead times
on orders and vehicles after chip shortages curbed availability of vital components. On a micro level, grand plans for home renovations hit snags
throughout 2021 due to supply chain and demand issues, including scarcity and delays of everything from kitchen appliances to home electronics components for some HVAC systems—compounding stress for people
who found themselves working at home. Automakers adjusted their supply
chains for chips, the US has enticed Taiwan Semiconductor Manufacturing
Company (TSMC) to invest in fabs on American soil, and European governments have gone knocking on Canada's door for minerals and energy
sourcing. Once trouble hits, it's easy to see the pinch points and fragility.
The trick is to stress-test and plan contingencies beforehand with a framework like FLP-IT, ideally supported by an ongoing, dynamic, and smarter
use of sensing and computing technologies we already have.

The impacts open themselves up to leaders who work through the FLP-IT
framework and go back to what Salesforce CEO Marc Benioff calls a "begin-
ner's mindset." This puts us in search of not just the emerging points of
fragility but the potential points for epiphany, progress, and growth. We
can't expect easy answers, mind you. In almost every case of significant
disruption and shift, leaders must go through a cycle in which they identify
the symptoms of socioeconomic and/or market fragility, develop solutions,
and, over time, begin to understand the side effects or unintended consequences of those solutions. Only then do they acquire the wisdom and
insight to recalibrate and develop processes or strategies that strike closer
and closer to the root cause of our problems and the points where we remobilize beyond them.

Inevitably, some stakeholders will fall by the wayside and lose power;
others will ride the crest of the new wave. This will happen across societies,
organizations, and our own local communities and networks. Who stands
to lose or gain, and how do we react? Even with using the FLP-IT process
to help identify these forces, logic, and phenomena, the way the impacts
of these can ripple through societies, industries, and economies can make
them difficult to decipher without time, imagination, and careful negotiation. Consider again the macro implications of the semiconductor supply chain example. While the US and the Netherlands hold sizeable IP

advantages on semiconductor and chip fabrication technologies, respectively, Taiwan remains one of the largest manufacturers of processors. The possibility of China seeking to fully annex Taiwan by force raises immediate geotechnological and geopolitical questions about supplies of this indispensable cog of the cognitive economy's machine. The 2022 CHIPS Act aimed to lessen US dependency on Taiwan's suppliers and keep the US safely ahead of mainland China's efforts, but it could not immediately relieve the political, commercial, and technological implications contained there.

Leaders in the public sector have vast experience with such power struggles, of course, but rarely do the implications of past challenges forecast the implications of present or future ones, at least not with the precision needed when the potential stakes include armed conflict. When interpreting the impact of complex forces and phenomena with little established structure or precedent—for instance, US-China relations as a competition between near-peer global powers—leaders need to be careful to find consensus where they can.

"I would engage with China on the boring and somewhat uninspiring middle ground, where you have the capacity to push back—and do—on the things you disagree with but would not go to war over those," said Thomas Pickering, former US ambassador to the UN, India, Russia, Israel, and Nigeria as well as senior vice president at Boeing and now senior counselor at Albright Stonebridge Group. The creative and careful use of military influence makes sense, Pickering said, "but not the notion that military influence has to be in one way or another engaged to get diplomatic answers." Rather, cooperation on existential issues, such as climate change, where both sides will suffer the negative impacts of our current trajectory, can provide the foundation for negotiations over other contentious impacts, including supply chain resilience. This way, the diplomacy of crisis management protocols can be a safeguard mechanism, or at least a safety valve, for the smarter systems-fragility diagnostic we propose for leaders across countries and at all levels of government or business.

It's not an easy balance to strike with such massive implications for global order and the lives of billions of people around the planet. Weighing the impact of collaborative openness against protective closure might prove to be the most difficult challenge that leaders will face at such a critical moment in modern human history. War, cyberattacks, bioweapons, autonomous killer drones, artificial intelligence, and viruses (unleashed by nature or people) raise the stakes for every action and inaction. The Cognitive Era requires a new level of vigilance to expand concentric and collaborative circles throughout an organization, an industry, a society, and the natural ecosystem that surrounds us. As leaders, we need to relax our local and global systems enough to sense and shift with the changing impact of the logic and phenomena we see evolving. But an open and productive vigilance about the impacts we all face—one that's built on trust assurance and supplemented by real-time diagnostic and verification tools—can provide an effective starting point for the final, triage phase of the FLP-IT framework.

Triage

Global supply chains and trade became ground zero for triage during the pandemic, with the abrupt restrictions on in-person contact and the widespread transition to online tools suddenly accelerating long-standing efforts to digitize trade. Countries grappled with the switch from traditional paperwork to digital tracking of trade across borders, explains Gosia Loj, the head of global governance at the UK Department for Digital, Culture, Media and Sport. Loj and her colleagues were already knee-deep in efforts to digitize trade regulation so as to increase efficiency and transparency. They had worked with companies, industry organizations, and other countries, such as Singapore and Switzerland, to modernize and streamline systems for the Cognitive Era. But this endeavor is not simply a matter of buying hardware, installing software, and following best practices, she explains. Decades of trade regulations across dozens of departments in different countries have to change to accommodate new systems and paradigms. "We're basically looking at the review of laws that apply solely to papers, to the procedures that entail paper," she says. The wording of those regulations must be changed to legally accommodate the use of digital technologies.

It seems so simple, but the tedious and expensive reengineering of even the most mundane processes lies at the crux of the triage phase of our current transformation, because even the most basic operations can form pinch points that result in system fragility. We might imagine an automated and self-organizing web of channels that responds quickly to massive disruptions, a concept we brainstormed during a project with students in a global venture development course. Manufacturers face enormous risk when their supply chains are threatened, so an equally enormous effort to develop such an advanced system might be warranted, especially since the basic components for it already exist. AI systems could recommend solutions to rejigger supply chains with agile contract renegotiation, preemptive and preventive negotiation of contingency plans and contracts, new futures markets that trade on prospective flows of goods and services, and insights into commensurate carbon-mitigation strategies.

Whether rebuilding supply chains, digitizing regulatory paperwork, or overhauling corporate cultures, leaders typically rely on a past or present snapshot to make decisions about what actions to take first. Loj and her colleagues in the UK can look to other countries, such as Singapore, which have already modernized and provide some signposts for future directions. But in the end, UK government officials have to align regulations and processes with those of every country with which they interact. They're working through the G7 to help develop some standards and then do the difficult internal work. "You need to look inside of your own structures and you need to decide what reforms you need," she said. They need to *triage* their processes, rules, and standards in light of a new operating logic in the international trade community. New priorities emerged; old ones had to be de-emphasized or dropped. "Then we can start engaging with countries like Singapore that are on the forefront of that and making it more of a global thing."

So, Loj and her colleagues have to channel their investments of time, money, and resources toward their top priorities—including the adoption of new digital technologies while still making mundane fixes of old regulations, perhaps at a slower pace. They needed to triage their resources between the forward-looking investment ideas such as distributed ledgers to track international trade and the unsexy but critical work of amending existing code to allow use of those innovations in the first place. "It's something that is being discussed and it's being shared as an idea," Loj said of distributed ledgers, "but it's not yet done because it requires a lot of, again, new legislation that would be put in place. And that starts with a review of what exists, what blockages there are, and then you need to go through the whole process of consultations and back and forth with the Parliament." Some new things get more attention while other existing projects get less, and some ideas and programs get dropped altogether.

These sorts of trade-offs and balances during the triage process can force leaders to abandon long-favored projects and programs in the name of progress. It's not easy, but it's almost always necessary, and the FLP-IT framework can provide the empirical and imaginative underpinning to justify those difficult decisions. We hope the combination of FLP-IT and the proposals we suggest will spark conversations and design activism that will lead to a more sustainable, resilient, and equitable world—one that can be a fertile basis for the next tier of healthier human, economic, and technological growth.

II Forces

2 Red Hot Cataclysm: Geopolitical Curveballs

The international expansion by Chinese technology company Huawei of its next-generation telecommunications networks raised alarms in the US and Europe, and tensions came to a head with the arrest in 2018 of Meng Wanzhou, who was detained nearly three years in Canada on US fraud charges. Meng, the company's CFO, was accused of having misled HSBC Bank about Huawei's business operations in Iran, but the case remained intertwined with concerns that the company's advanced telecom infrastructure could provide Beijing broad surveillance and intelligence capabilities if it contained "backdoors" for remote, covert access to the information flows it carried. The US and Dutch governments alleged exactly that, although definitive proof might never become public for national security reasons. Years of US sanctions against Huawei, which severely restricted the company's access to American software and semiconductors, crippled it. As chairman Eric Xu predicted in September 2021, the company's annual revenue that year dropped sharply as it was "getting used to U.S. sanctions," falling 28.5 percent from the prior year and marking its first sales decline on public record.[1]

While digital technologies have influenced geopolitics since the internet crossed borders and computer companies built global supply lines in the 1990s, the high-profile and public arrest of Meng and accusations against Huawei exemplified a new reality. Artificial intelligence, quantum computing, advanced semiconductors, and other cognitive "deep technology" applications no longer merely influence geopolitics and international affairs; they now play an absolutely central and inextricable role in global diplomacy, commerce, and relationships. Understanding this full integration of technology, geopolitics, and global economics has become so instrumental to every global system that it spawned the word "geotech" as its own term of art.

The set of forces a leader might identify while using FLP-IT to find a path through uncertainty will inevitably depend on their own circumstances. But the tectonic Five C forces—COVID and pandemic management, the cognitive economy, cybersecurity, climate change, and China—will affect virtually everyone and everything worldwide. These will change the global order as we know it, whether we fight them, ignore them, or, hopefully, try to guide them. Those who seek to understand which direction the major geopolitical trade winds will blow have to start with the following factors: China, cybersecurity, and climate change.

Already, China has aggressively pushed its geopolitical and technological reach outside its borders with the Belt and Road Initiative (BRI), the key driver of its next development frontier. The BRI's massive infrastructure investments in everything from ports to rail lines have given China and its companies a growing foothold in about a hundred countries, which together contribute more than half the world's gross domestic product. Experts have debated the effectiveness of the BRI, noting the backlash when China leveraged financial obligations on massive infrastructure projects in vulnerable countries, such as Pakistan and Bangladesh, to bend them toward its interests. But the BRI also made inroads into wealthier nations such as Qatar, Poland, and Switzerland, where Chinese technology companies are carving out market share, even in light of concerns about whether China can maintain the pace of BRI expansion as it hits lagging growth at home.

As the West and China oscillate between cooperation and competition in the decades to come, the changing vectors of these geopolitical and geotechnological forces will continually reshape global supply chains, the direction and speed of technological advancements, and the balance of economic relationships and power. The geopolitical tension between the major, tech-enabled powers will play out in the virtual world, as well, where cybersecurity will assume a critical role in national, commercial, and personal security. We have little hope of harnessing the power of these forces for progressive solutions and equitable redesigns without at least the selective cooperation of China.

But the effects of these geopolitical factors can strike at more fundamental human needs, too—as one can imagine after Russia's invasion of Ukraine. The critical ripple effects of the war-induced regrouping of global trade and security started with energy and food. Because Russia is the world's largest exporter of natural gas and is the third-largest producer of oil, the OECD's and G7's decision to step away from Russian natural resources set off frantic negotiations over substitutions.[2] The potential for a global food crisis throws even more uncertainty into the mix, given that Russia and Ukraine supply 28 percent of globally traded wheat, 29 percent of the world's barley, and a quarter of its corn.[3]

Still, looking long term, the primary geopolitical prospects still boil down to the contest between the West and China, due to the country's sheer size and its ability to project its military, economic, and technological capabilities. Even Russia's war in Ukraine will eventually switch back to the question of China's future relationship with the world, for two reasons. One, Beijing has been watching Moscow's brazen attempt to annex more of Ukraine's territory and the international community's reaction to it as a potential precedent for its own aspirations for Taiwan. Two, Russia is essentially defying the world's established economic, energy, food, and financial systems, providing valuable lessons for China's own dependence on these systems and its need for greater resilience via alternatives as its influence expands.

Around the time Russia marched into Ukraine in February 2022, Beijing's expanding reach had nudged US experts toward two competing perspectives. The first, gleaned from our conversations in Washington, sees academic, scientific, and entrepreneurial collaboration with China as dangerously naive. Proponents of this view cite numerous cases of industrial espionage conducted by Chinese cyber-agents and high-profile accusations of spying against Chinese scientists who reside and research in the US (despite the fact that many of those cases proved to be based on clerical errors, rather than illicit intentions). They also point to parallels with Russia, the original Cold War foe, with its election interference and social media manipulation. Between the infrastructure and intellectual property attacks of China and the psychological operations of Russia, Washington is squeezed into a defensive posture. Understandably then, this "East Coast" perspective sees the BRI as a power grab by a China determined to challenge the global order led by the United States in what some have dubbed a "Cold War 2.0." In contrast, the second, "West Coast" perspective tempers that notion, suggesting that the BRI expands access for Chinese companies to new markets in ways that could bring closed nations into the global economy. Those we met in Silicon Valley had a less restrained mindset toward

collaboration and the exchange of ideas and expertise. To West Coast innovators, Chinese talent is indispensable, bringing STEM expertise, entrepreneurial gusto and speed, and cash in the form of tuition payments to
institutions at a time when many of them have been strained by hundreds
of millions of dollars in budget shortfalls and COVID-related costs.

These perspectives aren't uniquely American. Germany has tradition-
ally taken more of a conciliatory stance, even though politicians like former defense minister Ursula von der Leyen, who became president of the
European Commission, admitted that China and the transatlantic alliance
countries are "system competitors." National postures within the EU often
shift depending on the domestic party in power, but the European Union
abruptly felt the pressure of Chinese aspirations when Greece announced
a major infrastructure collaboration with China. That project, launched
while Greece's economy was limping and memories of EU austerity measures were still fresh, revitalized the country's port in Piraeus by expanding,
upgrading, and linking it to railway networks. Container handling at the
port grew more than sixfold from 2010 to 2020.[4]

Nothing is as binary as either the East Coast or West Coast perspective on Chinese technology and geopolitical expansion would suggest.
Such black-and-white mindsets only obscure the critical technological and
political nuances that can foster mutual progress and security. Yes, American and Chinese politicians and companies will compete to expand their
influence and penetrate markets around the world, but this race need not
dictate every interaction. The competition over artificial intelligence, quantum computing, and other advanced technologies will not boil down to
simple winners and losers. In fact, while researching the book he wrote
with Mark Nitzberg, *Solomon's Code* (paperback title *The AI Generation*),
Olaf discovered an array of successful models pursued by countries large
and small, collectively seeding a diverse market of intriguing ideas and
products. These models often integrate the American market–led and the
Chinese government–led approaches to politics and advanced technology
development alike. And, in some cases, the emerging ideas have pushed the
boundaries of the prominent two-model system.

We might think of this new geotechnological world as a mountain range
with two highest peaks (US and China) and a whole range of other peaks
around them, not unlike Mount Everest and Lhotse among the Himalayas.
As geological forces move tectonic plates, some of these peaks rise slightly

or sink slightly. For example, Europe remains a seedbed for AI startups, with fourteen of the top 100 AI startups compiled in 2021 by CB Insights being headquartered in Europe, including eight in the United Kingdom.[5] While it's admittedly unlikely that many of these companies will scale to a very large size before one of the notable American or Chinese hyper-scale platforms acquires them, they are evidence that raw entrepreneurial AI innovation prowess exists in more places than a US-versus-China discourse suggests.

As with geology, true technological power shifts don't happen overnight. It takes decades to build the types of deep-tech innovation ecosystems that can foster a large tech platform or produce the top performers who shine across multiple scientific and technological fields. This critical mass, where the innovation ecosystem becomes robust enough that different fields intersect to generate game-changing innovation, is what elevates the existing leaders. However, because these advanced technology arenas fuel both economic-commercial and security activities, we will see intense global negotiations over new advances and a cross-fertilization of ideas from many countries. In contrast to the bipolar alignment of the first Cold War, various political and economic alliances will form and then reform—often around technological capabilities instead of political sensibilities alone. After all, programs that were conceived as economic in nature often morph into security matters over time—whether it's China taking over ports and other infrastructure when host countries are unable to repay its loans, or the US keeping an iron-fisted grip on its semiconductor advantage to control the pace of digital-technology advancement in other countries, especially China.

One might justify a dug-in posture from a national security perspective, but it becomes trickier from an economic one, as it leaves innovators in an untenable position. Consider the critical importance of research and development spending, particularly in basic science, which benefits from collaborations across cultural, geographic, and political boundaries. In a 2021 report, the US Chamber of Commerce noted that a strict cold war posture that decouples the two global powers would cripple R&D investment. The US had invested $511 billion in R&D during 2018, followed by China at $452 billion. Limiting cross-border collaboration would diminish private-sector R&D spending for companies that depend on operations in China, the Chamber argued. It would all but eliminate Chinese R&D investments in the United States. It would limit American investment in countries more aligned with Chinese ambitions. Even US companies without a presence in China would need to remove or reduce the growth potential of a massive market from their plans.[6]

Our current form of globalization, for all its faults, has created a symbiotic interrelationship between countries, one that neither side can abruptly sever without damaging its own interests. The United States remains superior to China at commercializing scientifically rooted "deep" technology, and that helps make it more resilient to the decoupling, whereas Chinese companies tend to be faster at iteratively improving on established consumer-facing tech innovation. Because of this, technological decoupling leaves Chinese firms worse off than US firms, according to a study by Stanford's Center on China's Economy.[7] While Chinese firms might file more patents initially, the study found, their productivity and valuation suffer later because they can't scale out into an American consumer market. American firms only suffer medium term on valuations, likely due to lack of market access in China rather than a loss of innovation edge, the value of which accrues domestically and globally over the longer term. However, it is unrealistic to assume that China will stay at its current levels of science and technology research and development. In the medium run, it will continue to become, albeit maybe more slowly, a dominant innovation power. Can we afford to merely play for a two- or three-year competitive advantage, at the expense of the critical social, security, ecological, and economic problems of the day?

The idea of a Cold War 2.0 is actively detrimental to potential cooperation on climate change, pandemic response, cybersecurity, and other global challenges. If the US attacks China on every aspect of its being, China will push back with equal or greater force. "It now has the size, the influence, the buying power, and the technology to be a country of long-term influence," said Denis Simon, clinical professor of global business and technology at the University of North Carolina's Kenan-Flagler Business School and the former vice chancellor at Duke Kunshan University. "Its ability to set the direction of the global economy is much more powerful than it ever has been." So now, he said, it can follow, break, and help make global rules. Both the US and China, along with each side's shifting affiliations and alliances, will pick the issues on which they disagree, the differences they'll tolerate begrudgingly, and the key areas where they can embrace effective collaboration.

A Thinning Margin of Error

Constructive yet vigilant engagement is never easy, and it might be even harder today because we need to forecast an unknowable future based on a turbulent present. We need to understand where China is going, not just where it has been or is now. An extrapolation from China's fast-paced development over the past forty years won't provide a realistic projection of its future trajectory, explained Nina Xiang, an author and tech expert. The country has started to bump into the limits of how fast it can build self-reliance in semiconductors, quantum computing, and other deep-tech fields, she said. Among those limits are active efforts by the US to control or even damage parts of the value chain. "US sanctions have produced strong consensus in China—from the government to the private sector—that they must become self-reliant in key industries," Xiang said. "No Chinese company feels safe that they can rely on the global supply chain as they once did. It's imperative that the Chinese supply chain is separate and independent."

The choke points to rapid development are too complicated to be solved with more and more money, she says. The lithography machines that fabricate microchips rank among the most complicated machines humans have ever built, and it will take a long time for China to develop the expertise to design and build them. Similarly, it's one thing to develop two or three top-tier universities to support those goals, as it has with Tsinghua and Peking Universities. It's an entirely different matter to develop dozens of these institutions, yielding hundreds of Nobel Prize winners and thousands of world-class scientists who move among these institutions, startups, and corporate labs.

The same holds true for China's global diplomacy and international investment policies. Aiming to be a superpower, becoming one, and remaining one are three very different undertakings. To become a dominant powerhouse in the global economy requires a complex interplay between carefully calibrated power projections abroad and openness at home. As preeminent hegemony expert Robert Keohane has explained, a hegemon needs to be able to forgive some of the infractions against it, like a beekeeper who accepts that a few irritated drones will sting them. At best, China has posted a spotty record of foreign aid and benevolence (its donations of its domestically developed, woefully ineffective Sinovac vaccine notwithstanding). The voices accusing Beijing of neocolonialism and environmental destruction have multiplied since the launch of the Belt and Road Initiative, forcing President Xi to admit responsibility and call for a softer projection of Chinese influence during the 2021 BRI summit. Last but not least, China's early siding with Russia over the invasion of Ukraine might send a signal of defiance, but does little to assure the global community that it stands for a more responsible, peaceful order. No doubt China will learn and will continue to expand its global presence, but it will be very difficult to consolidate hard and soft power leadership in the next decade—especially if it picks a substantial fight with the West.

Make no mistake, any armed conflict would not be an easy and quick brawl. Interviews with two dozen US-China experts on both sides of the Pacific underscored that the US retains military and cyberwarfare superiority, but even US military officials note that China has narrowed the gap. While Washington continues to pour money into defense, China has rapidly modernized its military capabilities—as evidenced, for example, by reports that China tested a nuclear-capable hypersonic missile.[8] According to a US Defense Department 2020 report to Congress, China's efforts to build a "world-class" military have already exceeded US capacities in shipbuilding, land-based conventional ballistic and cruise missiles, and integrated air defense systems. The Chinese Communist Party has asked the People's Liberation Army to develop the capability to project power outside the country's borders and secure its overseas interests and foreign policy goals.

To support these national rejuvenation goals, China pursues a military-civilian fusion development strategy that glues its economic, social development, and security goals. In a key pillar of that effort, China has pressed private firms, universities, and provincial governments to cooperate with the military in developing advanced technologies, including through the covert diversion of research, resources, and intellectual property from partners in the US and elsewhere. Needless to say, this does not contribute to the trust needed to increase collaboration, especially considering the broad array of retaliatory responses available to US presidents under the American War Powers Act. "If we can, at the pull of a cyber switch, devastate all electrical power production in the homes of our enemies, there's no reason to believe that a similar switch in the hands of our enemies can't bring down all of ours," said grandmaster diplomat Thomas Pickering. "So then we have a mutually assured destruction deterrence capability, and rational and reasonable behavior makes a lot of sense."

Despite the echoes of Cold War terminology, Pickering believes the existing impasses open opportunities for greater collaboration on threats such as nuclear weapons and climate change. Beijing has already shown considerable will, at times, to address carbon emissions within its borders, so a clearheaded approach to both the risks and opportunities could help restore some working trust between the countries. "Singing 'Kumbaya' will not get you there," Pickering said, "but hard-headed work might."

Yet, while Presidents Biden and Xi appeared to ease tensions in late 2021, the tenuous balancing act continues to leave little room for error and ample opportunity for miscalculation. The digital version of a Gulf of Tonkin event—a US frigate disabled by cyber weapons or a large regional electricity grid in China brought down by a cyberattack—could easily escalate into armed conflict because we currently have few, if any, valves to release the pressure. As Michèle Flournoy, former deputy assistant secretary of defense for strategy under President Bill Clinton and under secretary of defense for policy under President Barack Obama said: "We don't have any of the structures in place that we had with the Soviets. We don't have a hotline. We don't have strategic stability talks. We don't have an incident-at-sea agreement. We just don't have the risk-mitigation and risk-management structures that we had even in the Cold War in place for the Chinese."

In fact, we would argue that US agencies have only recently started to put in place clearly coordinated strategies on how to deal with China and its international initiatives. More coherent alignment on Chinese affairs with other countries in the Quad—the strategic security partnership between the US, Australia, India, and Japan—and efforts like the G7's $600 billion Partnership for Global Infrastructure and Investment in the Global South have started to solidify that much-needed collaboration with global partners. Yet, given the level of tension generated by the US security guarantees for Taiwan and the organized intellectual property theft by Chinese actors, these initiatives come late and are predicated on competition between the sides rather than collaboration. Competition of governance models is necessary, of course, but it also breeds potential misunderstanding and miscalculation—geopolitical, technological, or otherwise. Absent clear and open paths of crisis communication, those tensions could easily devolve into misinterpretation, or even a conflict that neither side wants.

Media and institutions in the US also tend to put blinders on when it comes to China, mistaking its moves as acts of deliberate hostility, said Chandran Nair, the founder and CEO of the Global Institute for Tomorrow based in Hong Kong and Malaysia. "If I write an op-ed criticizing China," he said, "the mainstream Western media will publish it. But if I give a more balanced and nuanced picture, drawing on facts on the ground, they're not interested." China doesn't necessarily seek to antagonize the US, he said, it simply doesn't seek or want Western advice or approval about its political system. It is happy to collaborate on other areas.

The rise of Beijing's economic and geopolitical power means it no longer relies on a hand to feed it. Conversely, though, it's not readily apparent that China has deeper insight into the US, either—President Xi's rhetoric on "inflicting pain" on America might bolster his standing domestically, but it will heighten resolve in the United States. The same holds true in the West, where the loss of power and privilege blinds many people to the growing global interest in a more malleable and multipolar model of governmental, societal, and economic life.

Of course, this reality clashes with the old belief that globalization would eventually lead to a convergence of countries' development paths. The promise of globalization and the internet making the world "flat," as political commentator Thomas Friedman once put it, never truly materialized. Even as trade, investment, people, money, and data flowed ever more freely, they coalesced into peaks and valleys. Economic gains accrued to most people, but disproportionately to an elite technorati, while tensions and misunderstandings grew more pronounced and complex.

Hence, we need to define a new model of engagement between the United States and China that flexibly designs and navigates key alliances with innovators around the globe. We need to maintain both engagement and vigilance vis-à-vis China in the dozens of worldwide research centers for artificial intelligence and other advanced technologies. We should train a new guard of deep-tech diplomats who can safeguard our projects and ensure compliance with guidelines for mutual safety. We also need to upgrade our multilateral institutions to engage with China on its technological development, lest China and the US regimes harden into a literal and figurative advanced technology arms race, à la the original Cold War.

To guide each of these important steps, we need a new *grand strategy* that integrates scientific, commercial, and security dimensions to ensure a vigilant yet constructive engagement between China and the West. "We can, for instance, agree with China on rules of engagement with countries in the BRI by defining a shared aim—the development of a host country for our respective investments and what exactly that means," Thomas Pickering told Olaf during a 2022 lunch in Washington. "Then, we define a mechanism for settling disputes and for monitoring for misunderstandings" to reduce the risk of escalation. To be stable and resilient, a G7-plus strategy for engagement with China should constantly adjust and readjust between the archetypes of the skeptical East Coast perspective and the cooperative West Coast stance. Indeed, the countries that smartly foster this model of vigilant but constructive cooperation will rise in the new world order.

The Russia Curveball

The Russian invasion of Ukraine in 2022 turned all the geopolitical expectations upside down. In response to its seemingly miscalculated invasion, a majority of countries united behind economic sanctions on Russia and in favor of military aid for Ukraine. With all but a small if potent set of countries—mainly China, India, and a few in Africa and the Middle East—now sanctioning Russia in both the physical and online spheres, it's clear that the rules of engagement have changed in a cognitive economy. Foreign reserves became the primary choke point, allowing outside countries to take at least some control of approximately $630 billion of Russian reserves, limiting the government's transaction capacity to a small number of trading partners. The ability to wield roughly $20 trillion in foreign reserves, approximately a quarter of global GDP, against hostile governments might suit hawks in favor of democracy and free-market paradigms. But nondemocratic countries that saw Russia ostracized by governments, private-sector institutions, and individual activist groups alike could begin to build joint alliances to prevent that from happening, as Thomas Friedman rightly hypothesized.[9] It leaves "strongman" leaders with few good options outside of building or deploying nuclear weapons capacity, destructive cyber warfare, or the creation of economic and political spheres of influence and transactions that evade the current liberal global order. In the worst case, it's all three, and a dangerous flirtation ensues by countries caught in between the parallel systems—especially nations too big to operate as satellites of great powers, but also too small or not yet economically advanced enough to exert the great powers' gravitational pull (e.g., India, Pakistan, Turkey, and Brazil).

These forces might ultimately cause a preemptive decoupling of autocracies from the rest, resulting in a volatile world where an awkwardly placed China drags Russia into alliances as a balance of power against the Western alliance. China's potential rapprochement with India alongside Russia also gets tricky, not least because India has only partially overlapping interests. It holds a decades-long détente with China and, reliant on Russia for weapons and oil and gas supplies, did not vote for sanctions after the invasion of Ukraine. But its democratic government model and quarrels over borders make it a rather tenuous partner. In addition, India is acquiring Western investments in growth-critical technologies, such as semiconductors, to ease global supply chain bottlenecks and to bypass China's threat to Taiwan and the largest global chip fabricator located there (TSMC).

While these forces and alliances will shift over the coming decades, China's massive gravitational pull will steer most of what develops among the autocracies and "swing countries" with one foot on either side of the fence. And Beijing will have a compelling reason to remain engaged with the broadest set of nations possible, rather than retreating too far into bipolar standoff. Neither Russia nor India is a suitable innovation partner for China, which needs to upgrade and accelerate its technological capabilities to escape the middle-income trap and take the path of Japan. That will be hard to accomplish without opening itself to the leading-innovation nations around the world and a more careful treatment of innovators and captains of industry within the country itself. Absent those interactions, it could miss out or have little influence on standards for significant global innovation waves, including the evolution of the Internet of Everything, Web3, and the metaverse.

Cybersecurity: A Virus in the Virtual Lifeblood

If outright physical conflict is too messy, cyberattacks are the cloaked method of choice to curb other countries' power and influence. The world has established institutions and regulations to govern conflict and armed combat. Nations and companies can take trade disputes to global arbitrators. Private-sector organizations like the Institute of Electrical and Electronics Engineers (IEEE) have created vast sets of standards for product compatibility and reliability. Yet despite the growing threat of cyberattacks from state and non-state actors—on targets both international and individual—we have only outdated laws and a patchwork of regional agreements on which to rely. The Budapest Convention on Cybercrime in Europe and the African Union Convention on Cyber Security and Personal Data Protection provide some deterrence and recourse against some of the most disruptive forces in the world today, but the lack of a binding, Geneva Convention–level accord should alarm everyone.[10]

It shouldn't surprise us, though, given the many shades of gray involved in cybersecurity. The civilian-military fusion of technologies, in which malevolent actors can weaponize commercially deployed applications, can make it difficult to draw a line between acceptable and prohibited capabilities and target spaces. Destabilization campaigns through fake accounts on social media networks, while unsavory, won't raise the same concerns as malware that brings down huge swaths of a country's electrical grid. Should both fall under the same set of cybersecurity regulations? And who would decide what actions fall under criminal law or global accords between nations? As William H. Harold of the RAND Corporation, the US-based security and defense think tank, notes in a 2016 essay, "China's economy, the commanding heights of which are controlled by the state, differs dramatically from a market economy, where the private sector and the government are cleanly separated, making the U.S. argument that private-sector actors are illegitimate targets an alien one to Chinese leaders."[11]

A 2015 cybersecurity agreement between the US and China marked a step in the right direction. Pushed after the indictment of five Chinese intelligence officers and the threat of sanctions, as well as the desire to reel in private-sector actors who got sloppy and strayed too far from the Party's mandates, China came to the table to sign an agreement that created a shared space between the two powers' opposing views. Broadening this accord by bringing in US allies might provide a first constructive step toward a multilateral solution. But we cannot pretend to remove cybersecurity accords from the realities of international relations on our analog planet.

"Cyber is just a reflection of the physical world dynamics that we encounter on a daily basis," said Dmitri Alperovitch, the founder and former CTO of CrowdStrike who now leads the Silverado Policy Accelerator. "So if we have polarization in our society, it's going to be reflected in cyber." If we want a stronger defense against nation-sponsored cyberattacks, Alperovitch says, geopolitical tensions must be mended. If we want to reduce misinformation on the internet, we must repair the polarization that pits people against people. If we want less cybercrime, we must figure out ways to encourage our primary adversaries to prosecute it within their borders. Relying solely on technological solutions provides little protection on such a massively asymmetrical battlefield of cybersecurity. There's always another hacker and another way in.

That "in" now includes your body, your cells, and your chromosomes. In a May 2021 paper for the European Centre of Excellence for Countering Hybrid Threats, Eleonore Pauwels raises a red flag about the potential threat of AI-powered cyberattacks on biotechnology.[12] Pauwels, a senior fellow at the Global Center on Cooperative Security and one of the world's leading researchers on the security and governance implications of dual-use technologies, warns that the integration of AI and biosciences creates a whole new cyber battlefield. It's not an especially comforting scenario. State and non-state actors alike have started targeting biomedical data sets and digital infrastructure for both adversarial and commodification purposes, Pauwels writes. Motivations behind the attacks include anything from falsifying clinical trials to sabotaging drug development, and from ransoming biomedical data to undermining trust in medical diagnoses. Such attacks will threaten national sovereignty, our trust in government, and our individual financial security. But what makes these attacks feel especially pernicious is the threat they pose to our physical and mental security. Hackers can now attack people "inside out," by either manipulating digitally stored information about our personal health or, perhaps in the future, finding ways to manipulate biomedical trials, produce drug-resistant pathogens, or hack into our digitally connected bio-implants.

Even the possibility of these unseen and invasive cyber-biosecurity attacks can undermine societal structures and cohesion. If the digital infrastructure that underpins biotechnology is a global public good, Pauwels writes, then the emerging threats will contribute to "a new geopolitics of inequality and insecurity that cuts across societies and borders." As such, the protection of information integrity, explainability, and public trust in biotechnology becomes crucial for the preservation of global security and national sovereignty. Failures here would erode people's trust in governing institutions, emergency data systems, industrial laboratories, food supply chains, hospitals, and critical health infrastructures.

It's almost enough to make identity theft and ransomware attacks feel quaint in comparison. Yet the same asymmetrical challenges affect virtually every security system, whether bio, digital, or physical. Security systems need to defend all kinds of possible vectors at every moment, but malevolent actors need only succeed in one way at one time. So IronNet, a cyber-defense company, has adopted an ecosystem security mindset, bringing together an array of private-sector companies and public-sector agencies to combat cyber threats. The company was founded by Gen. (ret.) Keith Alexander, who previously served as director of the National Security Agency, chief of the Central Security Service, and commander of the United States Cyber Command. Alexander has seen a wide spectrum of cyberattacks, but the emergence of a new class, what he calls "nation-state affiliated hackers," has unleashed increasingly successful ransomware attacks, whose purpose is to steal intellectual property and sell it back to their state sponsors. If a certain country needs IP to fuel its economic engine, it will reward hackers who bring in those resources, with few restrictions on where or how they get them. "You do that here in the [United] States, the FBI will catch you and you're going to jail," he said. "And that happens all the time. Over there, we show pictures of who it is, and nothing happens. They [the hackers] just can't leave those countries now, but they're doing all right. They're making a ton of money."

Given the breadth of the attack surface, the hackers won't stop making money anytime soon—which means, of course, that cyberattacks will continue unabated, as they did throughout 2021. Indeed, when we spoke with Alexander during August of that year, he noted two areas that had seen expanded fallout from attacks. The first was collateral damage that companies suffered from attacks not directed specifically at them. When Russian-backed hackers attacked the Ukrainian tax infrastructure in 2017, they caused billions of dollars in damage worldwide when the malware spread to FedEx, Maersk and dozens of other companies that did business with Ukraine. The second involved the software supply chain—that broad network of companies, government agencies, partners, and others that share connections through an ecosystem of partners. The attacks on organizations using the SolarWinds and Hafnium software systems fit this mold. These are the ones that Alexander and his colleagues worry most about. What happens if somebody who wishes us harm embeds malware in a widely used software ecosystem and pushes the wipeout button? "If every company is going to defend itself, every company will be defeated," he said.

"It's got to be companies and sectors working together—between both the private sector [companies] and the private and the public sector working together. We've got to figure out how to work together in cyberspace for the collective good."

Boiling the Frog

In this book, we harp on the idea of ecosystem- or community-based efforts like these because we need to work together to break down and rethink the paradigm of Great Power relations so we can redesign global systems in ways that address the biggest challenges we face. Nowhere does that collaboration become more critical than in our response to climate change. Absent a coordinated global response to reduce carbon emissions, our planet will become largely uninhabitable. The areas that remain livable will draw massive waves of migrants and grow overcrowded and conflict-ridden. There is no army large enough and no fence high enough to stop this major relocation.

So, we watched in hopeful anticipation as a host of global political and scientific leaders gathered in Glasgow in 2021 for the COP26 Climate Change Conference, optimistic that a breakthrough would activate serious global efforts to reduce carbon emissions. But as things wrapped in Scotland, we couldn't quite tell whether we should be encouraged or disheartened. As it turns out, the many climate experts we interviewed had varied opinions, too.

Wayne Visser, a fellow at the University of Cambridge Institute for Sustainability Leadership, took a fairly positive view. These conferences aren't where the dirty work of global agreements gets ironed out, he said, but where countries and leaders start to build the kind of consensus that leads to breakthroughs. By that measure, he thought COP26 and COP27 in 2022 went reasonably well. "What people should be thinking about is the flywheel process," Visser said. "Each time we meet globally and we bring new policy, we also bring a lot of innovation." For people who wanted to see bottom-line goals, progress made toward them and penalties for those not doing their part, many of the key, momentum-sustaining announcements went overlooked, Visser said. From a systems thinking perspective, he said, even the less-noticed agreements and conversations create an "enabling environment for convergence." For example, ongoing discussions raised the voice of indigenous communities at COP26 and resulted in an $8 billion partnership to finance clean energy in South Africa and a $1.5 billion plan to secure vital carbon sinks in the Congo basin.

But at this point, the many species at risk—one of them being us—might be forgiven for thinking that reaching goals quickly is all that counts. And on that front, Kelly Sims Gallagher, the academic dean of the Fletcher School at Tufts University and director of its Climate Policy Lab, was not as optimistic as Visser. "It's not a surprise, it's just a frustration," she said. "What is it going to take for people to really get serious?" The science and economics of climate change are clear, yet still we struggle to mobilize. We're caught in a political trap, Gallagher said, particularly in the United States. We will need aggressive political action on the national and international levels to create the sticks to drive countries and industries forward on decarbonization. But we need carrots, too, to entice more constructive action.

Absent one or the other, we risk changes in our planetary environment and systems that will force us to reorder civilization rather than make incremental adjustments. While people continue to leave failing states for opportunity elsewhere, climate-related population shifts have surpassed political migration.[13] "Unless the pace of global warming slows or we develop better techniques for adapting to climate change, we're going to see even more migration," said Janet Napolitano, the former US secretary of Homeland Security. "And that will put great pressure on both the countries that are being left and the countries that are being occupied."

The pandemic played a complex role in climate change and public awareness of it. On the one hand, many people began to realize how much waste arrives on our doorsteps from home deliveries, for example. A December 2021 study by Oceana, an international organization focused on oceans, suggested that as much as 23.5 million pounds of Amazon's plastic packaging waste entered and polluted the world's waterways and oceans during 2020, the equivalent of a delivery van payload of plastic dumped into the oceans every sixty-seven minutes.[14] On the other hand, the skies around the world enjoyed plummeting carbon emissions due to fewer commuters in cars, less air travel, and lighter sea traffic as trade volumes eased. The pause was short term and artificial, but it caught broader public awareness and provided a curious moment of pressure during which government officials, such as Germany's then-chancellor Angela Merkel, pleaded with the aerospace industry to take the opportunity to innovate.

Merkel's pleas to the private sector were especially critical given the increasing financialization of the global economy and the role of financial markets as a lever for change via investments in corporations that can mitigate the biggest risks to their operations. The four hundred fifty members of the Glasgow Alliance for Net Zero, a global coalition of financial institutions committed to accelerating the transition to a zero-emissions economy by 2050, collectively account for $130 trillion in net assets, but only $57 trillion had been tied to net-zero commitments as of early 2022. Those commitments didn't go far enough. At that threshold, we continue to exceed the 1.5-degree red line—the forecast temperature rise by 2100 that would result in severe climate disruptions and widespread hunger, drought, and conflict. Perhaps the tipping point for a deceleration of warming lies somewhere between $57 trillion and $130 trillion in net-zero commitments, or it could lie far beyond. There's no way to know for sure, which is why we need to push as far into incentivizing the decarbonization of assets as we can, de-risking these assets in the process.

Fortunately, we have seen a number of market and technological forces emerge to channel carbon back into productive uses, promising financial returns, but the bigger problem might be convincing people that there's no easy fix. Andrew Isaacs, a senior lecturer at UC Berkeley and the director of its New Management of Technology Programs, worries that far too few people grasp the urgency and scale of what's happening to the planet. Like a frog in a slowly heating pot of water, we have yet to feel the burn enough to act decisively, Isaacs said. We've altered the Earth's climate more in the past eighty years than in the previous three millennia, but 90 percent of the additional heat resides, at least temporarily, in the planet's oceans. The seas are now 30 percent more acidic than in the 1940s. The weather patterns, even if more severe, hardly indicate the level of the threat, Isaacs warned. The hope of hitting the 1.5-degree target is all but dead. So it's not a matter of installing a smart meter or some other home technology or software. "There aren't six easy things you can do to solve the problem with climate change," Isaacs said. "There's more like fifty hard things you can do."

As for technological solutions, Isaacs remains skeptical of radical carbon-capture breakthroughs or science-fiction-like ideas to shield the earth from the sun's energy. "Is there technology out there?" he said. "Hell, yes, and it's very familiar. It's not some nifty, groovy thing that involves lasers and nuclear fusion and stuff." By 2020, the cost to produce a megawatt-hour with photovoltaic cells had dropped below the cost to produce the same amount of power with fossil fuels, according to a report from the UN's Intergovernmental Panel on Climate Change (IPCC). As the cost dropped, adoption of solar power cells soared from 2000 to 2020, but photovoltaics remained about 3 percent of power generation, Isaacs said. Onshore wind followed much the same pattern, according to the IPCC—promising, but not close to offsetting our still-massive reliance on fossil fuels for energy.

Ultimately, transitioning away from that reliance requires hard changes in our behaviors, our consumption patterns, and our concepts of growth. "We already have all of the technologies we need to get to net zero, without a doubt," says Visser, the Cambridge fellow. Along with the usual presentations on solar and wind, promising innovations at COP26 and COP27 included green hydrogen, cellular and precision fermentation agriculture, and regenerative agriculture. But none of these solutions work if they can't simultaneously address challenges across the natural, societal, and economic realms. Without this kind of systems-level rethink, all of the focus on mitigation and adaptation seems for naught, as we are addicted to old definitions of growth that say "more is more." We are seeing the underlying phenomenon of untenable economic expansion inadvertently reinforced by our own efforts toward a sustainable global order, rather than changing the underlying structural elements that lead to the imbalance. As Visser said, "That's really what we are looking for—technologies that simultaneously solve a social problem and an environmental problem, or make us more resilient and healthier at the same time."

As the US and China expend north of $300 billion on clean energy and decarbonization technologies in coming years, they both face the specter of massive migration, civil unrest, and skyrocketing insurance and health-care costs. Collaboration to develop and scale out these green energy initiatives will be imperative. Too much is at stake, both in financial and human terms. We need to establish a doctrine of productive vigilance and safe experimentation spaces now, before rising tempers and temperatures bring our better judgment and our societies to a boil.

3 Flexibility or Feudalism: Digital Actors Adrift

By the end of 2021, the share prices of Facebook/Meta, Amazon, and Apple had more than doubled in a year and a half. Apple had blown through an unfathomable $2 trillion valuation mark—a first in the history of our global economy—and then reached $3 trillion in January 2022 before receding later that spring. Shares of Netflix and Alphabet (Google), two of the other dominant digital platforms, traded around all-time highs. Meanwhile, ExxonMobil, one of the oldest and most iconic members of the S&P 500 since 1928, left that index on August 31, 2021.

As pandemic restrictions forced people to move more of their work and lives online, the digital barons went on a shopping spree. Soaring share prices sent the cost of capital for the large digital platforms plummeting, making it easier to create even more value through investments. In 2020, Alphabet picked up $2.25 billion in ten-year debt at an interest rate of just 1.1 percent. In mid-2021, Amazon borrowed $1 billion for two years at just 0.1 percentage points more than the rate at which the US government could borrow. And that cheap debt made it even easier to accelerate the decades-long expansion of their innovation capabilities. Through 2021, Apple acquired twenty-seven companies related to its original business, but made ninety-six acquisitions in new sectors, according to data compiled by the *Washington Post*.[1] Google had made more than a hundred deals in areas outside its core search, advertising, mapping, and mobile businesses. Amazon acquired forty firms in its original e-commerce sector through 2021, but added seventy-one companies in outside fields—including more than a dozen acquisitions to expand Amazon Web Services, the company's most profitable business and the dominant force in the cloud computing market.[2] While much of the global economy suffered through the pandemic, the digital barons never had it better.

We still need these massive digital platforms to help transform and upgrade our economies, especially since we grew more reliant on them in recent years. However, their network effects and their hegemonic control over massive consumer data sets have accelerated the "platformization" of the economy, hollowing it out in much the same way the financialization of the economy did in the 1990s and early 2000s. By siphoning out productive resources, particularly capital, financialization gutted the core of the real economy, which collapsed into the Great Recession in 2007. Like financial services before, digital platforms have become an indispensable and often welcome part of our lives. The products, services, and connections created by the digital barons serve as vital lifelines for billions of people around the world.

But these companies no longer provide just digital services and infrastructure—they now have near-unilateral control over the marketplaces that are built upon that infrastructure. They determine the apps that billions of users around the world can access, and under what conditions. They extract hoards of data from users in hopes of triangulating, via AI and machine learning, the holy grail of marketing—predictions of future behavior.[3] And because of that, they enable vast disparities in consumer choice and privacy.

The outsized power of these companies dawned on us slowly, but we now see how these mature digital platforms tightened their grip on how we connect, find information, or buy goods and services—by exercising a virtual stranglehold on the production assets that are critical for the rest of the global economy. The concentration of advanced AI capabilities in these few corporate hands will lead to even more entrenched market dominance by these digital barons in the US and around the world. In China, for instance, Alipay and WeChat have dominated the country's mobile payments market, making it all but impossible for even large e-commerce companies such as JD.com and Pinduoduo to challenge them.

The pandemic only hastened these trends. While the internet giants and the broader digital economy had started to detach themselves from the Main Street economy already, the dramatic and unforeseen forces unleashed by the pandemic all but severed the remaining bonds between the digital and traditional economies. The platform economy cannot continue to thrive if it leaves behind the tens of millions of businesses and workers who comprise and rely on the "Main Street economy" and the productivity it drives.

Of course, we shouldn't mindlessly stunt the growth of platforms. Rather, we need to ensure that a larger network of stakeholders, not just the AI oligopolists, define how platforms function. For that, we need to craft balanced and thoughtful tethers to ensure that the same digital ecosystem that once nourished the evolution of everyday society and productivity doesn't break free of it entirely.

But make no mistake—even if we rein in the digital platforms, the accelerating cognitive economy forces will transform our systems and lives at every level. We saw the macro effects of China, cybersecurity, climate changes, and other tectonic shifts in chapter 2. But because these forces now permeate our economies, we need to also consider how they change the mechanics of our daily lives on a meso, industry, and market level— how we generate power in markets, safeguard the security and privacy of data, structure our work environments, and calibrate our productivity. Ultimately, we'll need to shape these technological forces to protect our livelihoods and make sure our economic engines can move us all forward.

Data Dreams or Delusions?

The data deluge already generated by the booming internet economy will look positively minuscule when compared with what's coming as the Internet of Things, ubiquitous sensors, and hundreds of millions of new internet users come together. The world generated 64.2 zettabytes of data in 2020, according to IDC, a global technology research firm. Analysts at IDC expect that figure to grow at a compound annual growth rate of 23 percent through 2025, which would mean 180.7 zettabytes of data generated in that year alone.[4] Given that volume, global cooperation on regulatory frameworks will only become more critical to ensure privacy and security. Increasingly, data and data authenticity lie at the core of trust, the most important and most overlooked currency of the Cognitive Era. But trust is a tricky devil—especially in an era of digital misinformation, deepfakes, and fraud—and it's not easily controlled by macro-level global policy.

The health care sector, for example, creates one of the world's largest and fastest-growing depositories of sensitive personal data—1.2 zettabytes in 2018 and forecast to grow at a compound annual growth rate of 36 percent through 2025.[5] All those medical records, test results, and other digitized health information place a high premium on privacy and security, but the sharing of these same data can drive radical discoveries to enhance human health. How do we find that balance? Data restrictions vary widely from one country or region to the next, making life more difficult for research teams, such as those involved in the cross-border efforts to generate a COVID vaccine. And our expectations about privacy often change from situation to situation, said Ayesha Khalid, the Chief of Division of Otolaryngology at Cambridge Health Alliance and clinical director of the Yale School of Medicine Center for Biomedical Innovation. People tend to be far more open to data sharing and digital surveillance when it can save their lives or increase their incomes, Khalid said, even if questions about the ownership of and access to that data remain unanswered.

Regardless of how we react to contact tracing, DNA testing, or any other medical and genetic data-tracking processes, the collection of more and more personal information plays into the hands of existing data brokers, analytics companies, and large digital service platforms. We can and need to debate legal and regulatory structures that can "surveil the surveillants" and keep tracking technologies from infringing on human rights, but we also need to gauge the value and security of our data in more benign places. After all, our heightened reliance on Google, TikTok, and any number of other digital connection platforms throws off data exhaust that becomes valuable input for all kinds of services.

How much value that data has remains a topic of much debate. Michael Schwarz, the former chief economist at Google Cloud, said there is an enormous difference between the average and marginal value of data. The production and processing of massive volumes of data for AI models and other applications make the incremental value of any one bit or byte virtually worthless, Schwarz said. "If you need to do face recognition and you need to train your algorithm, maybe a billion pictures would be plenty," he said. "If there are trillions of pictures out there, the market price of these pictures might be high if they belong to a monopolist. But if each user can sell their own image, the competitive price of the images becomes zero." The sheer amount of data exhaust we shed while surfing the web, exchanging code on GitHub, readjusting our thermostat, or engaging in the millions of other digital interactions makes the value of information from each marginal user virtually worthless, Schwarz said. Google, Facebook, and other platforms offer free services so they can channel huge rivers of data into their digital ocean.

But Schwarz was quick to acknowledge that not all data—and not all demand for data—is equal. "If I want to sell something to you, I want data about you," he said. "And that data is unique and could be very valuable," depending on who wants to buy it, what they want to do with it, how they combine it with other data, and an array of similar factors.[6] So, if you are training an AI model to read California driver's licenses and ID cards, one of more than thirty-four million isn't that valuable. But the first thousand pictures of licenses used to train a new facial recognition model could be extremely valuable.

Consider one possibility that Olaf and his colleagues at Cambrian Futures contemplated while researching data markets: an algorithm that can discern your age and general health status from multiple photos of you, such as old driver's license pictures. Then imagine a batch of those photos being sold to insurance or pharmaceutical companies so they can run actuarial models on your risk profile. In those cases, the only reason those data points don't command a higher price is because they're so easily accessed. They provide actual value to those companies, but nothing makes those individual data points scarce by protecting them or giving you agency over them. The same would hold true for most other use cases that are tailored to an individual user's profile. For instance, microfinance firms might acquire an array of data on your individual psychographics and behavior, correlate your information and patterns with those of thousands of other users, and then use what they find to calculate your personal creditworthiness.

The idea of data scarcity simply does not exist in current digital ecosystems, so all that data exhaust is essentially worth peanuts, according to researchers Jaron Lanier and E. Glen Weyl, who are colleagues at Microsoft. In a September 2018 essay in *Harvard Business Review*, they argue for an alternative perspective that demands "data dignity" as a replacement for the prevailing dogma of "dataism"—in which big data and analytics increasingly define our productivity, mold our mindsets, and dictate our decisions. Rather than a commoditized raw material, Lanier and Weyl suggest we consider data as a form of property, and then establish "mediators of individual data" (MIDs) to serve as a transparent bridge between the tech giants and individuals.[7] The not-for-profit MIDs would essentially act as labor unions for data, handling negotiations over royalties or wages, for example, or collectively bargaining on behalf of aligned individuals. In their arguably optimistic estimation, a family of four could make up to $20,000 in annual income.

Lanier and Weyl had no shortage of critics, but the notion of data dignity—and even a general, anecdotal sense that data is personal property and has value—permeates discussions of the digital and cognitive economies. The "free online services" model employed by digital platforms today has done more than simply shape the relationship between internet users and digital companies. By encouraging people to make personal data so readily available, it has created a vast imbalance between the volumes and value of data exchanged in virtually every kind of business model and digital transaction.

Mechanisms that make the value and use of our personal data more transparent would help reestablish trust in the data economy. Surveys regularly show that people would feel more comfortable sharing personal data if they received an incentive in exchange, but there's a sharp contrast between their vague perception of their data's value and its actual market value. Data brokers trade general information about a person—such as age, gender, and GPS location—for a fraction of a cent per person. Consumer estimates, though, are all over the place. In 2013, when researchers placed a diverse set of 168 people into an auction to determine the value of different types of personal data, the prices settled at roughly $10 for browsing histories and $36 for personal information.[8] In a 2017 survey, US and UK consumers estimated the value of their data at $244 *per year*. And a 2019 survey of US adults pegged the value of their geolocation data at $100 and passport information at $1,000.[9]

The lack of clarity into the value of data has ignited a race to develop transparent and trusted data marketplaces. Most of them seek to create some form of data scarcity and to transition control back to the individuals and businesses that create the data, both of which would enhance value. Some models frame data as labor, for which producers ought to receive compensation. Others have suggested a government-mandated data dividend that platforms would pay individual users. More recent proposals seek to establish market prices in a way that also ensures personal privacy preferences—with higher prices for more sensitive information, and some data not for sale at all. Either way, a trusted marketplace will need to provide a flexible and transparent structure that evolves as the market develops and balances the bargaining power between supply (the data creators) and demand (the data buyers). Whatever the shape a data marketplace takes, governments will play a vital role in determining the legal and regulatory guardrails for the security and privacy of our digital information.

Regulatory Blues

Whatever its faults, the European Union's General Data Protection Regulations (GDPR) established protection of personal data against some of the constant commercial abuses. Launched in May 2018, the regulations gave individuals more control over their personal data and what companies did with that information. While directly effective only within the EU's jurisdiction, the GDPR had ripple effects well beyond, especially on the massive digital platforms that do business there and across the globe. It came as a welcome human-centric signal, even if a bit ham-handed in its overgeneralized approach, and it set a precedent for similar regulations elsewhere, including California's Personal Information Protection Law. Along with experts such as mathematician Hannah Fry and UC Berkeley computer scientist Stuart Russell, we at Cambrian have called for the creation of an independent body (similar to the US Food and Drug Administration) that could test and supervise data and algorithms and limit the chance that these advanced systems would generate a wave of harmful second- and third-order effects.[10]

The EU built on GDPR since it was enacted in 2018, reaching a new transatlantic data privacy agreement with the US, helping create the 2021 US-EU Trade and Technology Council, and introducing the Digital Markets Act, a sweeping set of antitrust rules designed for the large technology platforms. But smaller countries haven't waited around while the EU and other global powers jockey for data policy leadership. New Zealand, Chile, and Singapore signed the multilateral Digital Economy Partnership Agreement (DEPA) in June 2020, establishing new rules and practices for digital trade between the signatories and promoting ongoing discussion about issues such as digital inclusion, inclusive trade, and support for small and medium enterprises in the digital economy. Based on trade agreements and designed to evolve as digital technologies do, DEPA covers everything from digital identities to electronic invoices to artificial intelligence. Among other things, it creates innovation and regulatory sandboxes where companies can safely try out applications to test for negative ripple effects. It also creates a mechanism for secure digital identities that all the participating nations recognize. The agreement has attracted interest from other countries, perhaps in part because it originated outside the established geopolitical trenches of the larger global powers. Canada officially expressed interest in joining the agreement later in 2020, and South Korea did so the following year.

The larger global powers have started to sound similar notes. The US had already started to discuss digital trade agreements with the Indo-Pacific economies, perhaps structured on DEPA. Then, on October 31, 2021, Chinese president Xi Jinping said China would apply to join DEPA directly. "China stands ready to work with all parties for the healthy and orderly development of the digital economy," Xi announced during a virtual speech to the G20 Summit in Rome.[11] Officials in Europe raised new calls for international cooperation on the data economy, in keeping with their interests in expanding at least some of the principles embodied by the GDPR across the globe.

But DEPA is not the only agreement of this kind. As countries recognize that digital and data trade is the future of the global economy—and that small- and medium-size enterprises (SMEs), the backbones of their economies, depend on cross-border frameworks to minimize transaction costs—they gravitate to these types of compacts. None of these agreements are global yet, but interoperability clauses will soon connect them. Already, efforts like the bilateral UK-Singapore Digital Economy Agreement (UKS-DEA), the Association of Southeast Asian Nations' (ASEAN) Bandar Seri Begawan Roadmap on its Digital Transformation Agenda, and the "connected economy" portions of the US-led Indo-Pacific Economic Prosperity Framework have started to link agreements across borders. The World Economic Forum has also launched a Digital Economy Agreement Leadership Group to facilitate best-practice sharing and dialogue around interoperability in Southeast Asia.

"There is a lot of fragmentation when it comes to national digital frameworks today, as countries have tried to understand digital economy dynamics, opportunities, and risks—not just for business but for citizens and national security," said Ziyang Fan, the head of the digital trade program at the World Economic Forum. "One example is the digital services tax, which includes taxation over digital transactions that involve a country's citizens. For some governments, it's a matter of digital sovereignty. It's my hope that we can bridge the fragmented digital policies to unleash the power of connectivity and innovation." Absent this type of bridging, we'll see parallel camps again. On one hand, Vietnam has already enacted regulations similar to China's cybersecurity law, despite their reservations about Beijing's power projection. On the other hand, the California Consumer Privacy Act of 2018 (CCPA) and some of the federal charters and bills in the US, such as the Blueprint for an AI Bill of Rights, read closer to Europe's GDPR and its forthcoming AI Act.

Whatever regulatory frameworks we create to control these increasingly powerful technologies and bridge their application across jurisdictions, we need to recognize, understand, and minimize the trade-offs that inherently come with technology regulation. For instance, policies that call for greater use of surveillance technologies to reduce terrorism could also compromise social, cybersecurity, or other personal protections. And given the varied perspectives on these trade-offs from one country to the next, it is imperative that we revamp our efforts to collaborate across jurisdictions, particularly through setting standards.

If we want entrepreneurs to source the best teams, capital, and data for the best solutions, and then scale successfully, they can't stay cocooned. We need to enable them to reach across borders. UK Information Commissioner Elizabeth Denham said it well during a September 2021 speech at the Oxford Internet Institute: "If we are to unlock the full potential of data-driven innovation, supported by public trust in how data is used, we need an international approach to data protection standards. We need an international solution. We need a data Bretton Woods."[12]

Virtual Identity Scramble

In this uncertain environment, the data we send off into the digital world will increasingly shape the projection of our individual political and human identity, said Eleni Kitra, CEO of the PeopleFirst Group and one of the White Page International list of Asia's 100 Powerful & Rising Women Leaders 2022–2023. Prior to founding PeopleFirst, which helps companies enhance diversity and inclusion in ways that directly impact how people function and perform, Kitra spent nearly a decade at Meta, including as its head of mobility and the culture lead for its Middle East and Africa division. As Facebook looked toward more immersive online experiences and eventually changed its name, Kitra realized the emerging metaverse will eventually force users to reconsider their perceptions of culture, community, and convenience, and different cultures will adapt in different ways. Individuals and organizations will find new ways to connect, resulting in different outcomes, some with troubling consequences, but the merger of physical and digital will not stop or reverse itself, she said.

As more and more workplace activity moves to these immersive virtual spaces, we will need to expand our measurement of work to include more than productivity and output toward an organization's key performance indicators. Especially in the metaverse, we need to include measures of belonging, inclusiveness, ecological health, and worker fulfillment as a whole, Kitra told one of Olaf's UC Berkeley classes in 2021. Our considerations now need to balance the needs of business, the environment, the economy, and humanity as a whole. Workers from anywhere can gain agency in the emerging metaverse, Kitra said, so employers need to give them more freedom to choose how they present themselves to their bosses, peers, partners, and customers.

Companies might encourage more worker contributions to productivity by rewarding effective suggestions and ideas on remote-work improvements, or for support of and bonding with others who bring new facets of remote-work environments or identities to projects. Similar to Toyota's TQM system, employees could be incentivized with status recognition or internal company tokens to improve what might otherwise digress or devolve into looser and looser networks or digital smallness. As Kitra pointed out, management could aim to increase new types of measurements, such as a "Belonging Index" or the "Work They Enjoy" and "Diversity & Inclusion" indices. For some projects or tasks, it may simply be important to drive for more engagement and to show a higher degree of stimulation or interactivity in meetings.

This will require a transformation, of course, and it certainly won't include all industries and types of work, but these multimodal workplaces will become increasingly commonplace. Many companies have opted to retain elements of virtual workspaces and remote work permanently. When we spoke with Liz Pellegrini in 2021, when she was the head of financial services solution engineering at Salesforce, she told us that nearly 70 percent of the staff at one of her tech-industry clients said they did not want to come back to the office full time. "Maybe one or two days a week, because human touch is important," Pellegrini said then, "but they don't need to do it full time."

We will see more and more companies develop tools and policies such as information technology budgets, virtual office space kits, "portal" type tools, sensory enhancement harnesses, upgraded internet connectivity, and new definitions of remote work and workspaces, she said. Talented and inventive workers from around the globe will have ways to interact with teammates and like-minded thinkers. Psychographics—the classification of people based on attitudes, aspirations, and other psychological criteria—will become an increasingly potent enabler of both work and personal pursuits. Our avatars will become our surrogates and, perhaps, our best projection of ourselves to colleagues and the outside world. But as that happens, they also become part of the edge-computing realm on the Internet of Everything, opening us up to psychological attacks on our digital identity and personal privacy.

Reach but Not Richness

When Michael Dell launched his company almost forty years ago in a University of Texas dorm room, he sold made-to-order PCs and shipped them directly to customers. It helped prime the fuse for an explosion of personal computing, putting PCs in the hands of the masses and ushering in the Digital Era. Now, as the Cognitive Era emerges, the distribution of computing power has gone farther than Dell himself might have imagined as a young entrepreneur. In this increasingly connected age, new technologies are bridging some of the most stubborn digital divides. Telecom infrastructure, new 5G and soon 6G networks, smartphones, and other connected devices are putting more and richer experiences at people's fingertips around the world.

Together with the rise in edge computing, which brings data storage and processing closer to the sources of data and the devices capturing it (e.g., smartphones or sensors), high-speed wireless data connections will decentralize productive activities across industries and workforces around the world, said Chuck Whitten, Dell's co-chief operating officer. Researchers forecast up to one trillion connected devices in use by 2035, Whitten said, and the combination of declining costs and accelerating speeds of data connectivity will allow companies and people to process, automate, and do more with the reams of data spilling from all those connections. "Research has shown that improved connectivity, not urban migration, is one of the best ways to help people in the world's rural areas advance economically and modernize their livelihoods," he said.[13]

Whitten and his colleagues argue that modern society has hit "peak centralization in terms of urban environments," so they have positioned the company to help facilitate the decentralization of work and business. This will allow employees and employers to view jobs more in terms of what workers do rather than where they work. For Dell and its peers, that opens up opportunities at all points in the digital ecosystem—from data centers to end devices—but it also puts a greater burden on cybersecurity and trust in those digital connections. "It's crucial that future business, tech, and government leaders work together to form the right global ecosystem around that [cybersecurity and trust], because it's a powerful enabler of improving livelihoods," Whitten said.

The "remote work 1.0" version of systems functioned well as millions quickly adapted to working from home during the pandemic. But in the future, we will see a much more hyper-personalized world where work setups look significantly different for different professions and workers. Whitten expects Dell to play a key role in that transition toward home and hybrid office-home models, but he also knows that critical cybersecurity and trust-assurance risks go hand in hand with that potential. "It's more than just connectivity," he said. "It's 'what are the echo effects of that connectivity?'"

The ripple effects of technology will only grow with the deeper integration of increasingly powerful technologies in our lives. For companies, that means leaders will need to rethink organizational culture—not just ping-pong tables and free lunch, but the fulfillment and welfare of their employees as people in full. So how does a company balance the cost savings and health improvements of remote working with the sparks of creativity and mental and emotional well-being that emerge from in-person interactions? During the pandemic, the cloud-based software giant Salesforce walked this tightrope as well as any large company. It hired fifteen thousand new workers from the onset of COVID through September 2021, when we talked with Peter Schwartz, the company's senior vice president of strategic planning. Schwartz and his colleagues recognized that tools such as Slack and Clubhouse would become integral components of workplace collaboration. Even prior to the pandemic, Salesforce had taken a sizable stake in Zoom, in part because the company believed improvements in digital tools would enhance interaction and productivity. "We're going to get much, much, much better at doing all the stuff that we do now, digitally," Schwartz said. "The tools, the behaviors, how we manage, how we organize, how we distribute work. We're in the early stages of a fundamental revolution in digital work."

Salesforce also took specific actions in 2021 and 2022 to ensure that its employees and key partners can still interact in more personal, fun, and fulfilling ways that spread and enhance the company's culture. For example, Schwartz mentioned the company's Trailblazer Ranch, where employees, customers, and families come together for events, horseback riding, camps, games—and a dose of training and cultural infusion, to boot.[14] "If you start at Salesforce," he said, "that's one of the first places you go."

Intentional measures to ensure that people physically connect, get to know each other, and experience their company and its culture will empower both personal authenticity and organizational flexibility. These measures could help bridge a widening gap that another tech giant has found among its workforce. Microsoft used data from the transition to remote-work arrangements during the pandemic to better understand organizational dynamics in a distributed workforce. Olaf's colleague, UC Berkeley Haas School of Business professor David Holtz, and a team of co-investigators at the company looked at how organizational interactions changed due to virtually everyone working from home. Using telemetry data collected by Microsoft, they analyzed how much communication occurred between workers within and outside their core teams both before and after the shift to company-wide remote work. In short, they found that the organization got more siloed and less dynamic. After going remote, workers within the same formal and informal teams connected and interacted as much as they did while working together in the office, but the serendipitous interactions with coworkers outside of those core groups occurred less often. Furthermore, the set of coworkers that employees interacted with grew less dynamic over time. People simply didn't add and shed outside collaborators as much as they did while in person. "The collaboration network at Microsoft sort of ossified and just kind of froze in place," Holtz explained. "When you look at the collaboration media that people were using to communicate, the main finding is that people shifted away from forms of communication that were synchronous and rich."

As these "bridging ties" between groups become rarer, access to novel information and perspectives diminishes, potentially making it far more difficult for workers to be productive and come up with creative, novel ideas. Workers have fewer opportunities for the types of fully synchronous communication that, by allowing rapid back-and-forth interactions, help groups converge on the meaning of complex ideas. These changes might reduce innovation, creativity, and productivity, Holtz said. And while more immersive real-time tools can help maintain some of those broader connections, flexible work arrangements, company gatherings, and other ways to rebuild some in-person interactions across teams could reestablish some of the lost dynamism. The reach is there. The richness is not.

No doubt key advantages exist in the remote-work environment. Dozens of studies and surveys suggest that, on the whole, employee happiness increased when working from home. The benefits of remote-work flexibility during the pandemic—to take care of kids, parents, or ourselves, for example—appear less well defined but equally important. Even executives and managers found some distinct advantages to not having teams physically together. But problems did arise, of course. An official at one of the world's largest credit card companies told us productivity at its critical call center operations dropped with the switch to remote work in 2020, with an agent's likelihood of solving a customer's problem declining about 20 percent.

Remote work also disrupted one of the most powerful forces in the modern workplace—the informal alliances, office politics, and gossip most white-collar workers rely on to advance their careers. It's not necessarily bad or good, just different. On the one hand, remote work opens up new possibilities for people with different skill sets to advance. On the other hand, many employees early in their careers lost the chance to rub elbows with mentors and engage in the social interactions that help build career-enhancing networks. Without five days a week at the office, at least part of young workers' social lives fell quiet. How might that affect their careers and lives?

Flexibility without Feudalism

Nicholas Carr began worrying about the effects of the internet on our brains more than a decade ago. Finding himself struggling to submerge his mind in long texts, the technology writer started to question whether the bite-size content of the web might actually limit our capacity to sit and think deeply. His thinking eventually morphed into his book *The Shallows:*

What the Internet Is Doing to Our Brains, which was a finalist for the 2011 Pulitzer Prize for general nonfiction. He wrote that when we consume a steady internet diet, we miss out on the meditative act that allows us to replenish our minds and engage more deeply with an inward flow of words, ideas, and emotions, and that loss begins to actually change our neural processes.[15]

Carr's thinking built on a long line of concern about how new digital media and tools affect our minds and mental health. Even technological automation—once promised as the way to relieve us from mundane work—added enough stress to noticeably impact mental health. A 2018 study found that a 10 percent increase in job automation risk correlated with a 0.6 percentage point drop in assessed mental health, with researchers tentatively blaming the dip on job security concerns.[16] The widespread transition to digital technologies appeared to exacerbate those stressors. According to a 2021 survey conducted by Robert Half, a human resources consulting firm, 44 percent of workers said they felt more fatigued on the job than a year earlier. The mental languor reached all the way to the top. Even the leaders of organizations struggled with mental health challenges, as entrepreneurs and top executives self-reported mental illness at higher rates than the general population.[17] One study referenced by Jan Beránek, Group CEO at the digital consulting firm U+, noted that 75 percent of top executives and founders have mental health issues and more than half of workers are disengaged on the job.[18] "The mentally ill leaders lead people who don't want to be there," Beránek said.

COVID delivered a double whammy for workers already struggling with stress and mental illness. Many employers responded with flexible schedules and eased expectations during the outset of the pandemic, as everyone struggled to come to grips with the unknowns about the virus. But as those initial fears mutated into enduring, low-level COVID anxiety—and the additional resources and flexibility started to disappear—even employees who transitioned to work-from-home arrangements started opting out. Headlines in 2021 and 2022 were peppered with references to the Great Resignation, the Big Quit, the Great Reshuffle. An increasing number of the workers who could take renewed agency over their careers removed themselves from cog-like jobs in the workplace machine.

For many white-collar, programming, and other creative types of creative workers, the migration to a "portfolio economy" accelerated in recent years, allowing people to take jobs on the side or cobble together projects and contracts in lieu of drawing a paycheck from a full-time employer. For young people, especially those in Hong Kong and other entrepreneurial parts of Asia, virtual portfolio work became a side economy to boost incomes. But in the coming years, employees who might otherwise stay with a company because of their physical interactions with coworkers could lose those connections in virtual and metaverse work arrangements. Out of sight and out of mind, their loyalty to traditional employers deteriorates.

So does the future of work become an exercise in flexibility, with people free to pursue and secure the work that fulfills them? Or will it descend into feudalism, with oligopolistic platforms and AI algorithms dictating how workers are compensated and what rates users should pay for their services? The $100 billion "creator economy" provides an outlet for some fifty million individuals around the world to share content with others, but these creators still depend on the global tech platforms to find their audience and distribute content. "Despite directly contributing to the value of platforms by uploading content that engages users, creators resemble an underclass of workers, lacking the benefits and protections of employees or the share options that would let them benefit from platforms' success," Li Jin wrote in a 2021 essay in *The Economist*. "I've called these dynamics 'taxation without representation' or '21st-century serfdom.'"[19]

Technology and automation might still help many workers find more fulfilling and productive pursuits on their own terms, but they also open a more dehumanizing possibility. At the height of prewar industrialization in America, the management theorist Frederick Taylor posited his idea of scientific management, which saw humans as production assets whose work could be parsed into discrete tasks—the humans themselves interchangeable. Subsequent theories of work and management pushed the concept into the background, but workplace roles grew increasingly standardized—to the point that many are now replaced by automation, or with AI-powered technologies prone to automation in the near future. The gig workers of these digitized times, and likely those of a metaverse future, might become all the more Taylorized—completely measurable, trackable, surveillable, and interchangeable. They become a set of numbers beholden to an algorithm. They become little more than biological machinery.

It doesn't have to be that way.

Seeing More than Just Biological Machines

Becoming a licensed taxi driver in London means far more than hopping behind the wheel and stepping on the gas. The job requires an extensive knowledge of the city. Drivers have to train for three years, and then they have to pass an exam to prove their grasp of it. In fact, the job requires so much navigational awareness, it changes the makeup of drivers' brains. A study published in 2000 found that London taxi drivers had a "significantly larger" posterior hippocampus—the area of the brain that stores a spatial representation of the environment. Furthermore, the size of different sections of the hippocampus of taxi drivers changed with their experience—the posterior growing larger and the anterior, which mediates anxiety-related behaviors, growing smaller in those who had driven for years. The synapses and connections of those who passed the exam looked far different from those who hadn't taken the test.[20]

The fact is, our biology makes us more than machines—or at least makes us far more adaptable and our thinking far more generalizable than any other machine in existence. Cognitive technologies can surpass human capability in certain areas, but they cannot yet excel in multiple areas concurrently. But while human mental and physical capacity can stretch far and wide, we too often fall into a trap of narrow, machine-like work. Investigators who studied the 2009 Air France disaster, when a flight bound for Paris from Rio de Janeiro crashed and killed 228 passengers and crew, found that the pilots did not respond properly because they had lost touch with previous practices that machines had automated. The pilots had essentially become IT experts with an understanding of aerodynamics and flight mechanisms, and that dulled their ability to respond when the machines failed or provided contradictory information.[21]

Humans have an incredible capacity to expand or shrink to fit their roles. We also have the power to use cognitive technologies in ways that either scale or diminish our capacities. As we found with one bank client, it's not hard for companies to strike a far better balance of human and technological machines. When it hired us, the bank needed new ways to meet "know your customer" compliance standards, which had long relied on humans to review a customer's submitted information and ensure that procedures were properly followed. Bank employees would look at bank statements, driver's licenses, and declared information to ensure applicants' statements were accurate (e.g., for a mortgage application, making sure salary claims matched actual pay). But because humans make too many mistakes, cost too much, and move too slowly, the bank told us, it had switched to algorithms that reduced processing time from two weeks to just four hours. They claimed a return on the investment ten times over.

But rather than simply firing the workers, the bank upgraded their jobs, promoting them to supervisory roles and giving them new assignments. First, they became the critical "expert in the loop" or "human behind the curtain," checking anomalies and making sure that mistakes didn't slip through the cracks. They could interpret or follow up on obscured text or poorly taken photos to decipher information that the algorithm couldn't parse. As part of that, they could annotate the data, essentially improving the machine's ability to interpret a similar problem the next time around. Second, they could handle exceptional cases. For example, the algorithm, built to handle European driver's licenses, could not process a Japanese customer's license. It would make little sense for the bank to develop algorithms for isolated cases, so the bank retained their longtime employees to flex their acquired skills.

This *symbio-intelligent* model of human-machine augmentation undercuts the tendency businesses have to re-Taylorize jobs and boil their measures of productivity down to the lowest common denominator. It imagines how workers can expand to fill new roles and new ideas, rather than locking the box into which they shrink. Unfortunately, though, the most businesslike of dynamics continue to incentivize the reduction of humans to biological machines. Profit motives and accounting practices default to what we can objectively measure, track, or count, so current standards reward investments in machines and software that companies can depreciate, rather than human wetware that usually shows up as an expense. Especially when growth slows, companies begin to view people as a drain on financial resources, rather than an investment that provides accounting and possible tax advantages, so the profit-seeking inertia of business drifts toward automation.[22]

While humans and the innovation and processes they create often generate tremendous business value, that value only reaches the bottom line of the income statement (via increased earnings) and enhances the balance sheet (via greater shareholder equity) when an arm's-length transaction establishes it, explained Larry Louie, an accounting professor and our colleague at Hult. When one company seeks to acquire another, it can see the book value—the assets minus the liabilities—but in most acquisitions the value of the company exceeds what's on the books, Louie said. So, acquiring companies set out to merely estimate the incremental value that the books don't capture, which often includes the value of the human creativity, effort, and passion that makes the company a valuable acquisition target.[23]

The difference in accounting treatment for Mickey Mouse and Spiderman is a classic example, Louie said. Take a look at Disney's accounting books and you can find Spidey swinging through, but you will not find Mickey hiding there. When Walt Disney hired artists to draw Mickey, he paid them a salary, and the company expensed their work. Spiderman and the Marvel universe, on the other hand, came to Disney through the acquisition of Marvel Entertainment, so the less tangible value of all that human ingenuity and creativity to create those brands and characters took on a discrete financial value. Disney had to pay an actual dollar amount for that talent, and that event—the acquisition—provided a quantification of that value. "Any arm's-length transaction creates an event that is deemed more objective," Louie said. That outside event made the value quantifiable and objectively measurable.

Absent such transactions, the less tangible value of human ideas, inspiration, community, and relationship formation within organizations is not always captured. We all know or want to believe our daily productive activity creates this intangible value, but the predominant mantras we teach in business schools and formalize in corporate practices only underscore the tendency to pigeonhole people as human machines. We often say, "You can't manage that which you cannot measure," but how do we measure a person's innate, softer, or more qualitative skills? These less tangible human capabilities that we should encourage in workers as AI and other advanced technologies automate many cognitive processes become afterthoughts in actual practice. We resort to using humans as biological machines because we can measure how many packages somebody puts on the shelf or conveyor belt each hour. It is a short-sighted way to use a human being, but it's what we know, and our accounting and tax policies encourage us to do it. So we create a vicious circle for the bulk of workers whom finance does not recognize as generating value in R&D or brand building. The vast majority become cheaper for the company than a machine, or they become disposable in favor of automation, especially now that advanced AI systems are creating and inventing new content, technologies, and products on their own.

We need a new way to measure the value of humanity in the workplace.[24]

Measuring the Unmeasurable

The pandemic lockdowns and social-distancing measures elevated awareness and empathy for the "essential worker," but they exposed a painfully obvious truth we long chose to ignore—some of the jobs we feel are so indispensable pay terrible wages. These jobs remain in existence and their numbers expand not because we can't do without them but because companies can save money by hiring low-wage workers instead of investing in machines. Full-time workers such as hotel housekeepers make paltry wages, while replacing their tasks with machines would require millions of dollars of intricate technological development.[25] The prohibitive cost of automating housekeeping, restaurant service, and other low-paid service jobs pushes companies to hire humans, who compete with each other—and eventually also with cheaper machines—for those jobs and deflate wages. For workers, it's a race against time, during which they're treated like the machines that eventually compete with them. And while shifting to gig economy arrangements might give workers in these types of jobs more flexibility, perhaps even more income, such job changes don't always address the dangers and hassles of work.

The laser focus on the measurable precludes our opportunity to value humanity for its intrinsic worth. Ironically, though, machines might help us escape the narrow focus on hard data, allowing us to better measure the unmeasurable. Perhaps the ability of AI models and brain-computer interfaces to discover intricate and extremely complex patterns will reveal ways to calculate the concrete value of innate human capacities. If so, we might find ways to integrate both human contributions and human needs into an intelligent paradigm that transforms the human-plus-machine equation into something greater than the sum of its parts. We might just prove that we operate on a higher plane of productivity when our measurements encapsulate what we otherwise perceive as a weakness, foible, or shortcoming. But how do we come up with the right algorithm and data set to capture the value of human skills if we can hardly explain them to begin with?

The emergence of systems that use biological markers and other tracking metrics to measure worker readiness and well-being raise their own concerns about surveillance and privacy. Because most companies still rely on surveys, managers' assessments, or consultants to gauge the well-being of their employees, Beaconforce, a tech company focused on people management, created a system that measures an array of data from employees in real time, including biological vital signs and online interactions with coworkers. The platform uses a combination of tools and practices from psychology, neuroscience, gamification, and behavioral economics to encourage worker productivity and health. As the company notes on its website, its AI systems can "measure employee satisfaction, quantify the underlying emotions, and provide prescriptive actions to decision makers." Most companies deploy these types of systems only with a worker's consent or awareness, but other observational applications keep a constant watch over an employee's proverbial shoulder, often without their knowledge. Workplace monitoring and productivity-enhancing tools have gone well beyond the boss taking a walk through the office to see who's napping at their desks.

Beaconforce, DeskTime, and many similar applications are increasingly useful tools to help monitor employee well-being, protect against human foibles in hiring, or find subtle patterns that could enhance worker productivity, but we cannot forget that they are only that—tools, with inherent limitations. While human judgment is never perfect, it's still the best method we have for processing the rich array of factors we encounter in our businesses and lives, including insights generated through cognitive technologies. If we can use them to recognize and reverse our own biases—whether they overly favor our gut or big data—we open up new ways to measure the value of the human in the loop. We need to take care to tune this balance in ways that encourage the well-being of the organization and the individual. We have an opportunity to embrace these new tools to transform our present leadership challenges into resilience, prosperity, and health for our people and our companies.

Physical Reality in the Digital Economy

Our rapid and widespread transition to digital tools raises demand for better digital experiences, but it also provides a striking reminder of how deeply we cherish the physical, the tangible, and the human-made forces around us. Business at Siemens, the largest industrial manufacturing company in Europe, was extraordinarily strong during the pandemic, said Nicolas Petrovic, who was the CEO of Siemens France at the time. The separation and isolation brought by COVID accelerated the realization among many industries that they needed to transform, Petrovic said, and that real solutions to most of our issues rely on traditional industry. Need more masks or vaccines? Industry delivers. "It's great to have a website or an app, it makes life easier, but you need goods," he said. Home office equipment, gardening tools, noise-canceling headsets, and even that invaluable toilet paper—more often than not, industry will ship it.

The demand for physical equipment and goods began in China but soon spread worldwide, Petrovic said. In the US, for example, consumers sought goods (e.g., a Peloton bike) to replace experiences (e.g., riding the Pacific Coast Highway), so companies hurried to get their factories reconditioned and running. By the middle of 2021, he said, Siemens recorded "amazing sales" as industries invested to replace older equipment and expand production capacity. It was all part of a recalibration of industry and manufacturing that he called the "post-digital world." Such a world doesn't mean we move away from digital technologies, any more than the dawn of the postindustrial society meant we'd abandoned manufacturing. Rather, traditional industry, existing digital tools, and emerging cognitive technologies will build upon one another, bringing together the digital-virtual, biological-ecological, and physical-infrastructural. The post-digital society is the truly cognitive society, where AI, data, quantum, and other advanced technologies allow people and businesses to go into and beyond physical limitations, gain much deeper insights into the structure of the now, and craft better strategies for the future.

One can see this at play as more and more companies build intelligent twins that mirror real environments, running them through simulations to test new market ideas, supply chain designs, or other hypotheses. According to the 2021 Technology Vision report from Accenture, 87 percent of executives agreed that digital twins are becoming essential to their collaboration and strategic partnerships.[26] "Intelligent digital twins are changing how businesses operate, how they collaborate and how they innovate," the report said, "and enterprises that get left behind will struggle to participate in the markets and ecosystems of the future." The advent of digital twinning, edge computing, genomics, and other dynamic technological forces will transform industries in the Cognitive Era. As Petrovic notes, the coalescence of the ecological crisis, the importance of speed, agile factories, the pursuit of perfection, and the use of data and connections will force companies to overhaul their operations.[27] While our human affinity for creation and construction in the physical world will not fade, we will continue to move toward the virtual and digital, especially at the level of global interactions and networks. Businesses will need to shape and live up to new physical-digital hybrid identities as they integrate rapid technological change into their internal operations.

Companies will experiment more with 3D manufacturing, onshoring, and supply chain reconfiguration to develop antifragile practices. As *The Economist* noted in its May 14, 2021, issue: "The way to make supply chains more resilient is not to domesticate them, which concentrates risk and forfeits economies of scale, but to diversify them." Multi-shoring with production facilities at home and abroad provides a layer of resilience and flexibility that allows companies to adapt to disruptions, but it only works if we keep an eye on efficiencies everywhere. Those layers of complexity will require new cognitive technologies that optimize the multi-shored whole continuously. New technologies like 3D printing, for example, will allow for more cost-effective configuration of these new webs of channels. Companies will also look beyond Zoom to develop virtual experiences that feel more immersive and ease the friction between physical and digital interaction. Social distancing, cost pressures, and the resulting changes in our geography of work will accelerate the convergence of videoconferencing platforms, game-rendering engines, and augmented reality technologies in systems that foster deeper collaboration and richness of experience.

Indeed, cognitive forces will spark all kinds of new innovation in technologies and platforms that aim to enhance or complement our personal and professional lives. Nowhere is that as evident as the emergence of new ways to collaborate with and pay each other for our productivity. Blockchains, Web3, and some flavor of the metaverse might well take their place among the primary underpinning technologies on which we interact and transact in the cognitive economy. (We discuss these and the other operating logics and phenomena that various forces are sparking in part III.) But as the workplace drifts further toward the virtual, we will find it increasingly difficult to maintain the current sensory and intelligence capabilities that feed how we learn and relate—as well as the socioemotional satisfaction and relationships that physical interaction fosters. We, as individual workers and people, will need to strike a similar balance between the potential of the digital and our persistent need for the physical.

As businesses adopt these new technologies, people and the machines they design will need to adapt to new ways of relating and building trust, and workers will need to acquire the relevant skills these new types of jobs and work environments require. But as humans, we will also need physical closeness or rich multisensory experiences to create the intimacy and understanding on which deeper trust, beyond a few transactions, is built. If we can imbue our human-machine partnerships with that kind of trust—one that is based on caring and that holds communities and societies together—cognitive technologies could transform the intimacy of our interactions with friends and colleagues across the globe.

4 Inside Out: Tech on the Brain

Bryan Johnson is on a quest for zeros.

The enigmatic founder of Braintree, former CEO of Venmo, and founder of Kernel, which develops brain measurement and imaging systems, Johnson has made it his mission to discover the kinds of once-in-a-generation factors that radically alter the way we understand the world. He seeks "zeros"—the discovery of fundamental building blocks, tenets, or rules that previously seemed impossible or beyond our vision.[1] They're the discovery of something that didn't exist in our limited minds, lingering in an alternate dimension until finally pulled out of the ether and into our field of perception. Albert Einstein's theory of relativity, for instance, set scientists on a new path of stunning breakthroughs in quantum mechanics, astrophysics, and cosmology, but none of those subsequent discoveries opened up the same step-change in scientific thinking as $E=mc^2$. As these types of life-altering building blocks get defined, new ways of thinking emerge. In the cognitive economy, powerful forms of computational intelligence will accelerate them. For example, the AlphaGo system's radically unexpected moves in its victories over Go world champion Lee Sedol hinted at how deep learning systems could offer other step-change departures from the forces, logic, and patterns we take as gospel.

We struggle to identify extraordinary new forces because our existing biases and expectations belie their existence. Johnson endeavors to clear away those boundaries with what he calls "zeroth-principle thinking." If the concept of first-principles thinking boils considerations down to the fewest number of assumptions possible in a given time frame, zeroth-principles thinking doesn't exclude any possibilities.

One of Johnson's zeroth principles is the idea that the human body and mind do not reside in an exclusive plane "above" the natural environment that surrounds us. In fact, with the advent of AI, CRISPR, and other "inside-out" technologies, we have even begun to blur the distinction between wetware and software. The integration of digital technologies and human and other biological material has created what Johnson describes as "programmable molecules and organisms." We will face a reckoning with what it means to be human in the biological, technological, and virtual worlds.

As artificial intelligence and biological sciences evolve, Johnson argues, the human conscious mind will lose its "preeminent position of unquestioned authority and be supplanted with a much broader distribution of agents in negotiation" with one another. If these zero-type discoveries arrive faster and faster with new computational intelligence, they might exceed our ability to understand and integrate them into our lives, our societies, and our economies. But we can grow and change with the new realities and empower ourselves with new technologies and knowledge, as well. "We are the first generation that has ever been confronted with the situation that we will evolve into a different form of conscious existence," Johnson said. "No other generation has ever had that possibility, and we do. And therefore it invites us to think on that scale."

Doing so requires the imagination and willingness to engage in a far more comprehensive partnership with the world around us. Whether COVID or climate change, Johnson said, the problem comes down to a matter of goal alignment. We don't talk about most natural organisms as having goals, but a virus exists and has an effect on biological life. What if, Johnson asks, we could align the "goals" of those organisms with our own? Imagine, for example, a distributed environment of intelligent agents throughout all spheres of the environment, a mesh of intelligence that could form, say, a global biological immune system. In theory, we could program fundamental elements to recognize and respond to new viruses in real time. A monthslong timeline for vaccine development would seem painfully slow, rather than shockingly fast. We can and should seek to develop the capacity to detect a viral threat, manufacture a vaccine, and distribute that vaccine globally in almost real time, he said.

It sounds like science fiction fantasy, but all the scientific elements to accomplish these kinds of breakthroughs already exist. For example, Johnson is refining an algorithm that would help him care for his health better than he can on his own. His Project Blueprint measures more than seventy of his bodily organs to routinely generate data on hundreds of biomarkers.

Having weighed that data against the results from more than one thousand peer-reviewed scientific reports, Blueprint generates a plan to improve his health. "The process [has] enabled my heart, liver, kidney, and all my other organs and biological processes to directly speak for themselves," Johnson said. He has built what he calls his "Autonomous Self." The result: in 2022 he set a world record for epigenetic age reduction, effectively reducing his biological age by 5.1 years in just seven months. According to one measure, his biological calendar flips at just three-quarters the speed of actual calendar time.

These types of intersections between digital and biological forces will transform humanity at the most micro levels, changing us and our identities from the inside out at a time when identity politics is already testing capacity for tolerance and adaptability. This is the essence of the cognitive economy, where cognification injects cybernetics functions into the global economy. New advanced technologies connect the dots across infrastructure, ecology, biology, and psychological systems, transforming perception into sense-making and sense-making into automated action. That shifts the dynamics of power and income in favor of those who can enable, gatekeep, and optimize these emerging human-to-everything relationships, and it makes trust the most important currency going forward. Naturally, then, some of this chapter's examples of how emerging forces meld the digital, biological, and environmental might give us reason to pause: innovations in brain-computer interfaces (BCIs), generative AI, organoids, genetic engineering through CRISPR, and the use of psychedelics in treating mental disorders. But with the possibility of transformational benefits in a cognitive economy, we will not stop for long.

"Humans have never stopped, ever," Johnson said.

Technology Turning Us Inside Out

Remember that moment you first fell in love—the invigorating, giddy feeling that made the sun on your skin just a little warmer? Imagine feeling that same sensation on demand, by pressing a button. Or perhaps you might prefer ending your conference call forty-five minutes earlier, because you plugged into a system that allowed everyone to communicate simultaneously. In the coming decade, breakthroughs in quantum computing, artificial intelligence, and brain-computer interfaces will enable machines and humans to model and understand entirely new dimensions of the world and significantly augment our capabilities. Already, each of these fields has developed applications that hint at futuristic scenarios. But as those technologies and trends converge, interact, and integrate, we will see an even deeper symbiosis of human and machine that alters the fabric of our economies, our societies, and our everyday lives.

Unlike the classical computer, which can only run one path after the other until it finds the way out of a two-dimensional maze, quantum computing can run all the possible paths at once. The result: computing power is increasing substantially. While "quantum computing" remains in its infancy, we've already seen instances of "quantum information" analyzing new molecules for drugs; banks developing powerful fintech applications; and automakers testing ways to improve traffic management.[2] Indeed, even if we are still years away from having the hardware for quantum computing available for popular use, the immense potential of quantum lies in the combinations of classical computing (which runs machine learning) and quantum. We can see this combination being expanded even further when you consider these developments colliding with yet another key technological development: brain-computer interfaces, which connect a human or animal brain directly to an external device for recording or stimulating brain signals.

Plenty of work remains, but technologically speaking, scientists have solved many of the most difficult barriers to making at least noninvasive BCIs work. Companies like Neuralink and Kernel are now testing technologies that are intended to cure a range of mental illnesses. BrainQ, an Israeli startup, already combines machine learning with neuroscience, following the maxim "cells that fire together, wire together" to train damaged neural tissue to refire. General Electric, Kernel, and other private-sector members of the US-backed BRAIN Initiative hope to take this confluence of technologies to the next level, aiming to augment individual patients suffering from epilepsy, Parkinson's disease, or posttraumatic stress disorder.

The potential benefits of integrating these and other technological fields establishes an almost moral imperative to keep pushing the frontiers of research. Opportunities to heal trauma, learn more about our world, and increase human well-being and happiness around the world should compel us to drive these innovations further. But let's not be naive: the widespread adoption of AI-powered BCI technologies comes with considerable risks, as well. Jaan Tallinn, one of the founding engineers of Skype and Kazaa, is well aware of this dichotomy. As cofounder of the University of Cambridge Centre for the Study of Existential Risk, Tallinn can wax philosophical about the art of the possible. Yet he's also keenly aware of the potential ripple effects from the deployment of existing technologies. "We talk about a drastic difference in topics between what exists and what might exist five years later," he said. A poorly designed AI might decline a credit card application this afternoon, he said, but it might start a nuclear war tomorrow.

How do we balance the immense potential with the existential risk?

Taming the Beast

Researchers have seen unusual human-machine interactions derive from loneliness, according to Matt Johnson, a colleague at the Hult International Business School, where he is a professor and researcher specializing in the application of neuroscience and psychology to the business world. The pandemic, Johnson said, has created a "market opportunity for loneliness," but researchers had long since found that humans often turn to technologies to fill their emotional voids. "When people send in their Roombas for repairs, they don't want just another Roomba back," Johnson said, citing a 2007 study by researchers at the Georgia Institute of Technology.[3] "They want *their* Roomba. They build actual emotional attachments to these things."

In normal circumstances, Johnson explained, people naturally engage in "social cognition," a process through which they form an internal model of another person's consciousness—a sense of what it's like to be them at that moment.[4] When people become lonely, they can turn this social cognitive mechanism toward inanimate objects. "Roomba didn't try to be a companion product, but we see this in terms of people getting more and more attached to their Siri or their Google," Johnson said of his own research. "And now there are new products which are designed to be companions, and they're galvanized by this general effect that when we don't have human contact—when we are experiencing loneliness [or] we don't have close friendships—this distorts our social cognition, such that these appear to be more real."

Loneliness doesn't just mean social isolation, distance, or exclusion, either. As explained by labor economist Noreena Hertz, it extends to a feeling of disconnection from politics, the workplace, and coworkers that leaves people feeling powerless, voiceless, invisible, forgotten, and forsaken.[5] In

Japan and the US, lonely people can now rent a friend or family if they need it, Hertz writes. Even when we're constantly connecting through videoconference platforms, we can't decipher social context as fast or as deeply as we can in the physical world, according to research by organizational psychologist George Kohlrieser, a professor at IMD Business School in Lausanne. As tech dependency takes deeper root in the years to come, it will likely become a cause of new, currently undiagnosed mental health issues, Kohlrieser said.

Malicious attacks on mental well-being will also grow increasingly dangerous as the biological, environmental, and digital fuse more fully into our lives. Nicholas Davis, industry professor for emerging technology at the University of Technology in Sydney, Australia, cofounder of the Human Technology Institute, and an expert on the Fourth Industrial Revolution, suggests we consider plausible ways that discontinuities could merge. For example, an illicit actor could create an artificially intelligent agent to propagate social media abuse at scale, targeting people with existing mental illnesses to cyberbully them into self-harm. In essence, Davis muses, a malevolent actor could use the sophisticated targeting methods embodied in the social media platforms' algorithms to find entry points with an initially willing, at-risk audience—and then bombard them with abuse that triggers a wave of suicides.

Pain and Collaboration

The influence of existing digital technologies on our mental health and physical well-being only amplifies when cognitive technologies tie directly into our brains and bodies. As the biological, environmental, and digital merge, we will see incredible AI-powered advances in genetic engineering and tailored pharmaceutical designs (e.g., mRNA vaccines). We will grapple with the intersection of cybersecurity, biological, and environmental upheavals (e.g., a combined cyber and biological attack during a natural disaster). And we will marvel at the technologies this cognitive confluence produces to heal, augment, and enrich our lives (e.g., BCIs that ease neurological disorders). And as technology helps us gain a greater understanding of the complex world that surrounds us, we will find more and more radical breakthroughs at the intersection of different fields (e.g., psychedelic drugs and psychotherapy).

The emergence of new cognitive technologies, which can plug digital directly into our physical existence, will only accelerate the biological-environmental-digital integration. BCIs have accelerated faster than anyone would have predicted a decade ago, said Matt Johnson, our colleague at Hult. Back then, almost all the work on these implants focused on medical treatments, such as ways to stimulate dopamine production in patients with dementia or Parkinson's. Now, Johnson said, researchers are tackling other uses, such as language acquisition chips that allow two people to speak in their native tongues and automatically understand each other. Language-processing functions occur across multiple locations in the brain, he said, so these applications will probably remain well into the future. But the promise of BCI technologies has made companies like Neuralink and Paradromics magnets for money. Investment in the sector hit an annual record within the first eight months of 2021, tripling the $97 million raised two years earlier, according to a VentureBeat report.[6] Around the same time, an analysis by Allied Market Research projected the global BCI market would grow from $1.5 billion in 2020 to almost $5.5 billion in 2030.[7]

It's easy to see the excitement, especially given how tantalizingly close some applications are today. For example, vision is mainly localized in one area of the brain, so researchers are testing systems that route visual information around damaged optic nerves and, using BCI implants, stimulate the occipital cortex directly. With a pair of glasses or implanted lenses connected to a brain implant, researchers might restore sight. Like most BCI ventures, this one is only starting to emerge from the deep science stage, and many struggle to find the right business model and product-market fit that will allow them to scale. But that will happen as the hype recedes—even Google Glass, the much-maligned smart glasses introduced to the public in 2014, found focused applications. The idea of BCI lenses that process physical and digital signals simultaneously could seamlessly integrate machine augmentation with both the human and the natural environment.

Kenneth Ford, the founder and CEO of the Institute for Human & Machine Cognition, spends his days focused on these confluences, particularly on machine augmentation of human capabilities. People have a long history of enhancing themselves, Ford explained, but those enhancements are beginning to replace more of what we considered innately human. Rather than just donning eyeglasses so we can see better, Ford says, we can now add "cognitive orthotics"—systems that help us process the world or make rote decisions so we can concern ourselves with more important things. Virtual reality and the metaverse could lead to a new renaissance and a period of material abundance, but we could just as easily evolve into a chairbound species living in our own virtual sphere of fear. "It's up to us," Ford said. "For the first time in human history, we get to choose. Up until now, we didn't get a choice."

This dawning of cognitive orthotics and deeper human-machine augmentation gives Ford both hope and pause. For one, he asked, who benefits from these advancements? Serious questions of equity arise when some people can afford and/or access a technology that others cannot. Second, he said, we tend to underrate the power of human choice and autonomy in these relationships. Early on in the development and thinking about AI, Ford said, he and other researchers spent too much time talking about whether AI was possible. They viewed it as outside the human, as a truly independent thing, rather than in a framework of human-machine interdependence. "If we're working on a project together, we have a shared mental model of the project [and] ways to work together," he said. "We can direct each other in concert. With machines, currently, it's at an incredibly primitive level."

Today, people bring virtually all the adaptability, learning, and fit to the human-machine equation. In the future, the machine might learn and adapt to the peculiarities of the individual, potentially closing some of the skills and job-training gaps in the workforce. Maybe the factory robot will learn how to work with the human worker, rather than the other way around.

New Tech, New Life

Similar questions about the interplay of human and machine gnawed at Chris White in recent years. White and his colleagues at Microsoft Research Special Projects, where he is general manager, shifted significant resources and attention to the pandemic—and, in particular, to the inevitable future disruptions that viruses were bound to cause. His "mad science department" in Microsoft's research arm quickly realized that these societal crises would come more frequently and be more severe, so they shifted their focus to concepts like "societal resilience," "sociotechnical innovation," and efforts to convene public- and private-sector collaboration around the role technology plays in solving major societal problems.[8] The heads-down lab bench approach will no longer work, White said: "If we want to address these very large issues of coming crises with climate and health care, with political instability, and with the rise of an AI era, then we have to be planning for it from a research perspective—on what technologies are needed to fill the gaps, and what relationships are needed to be robust."

We might create resources similar to the US War Powers Act, which gives the president authority to summon industrial capacity for grave national security threats. A similar mechanism for existential climate, health, and education crises might corral R&D actors that haven't already stepped up as Microsoft did. Connecting these actors with digital and other infrastructure that helps coordinate resource and knowledge flows could deliver an immensely potent platform for speeding up and coordinating responses in ways that keep pace with infection rates or supply chain pinch points. (Of course, we probably want a central policy-steering body to ensure it happens in the interest of the general public, not corporate stock prices.)

We can't solve every problem with technology, White said, and we limit ourselves by trying to do so. But technology can contribute incredible and critical components for the solution. By way of example, White described two intriguing possibilities opening up with our expanding understanding of organoids. Organoids are like tiny brains, hearts, or other organs that scientists can grow using stem cell techniques. With mini brains developed from someone's stem cells, for example, researchers could better predict whether new neurological drugs will work in clinical trials. And by modeling the dynamics of an organoid's structure with AI and quantum computer systems, White said, we might accelerate our understanding of neural, biological, and chemical interactions without experimenting on live animals or humans. Eventually, we might implement that understanding to create new types of computing models that more closely mimic the beautiful complexity of human bodies and brains.

We have gone from incredibly powerful and fundamental technological innovations that helped us manipulate the outside world—the wheel, the lever, the pulley, the robot—to breakthroughs that allow us to manipulate more and more of the internal—BCIs, nanotechnologies, mRNA vaccines. We might even come to accept the more beneficial biological manipulations as part of our very "selves" and our subconscious minds, as something that becomes of us rather than in us. Consider, for example, the increasingly accepted emergence of psychological therapies that use psychedelic substances, mainly psilocybin and MDMA. The introduction of these drugs into an intense and hands-on psychotherapy regime has shown remarkable effectiveness for treating deep-seated temperament and personality patterns in patients, explained Richard Roston, a psychiatrist at the Oakland Medical Center in California. The combination has gained more credence with US regulators, too. Rather than relying on traditional forms of medication and talk therapy programs over the course of years, if not indefinitely, these new approaches combine psychedelics with a regimen of roughly eighty hours of rigorous psychotherapy over a few weeks or months.

The treatment can trigger bursts of anger, sadness, and other intense emotional states, Roston explained, and the sessions can last for hours, with therapists needing to work directly and continuously with patients as they go through the therapy. In these altered states, patients begin to disconnect from existing patterns and piece together new ways of understanding themselves. "It's not like you come out a different person, but a lot of the neuroses—a lot of the places people get stuck—are no longer there," Roston said. "In a sense, they become *more* themselves. They become more settled in who they are, because they're less identified with who they were."

The potential of these therapies, BCIs, and other cognitive capacities to cure neurological diseases, enhance cognition, and even improve general physical health is tremendous. And yet, as with anything new and unproven that goes inside our bodies, the introduction of these digital, biological, and genetic technologies into our most intimate selves still feels invasive. Digital technology always reshapes and sometimes erodes our identity as humans, because our brains and bodies don't operate in narrow, binary economic terms. So, what would technology look like if it were shaped around the whole brain, not merely as an extension of the brain?

Designing around the multiple experiences of life—making machines that are brain friendly, body friendly, and environmentally friendly, for example—would transform what technology looks like. After all, human intelligence is a function of the entire human organism, not just the brain, and our entire human experience is fed by that. But to do that we need to flip our relationship with emerging generations of inside-out deep tech. Instead of it being a one-way street on which we learn and adapt to technology, technology should also learn from us and adapt to us. Human technology needs to mold itself to our makeup, whether physical or psychological. Our identities and capabilities will and should still morph, of course, as humans have always evolved through our use of tools. But this time around, the power over the power tool needs to rest in the collective of individual hands, not the dopamine-stimulating algorithms of digital platforms.

This will undoubtedly require safeguards. As technologies reach deeper into our brains and biologies, we need to take special care. Already, we've seen how the algorithmic narrowing of our social media feeds can lead people toward more fragmented and extreme perspectives, robbing us of the diversity of views that help forge commonality. We have called for the creation of regulatory processes similar to the Food and Drug Administration's drug testing to review algorithms that have far-reaching social impacts, as well as the creation of sandboxes where social media algorithms can be tested for unintended consequences prior to mass release.[9] And in chapter 9, we discuss some additional safeguards for a variety of innovations.

If we get this right, the combination of human and machine can produce powerful results. Human chess players regularly practice with and play against computers to hone their skills, but some of the most sublime playmaking emerges from "advanced chess" or "centaur chess" tournaments that pit human-computer teams against each other. But we need to think carefully about which technologies we adopt, and then anticipate and prepare for their second- and third-order effects. We need to enhance human experience and judgment, rather than replacing them. And we need to create the feedback and regulatory loops between digital, biological, environmental, and human systems that allow us to capitalize on opportunity while safeguarding against unforeseen consequences. If we fail to create those loops, the imbalances will lead to greater technological disruption of our minds and bodies—as well as our economic, geopolitical, and societal systems. But if we get it right, we will enter new frontiers for human growth.

III   Logic and Phenomena

5 Connected, Not Convergent: Integrating a Fragmented World

A family cannot build a loving home when factions feud. A company cannot maximize success when employees do not share a common purpose. A community cannot maintain playgrounds and parks when its residents don't share a sense of collective responsibility. Convergence does not make everyone the same. It is a confluence of purpose, resting on the recognition that our paths cross, intertwine, and overlap—and that all our journeys are safer and more rewarding when we work together to dismantle the barriers in our way. Convergence focuses on shared solutions that work in our collective interest. While the forces that transformed the world in recent years made us more connected than ever, they did not lead us toward greater convergence. Rather, they established a new operating logic: connected, but not convergent.

The first wave of globalization generated significant convergence around trade, connected most national economies, and created a freer cross-border flow of people, commerce, and information. In most circumstances, globalization occurred as a consequence of a fledgling trade model, a network of suppliers organizing themselves around shared production and becoming the primary driver of global manufacturing and distribution. Technology enabled this, and then itself became the world's main connective conduit as the internet expanded and billions more people connected to the web. Despite all the recent trade wars, tariffs, and talk of decoupling between the two global powers, US exports of goods to China had hit a record high in 2021, and imports were at near-record levels, according to US Census data.[1] As China quickly recovered from the initial pandemic lockdowns, US and European companies were understandably eager to restart the flow of supplies for products that were stuck in their pipelines, most notably in the automobile sector.

Under the surface of this economic globalization, however, societies and their institutional ecosystems remained highly fragmented. In an interview for this book, Parag Khanna, the author of *Move: The Forces Uprooting Us*, compared the world's heightened connectivity to a rope.[2] The rope connects people, groups, and nations, and the expansion of the internet extended that rope to billions of people who never had a handhold on it before. We can use that rope as a guide to new people, markets, and information. We can use it to tighten the bonds between our existing friends, families, and communities. And we can use it to pull people toward our products, our expertise, and our beliefs. We currently use that rope in a great global tug-of-war, Khanna said. It's not your usual tug-of-war, though. Yes, the two great world powers and their allies often pull in opposite directions, but in some cases they pull in similar directions. And, increasingly, small groups are finding one another and trying to pull their own way. With so many strands being pulled in so many different directions, the rope begins to fray. Some use the rope as a weapon, actively or inadvertently pulling apart the connections forged by others and undermining global efforts toward a common purpose, such as coordinating pandemic responses.

In geopolitical terms, this tug-of-war has raised the stakes on the effectiveness of governance models, pitting one against another in a battle of influence over data, information, and the infrastructure that channels it around the globe. When infrastructure meant a bridge that connected two countries, the neighbors shared a common interest in maintaining the span. But the vast network of global digital and data connections doesn't foster shared interests. And when countries don't see as much at stake, nothing really prevents them from steering away from or disrupting the existing order. Regardless of whether that turbulence will move us toward a better or worse world, our increasing connections and decreasing convergence make it far easier to pick a fight, to isolate, to alienate, or to actively attempt to break down our collective humanity. So while our economies remain globally intertwined, our politics and identities diverge.

However, regionalization is not necessarily antithetical to globalization. It's not a coincidence that at the height of the pandemic, when we were all supposed to be retreating into ourselves, the US, Mexico, and Canada passed three major migration measures and the European Union's monetary union continued to bind much of the continent in a regional order despite Brexit. It's no coincidence that China and fourteen other Asia Pacific countries signed the Regional Comprehensive Economic Partnership, and the US orchestrated the fourteen-member and growing Indo-Pacific Partnership, setting standards on supply chain security, clean energy, labor conditions, and the environment for roughly 40 percent of the world's economy.[3] "It's fundamentally human at times of crisis—you just look over the fence to your neighbors and say, 'Hey, can you help me out?'" Khanna said. But of course, creating spheres of influence is also deeply geopolitical. As tensions and uncertainty flare, new tribes and clubs form.

We have split into spheres—in some cases guided by the idea of "locally physical, globally digital"—but fragmentation can appear within those spheres, as well. The layering on of more political, digital, cultural, and individual complexity drives us toward divergence even on an intraregional basis. If we once believed that technology would simplify our lives into easier-to-process binary options, we can now see the full extent of our naivete. Technology has created ambiguous choices, not either-ors. We have a hard enough time with our individual preferences—balancing convenience against privacy doesn't come down to one simple answer. The same holds true for global interactions among dozens of regions, hundreds of national governments, and billions of people.

Meanwhile, in an interconnected world where small biological flutters can bring down global economies and systems, our dependence on complex, shared solutions has become more vital than ever. Pandemic-scale viruses require an interdependent response, but we won't agree on those collaborative actions unless we discover a form of interdependent and interoperable tribalism that allows most of the strands on Khanna's globally connected rope to pull in concert when necessary. The simplicity of "best practices" no longer works as effectively, because the people and institutions in one country might reject, or even take offense to, something that works in another. On almost every level of human organization—governments, businesses, social networks, and neighborhoods—our connectedness has made it easier to share products and ideas with others. But in our search for simplicity and efficiency within the global complexity, the same connectedness has helped reinforce the walls we've built around ourselves.

Rebuilding Value Chains in a Multi-Crisis World

When Sven Egyedy, the chief digital officer of the Federal Foreign Office of Germany, hunkered down at the start of the pandemic, he and his wife had three children, a cat, and a small garden plot in the yard outside their home near Cologne. By the time he spoke with us in September 2021, his brood had expanded to include six chickens, a fully grown garden, and a dog. They now had a very dense network of neighbors—"like going back to an old village," he said—and a lot of them now owned what they called "Corona chickens." Some in the community had concerns that they might have problems getting enough basic food items because of supply chain problems, Egyedy explained. Groceries such as flour and yeast had been rationed by supermarkets, and people wanted to gain independence when it came to their nutrition supplies. Corona chickens became popular "within weeks" of the quarantines, he said. And now he hopes they never go back, on both the community cohesiveness and the poultry. "Will we have more local sourcing on food?" he asked. "I hope so, because self-produced chicken eggs are really good, I can tell you."

The pandemic's sudden, stark reminder about the fragility of global supply chains shocked governments, businesses, and individuals alike. Months after our conversation with Egyedy, fully loaded ships lined up outside of US ports, waiting on truck drivers with empty rigs to haul the growing towers of containers into the heartland. All the advanced technology designed to streamline and track products from factory to farmhouse could tell you exactly where your product was, but couldn't do a thing to convince more truck drivers to hop in their cabs and head to Long Beach or Oakland. A family in Texas refurbishing their kitchen could find out exactly where in the world their delayed shipment of cabinet door handles was, but no one could predict when the shipment would arrive at its final destination. So, like Egyedy and his neighbors, people turned to the connections and supplies they could trust.

Someone like Egyedy, in his role at the Federal Foreign Office, will inevitably maintain a global network. But even he noted that his office lost something as the worst of the pandemic limited travel and forced some of the office's staff to return home. Whereas before he might meet Ruslan and Mitra on one day and Fatima and Evanson the next—what he called "this really vivid exchange of ideas globally"—he now needed to rely more extensively on his German colleagues' retelling of their interactions overseas. The initial physical limitations imposed by the pandemic lockdowns prompted a deglobalization, which accelerated as countries adopted different responses to the COVID threat. "Something that was broken, really broken, by COVID-19 was this exchange of cultures, of ideas," Egyedy said. "All these networks that you have globally have been broken down or at least have been disturbed."

The restrictions on physical interactions affected more than human networks, of course. With people isolating, logistics and supply networks also started to fracture, as factories closed down, customs and export-import offices went unstaffed, and brick-and-mortar store traffic waned. Global supply chain expert Richard Wilding used to advise retailers that people wanted fun, ease, and control over their shopping experiences. When the pandemic arrived, he added safety to that list. Going to the store was no longer fun and easy, and shoppers didn't feel in control or safe. E-commerce and digital services boomed, accelerating an ongoing shift to "servitization," said Wilding, emeritus professor of supply chain strategy at Cranfield University. Consider the morning coffee drinker. Nespresso sells them a Bluetooth-enabled coffee maker for a relatively low price, and then seeks to deliver the coffee they want directly to their doorstep—easy, fun, consumer-controlled, and safe.

Only one problem: Nespresso had to revamp its supply chain specifically for home delivery of their coffee servings. While it had managed to reshape its distribution prior to the pandemic, most big retailers ran into this problem once COVID struck, Wilding explained. Sales went through the roof, he said, but profits shrank. "They were using their old supply chain structures to operate in the new world," he explained. "And therefore, a big area we have to look at is cost to serve." Some companies have sought to onshore, with automation making cost of labor a smaller factor in their calculations. Some of the more forward-looking companies have started to "multi-shore," Wilding said, retaining multiple suppliers but in different areas, so blockages in one artery—a container ship stuck in the Suez Canal, for example—don't shut down flows. Yet, like Egyedy and his neighbors, businesses might also start to look increasingly local for the physical production of goods.

Spheres of Influence: Ascending Powers?

The combination of multi-shoring and other new supply chain strategies will alter the variety of goods consumers can buy, particularly in developed economies. Yet the adaptation of global systems to the reality of "physically local, digitally global" could restore stability and trust far beyond the value chain itself. For all the pleasure of Egyedy's home-raised chickens, the disintegration of global networks moves us in the wrong direction. We will need to develop grand strategies that advance collective welfare, but also carve those complex game plans into digestible pieces upon which individual people and businesses can act—smaller, smarter, and interoperable so they generate more trust.

As one might expect, proximity and familiarity have played the strongest roles in the clustering of regional spheres around the world, as cultural or geographical affinity shows the clearest correlations and congregations. The myriad forces that bind these spheres together shift and sway across different sectors and different times, but two spheres have ascended to greater prominence: Africa and Asia. Africa and the rest of the Global South are poised to take a dynamic new role in the global economy. With its massive, digitally native young population and their greater access to local startups in AI, blockchain, and decentralized finance, the continent's economic development and global influence are on the rise. Countries in Africa will become larger and more important data creators within the next few years. Consider that Pew forecasts Nigeria to grow to a whopping 733 million people by 2100, becoming the third-largest country.[4] Given the huge potential for internet expansion—eight of the ten countries with the lowest internet connectivity rates in 2019 were in the sub-Saharan—data volumes will almost certainly skyrocket in the coming decade. Already from 2012 to 2020, the number of IPv6 address registrations in Africa grew by 3,400 percent, compared to 300 percent growth in Europe and 200 percent growth in North America and Asia.[5] As Kai-Fu Lee, the prominent Taiwanese-born AI scientist and author, has noted: "Whatever company wants to lead in AI and wants to become the next Facebook or Google needs to have a strategy to tap into the markets of developing countries—this is where the consumers of tomorrow live."[6]

Given Africa's size, the number of countries on the continent, and their internet-enabled economic growth rates, African nations should have a more prominent voice in global economic and technological decision-making, said Monica Kerretts-Makau, a professor of practice and academic director at Arizona State University's Thunderbird Center for Excellence for Africa. "The way Africa is constructed with fifty-four countries, it really should be sitting at the table more in almost all the different (international) agencies, but it isn't," Kerretts-Makau said. "It is always still being boxed into this continent, Africa, as one country." She hopes that better communication between African countries gives rise to more influence on technological and geopolitical matters for 1.2 billion culturally heterogeneous people, rather than an underweighting of the continent as one disadvantaged sphere.

The ascendancy of the Asian sphere, meanwhile, had already become clear in the rise of China and the other "tigers" in the early 2000s, but the region's global reemergence from the COVID-19 pandemic, at least at first, accelerated the sense that the profitable center of gravity had shifted there. In several key ways, China and other Asian countries initially managed the crisis better than the West. Their economies rebounded sooner, and their citizens worked more collectively to manage the crisis. The Asian style of "mixed capitalism," unlike the purer capitalistic liberal democracy in the US or the half social capitalism in Europe, involves the active participation of the state in the private sector. "You don't have a corporate sector that almost actively tries to circumnavigate regulation or tries to circumnavigate the government," said Paras Anand, chief investment officer of Artemis Investment Management. That mindset proved especially effective during the early days of the COVID-19 pandemic, keeping a number of markets open while allowing governments to close off the biological flows of the virus. The populace in many Asian countries more readily accepted the data and other surveillance tools that helped authorities track the spread of the virus, and they more readily complied with the government orders to mask and isolate.

Whether one defines that as success, especially over the long term, depends on political perspective and philosophy, but it no doubt proved effective in economic and, for many countries, political terms—and that success has contributed to the sense both within and outside the region that Asia is the proverbial place to be. "You've had a more successful management of the pandemic, which means you can create a shorter path to recovery," Anand said. "But the second issue, which I think is really interesting, is . . . the much closer integration within Asia as a region." The general perception of Asia as the "factory floor of the world" bears some truth, but most Asian trade flows within the region itself. With its economic recovery, Asia proved more than just its resilience, Anand said. It "has proven its lower dependence on the rest of the world for its economic growth."

Anand noted that the looser alliance of ASEAN countries, particularly as compared with the stricter integration of the European Union, might have helped those countries to react quicker to the pandemic and economic crisis. At a time of fragmentation, when the nation-state has gained importance and borders have become increasingly important—as we've seen with the nationalistic Brexit vote—the combination of cooperation and flexibility in these looser alliances could prove more effective in adjusting to economic, technological, climate, biological, or other types of shocks. This is especially true in a region where responses from autocratic and technocratic regimes move fast, compared with the politically slow democracies in Europe. But this doesn't necessarily mean that Asian, and especially Chinese, modes of governance will ride an easy wave of ascendancy over the coming decade. "Authoritarian systems are better placed to set and pursue long-term goals," said Bilahari Kausikan, the former permanent secretary of Singapore's Ministry of Foreign Affairs. "However, that is only an advantage provided the decision was a correct one in the first place." That's the weakness of an authoritarian system—there is a single point of failure—and Asia's ascendence will rely on its governments' abilities to accommodate debate about decisions and directions. At the moment in China, for example, President Xi has "created a tiger and he's riding it," Kausikan said. "He can't get off because it will eat him."

Spheres of Influence: Fading Stars?

The US, Europe, and the Westphalian systems of global governance remain primary forces around the globe, but they have shown signs of strain. The American Dream that offers hope for both economic opportunity and social integration retains tremendous gravitational pull, but it has weakened as opportunities increasingly accrue to the fortunate few, rather than the masses. The EU's progressive social values have come under their own pressures, with the Schengen agreement that allowed freer movement between member countries suspended during COVID, and the economic and common data markets showing signs of splintering. We now have a stratification of "principal agent dilemmas," with politicians serving parties rather than people, and nations pursuing their own interests at the expense of global cooperation. We went from a language of alliance to one that occasionally sounds global but leads toward fragmentation and nationalism.

"COVID has seen the revenge of the nation-state," said Anja Manuel, a former diplomat, the cofounder of the consulting firm Rice, Hadley, Gates & Manuel, and the author of *This Brave New World: India, China, and the United States* (2016). At a moment of great global crisis, attempts at broad cooperation took a back seat to national interests. Everybody scrambled to shore up their national supply chains, and a sort of vaccine nationalism emerged. "When push comes to shove, the structure of the international system is still dominated by the nation-state," Manuel said. "We've seen through the pandemic that the international institutions are only as powerful as the nation-states that make them up."

While the UN and other global institutions still play a vital role in coordinating worldwide cooperation, the effectiveness of regional alliances such as NATO, the Quad, and others has chipped away at the dominance of some international organizations, allowing for different governance regimes that are less focused on the traditional concept of globalization as we think of it in the West. The complexity of this multipolar world exacerbates the divides and blocks the flow of people, information, goods and services, currency, and other resources. Nothing illustrates this better than the backlash against cross-border migration: Little has changed for wealthier elites with the resources and options to live in dozens of different countries, but US and European attitudes have shifted against those who would migrate in search of relief, safety, or opportunity. The owner of a Vietnamese restaurant we visited in California arrived thirty years ago with no money, but he built a business and sent his kids to college. That classic narrative of coming to the US to build a life has changed; significant shares of the US and EU populations view migration as a problem at best or demonize it outright, rather than seeing it as a growth opportunity.

Perhaps the most remarkable aspect of the American Dream isn't that it's fading, but that it existed as long as it did. The US ranked twenty-seventh out of the eighty-two countries on the World Economic Forum's Social Mobility index in 2020, below Scandinavian countries, Malta, South Korea, Japan, and the United Kingdom.[7] But given the comparative social, political, and economic complexity in the US—and the fact that few countries want to even play the role of being a destination country at all—the US model remains extraordinary.

As these Western values and geopolitical systems come under attack by mostly internal economic, political, and social forces, less liberally democratic countries in Asia have done a better job of delivering the goods for their citizens, increasing their standard of living instead of growing blunt economic measures like GDP. And in many cases, they have delivered those goods on a national or subnational level, which is more tangible and moves the needle more than global mechanisms. So, the prevailing global coordination mechanism, whether the Bretton Woods agreements or far-flung industrial supply chains, have been replaced by regionalization in some domains, most notably trade.

No doubt nationalism, populism, and protectionism drive much of this. As we wrote in early 2022, the UK had ordered 367 million vaccine doses—more than five times enough to vaccinate its population. Canada, Australia, and New Zealand had enough stocked for at least four doses per citizen.[8] While many residents in those countries opted against the vaccines, many countries in the Global South could only get enough to vaccinate a fraction of their populations. The results only accelerate a rising anti-globalization sentiment, particularly among the many people who haven't reaped its benefits (or have seen elites reap an unfair share of them), shifting the balance of parochial versus collective interest, even in countries that have reaped the most benefit. A recent study found that 44 percent of the EU-wide respondents are against globalization.[9]

Of course, most Americans and Europeans who decry globalization as a concept don't buy domestic goods merely because they're domestic. When they do buy domestic, it's because they believe those goods are comparable or higher quality—someone who can afford Cartier will not buy a cheaper local brand. Yet, affluent Western consumers show no signs of flocking to the latest luxury fashions from China, which they perceive as substandard despite the culture's rising global influence. As Jeffrey Sachs, the director of Columbia University's Center for Sustainable Development and former director of the Earth Institute, has noted, both American culture and politics are poorly attuned to national and global realities. Whether it stems from unfounded cultural stereotypes or fundamental political differences, misguided attitudes in the United States inhibit the deep systemic changes we need in financial reform, regional integration, global cooperation, and technological transformation. As Sachs has often suggested, including in his book *The Ages of Globalization* (2020), the US political effort to hinder China's development is just one example of a short-sighted perspective that makes it more difficult to foster the kinds of global cooperation necessary to work toward true sustainability worldwide.[10]

Yet, despite the retrenchment and weakened credibility of US leadership in many parts of the world, people are still drawn to the freedom of the United States' markets, the freedom it offers to elect leaders, and the freedom to shape one's own narrative and path—not to mention its relative safety and stability (albeit with periodic convulsions). It is still the leading global power, and it will remain so in tandem with China, with Europe and India as critical partners. But its current strength lies not in the state and image of its democracy, which are damaged, but rather its resilience and recoveries, its long record of personal and economic freedoms, its rule of law and due process, and its range of opportunities to build life paths. It continues to bolster that standing with a long and growing list of iconic innovations and companies, legions of cutting-edge entrepreneurs, and brilliant scientists and artists, all while projecting its soft power of culture and narratives through the media and entertainment industry and its economic power through a transparency that makes it a safer haven for investors. Combined, all these factors have created trust that, while fragile, remains higher than in other places that may have fewer oscillations but offer less opportunity. This is especially true for the US deep-tech economy, which is more vibrant but also more vulnerable than in other countries. As the global economic order reincorporates around a new flow of capital, talent, and resources with an ever-stronger emphasis on data and DNA, the US could either widen its lead or have it all come crashing down, depending on how well it generates trust.

Digital Smallness

Most developing countries still lack the infrastructure, resources, and talent base to capitalize on the multimodal work paradigms that will define the cognitive economy. If systems or programs cannot bridge that divide faster than they are now, these economies risk further bifurcation between an elite technorati and a population of digitally marginalized, environmentally and biologically exposed outsiders. Digital technology drives GDP more than ever, and that will only continue as the cognitive economy further automates our lives, changes the sets of tasks required of various jobs, and creates new deep-tech careers. By 2028, the developed economies in fourteen of the G20 nations risk missing out on as much as $11.5 trillion in their cumulative GDP if they don't address the skills gaps within their borders, according to a 2018 report from Accenture.[11] That amounts to 1.1 percentage points of lost growth. But the loss rates will be even higher for developing countries *during each year of that span*, the report found— annually, 2.3 percentage points in India, 1.8 in South Africa and Mexico, and 1.7 in China and Brazil. Contrast this with the approximately 0.5 percentage point losses for the developed G20 countries included in the study.

Disconnected workers could lose out even more, as jobs that incorporate higher levels of digital content pay better. For every 10 percent increase in the intensity of information and communications technology tasks in their job, the average US worker's salary increases 4 percent, according to a November 2021 report from the Washington-based Information Technology & Innovation Foundation.[12] Those findings underscore just how technology skills have reshaped the job market. A long-term study by MIT labor economist David Autor found that middle-skill jobs declined sharply from 1970 to 2016, while both high- and low-skill jobs boomed. This barbell shape—with the middle hollowing out as automation replaces human labor in production, clerical, and sales roles—is what the divide between the technorati and the disconnected looks like.[13]

This trend will likely increase. A 2020 World Economic Forum report, for example, estimated that automation processes will displace another eighty-five million jobs worldwide by 2025. Yet technologies don't only polarize people's income within countries; they can also widen the gulfs between countries. The evolution of the immersive metaverse, with its intense demands on data, compute power, and bandwidth, would become an alternative universe of wealth, digital creativity, and innovation that might capitalize on but almost certainly not include the digitally disadvantaged. Does anyone believe Elon Musk will take the least skilled, lowest-income Earthlings along to Mars? Will Mark Zuckerberg decide to pass up on that next billion dollars in favor of eliminating rapacious facial recognition systems from *all* of Meta's products? No wonder connectivity has not led to greater convergence.

The earliest imagineers of the internet dreamed of a network that could connect our disparate selves and broaden our minds, and in many ways the web did that. But algorithms that stuff us into filtered bubbles, especially on social media platforms, narrow our minds—even among the digital elite. The "like" button that was conceived to promote connection among users now feeds into animosity and opposition. Toxic tweets are retweeted significantly more than benign ones, while pupils in the UK humiliate their teachers as part of a TikTok challenge.[14] We no longer leave space for tolerance. As Theodore Roosevelt proclaimed, "In a republic, to be successful we must learn to combine intensity of conviction with a broad tolerance of difference of conviction." Instead, we're opting to devolve into cancel culture, or cries against cancel culture. We need to have honest conversations about who should be allowed to fail, which jobs we should automate, and how society should support workers who bear the brunt of decisions that lead to "digital smallness."

In many ways, the idea of the internet's long tail went to its logical end, creating smaller tribes with narrower interests. These tribes devolved into in-groups connected by small ideas, defined as much by what others aren't as what they are. It's natural for human groups to develop this way, coalescing around a "we're this" identity and a "they're not us" out-group identity as well, said Matt Johnson, the Hult professor who specializes in the application of neuroscience and psychology in the business world. Research suggests that oxytocin—the "love hormone" that stimulates many of a mother's bodily reactions around childbirth and that impacts bonding behavior, the creation of group memories, and other social functions—might also play into broader in- and out-group tribal affiliations. "There are more and more ways to engender this sort of great in-group comradery, which I agree we don't want to just dismiss," Johnson said. "We're social creatures. We're tribal by nature. But there are ways of inculcating this in-group comradery and this sort of shared identity without relying on a clear enemy to build up hostility towards."

Social media platforms undoubtedly provide value in keeping us connected, and many have fantastic potential to broaden our perspectives and forge new relationships and networks. Instead, their algorithms and our own myopic decisions have made us increasingly paranoid and parochial, focusing our attention on overly curated (and often fake) messages, moments, and snapshots. The tools squeeze us into keyhole-sized point-to-point lines of sight, devoid of any context that could create empathy and connection. And with the transition of office work into virtual spaces, digital smallness spreads anew in the realms of workplace collaboration, creativity, and productivity. In a February 2021 report, Daisy Fancourt and Alex Bradbury at University College London reported that 23 percent of the workers they surveyed said that their relationships with colleagues or coworkers got worse over lockdown. We are gradually losing the so-called theory of mind of others with whom we are supposed to collaborate— building a story in our heads about what is going on in someone else's head. Empathy gets lost in noise.

Digital smallness does not just limit our thinking and empathy skills, though; it reshapes our behavior, as well. For example, a 2017 study by researchers at Stanford and Cornell found that some people are born with a predisposition for "trolling" behaviors, but other social media users will also engage in these behaviors when the mood and context of the discussion prompt it.[15] We don't yet know how severely this narrowing of tribes will impact productivity in organizations, for example, but the very justification for building organizations is to maximize trust while minimizing transaction cost, and digital smallness threatens to erode both if we can't engage beyond the confines of the narrow workgroup "tribe."

Identity Meets Equity

The confluence of advanced technologies offers so much potential to improve the world, so we need to allow fresh ideas to bloom. But we must also acknowledge that the broad societal masses might not be equipped to benefit from these advances—even if they have the expertise they need. When we had to teach remotely, one of us taught an MBA student from India who was sharp and clearly possessed the skills to handle digital learning. She had high-speed broadband access, but she asked if she could access the recordings of the class anyway. Asked why she'd want to spend all that time rewatching the lectures, she explained that electricity outages often disrupted her ability to attend class in real time.

These kinds of equity issues continue to confound even the digital titans and the richest countries. The share of the global population that used the internet only topped 50 percent for the first time in 2019, according to data from the International Telecommunications Union.[16] Efforts by Facebook, Google, and others to expand access to high-speed data have helped nudge that figure higher, but their initiatives continue to fall victim to cost or government intervention. And while a larger share of the population in more affluent economies have high-speed access, significant gaps remain there, as well. President Joe Biden's Build Back Better plan included more than $1 billion to expand broadband access in both rural and underserved urban areas, but even that is only a fraction of the trillions of dollars needed to build out 5G and other broadband infrastructure.

Equity concerns only begin with digital access. We have seen the bifurcation between the technorati and the merely connected developing for years now. The isolation experienced during COVID took that to new extremes. Frontline workers risked far more exposure to COVID than office workers who switched to remote working arrangements, and illness only widened the wealth gap between the digitized and the disconnected. The charity group Oxfam called it the "inequality virus," noting that it took just nine months for the fortunes of the top thousand billionaires to return to their pre-pandemic highs, but it could take more than a decade for the world's poorest to fully rebound.[17] Broad elements of society fed off those divides to foment greater dissatisfaction, using the increased digitization and "data-ization" to vent their frustrations about the lockdowns and challenges of life.

Religion infused many of those questions about identity and equity, said Shreya Nallapati, the founder of Neveragaintech. The organization, which Nallapati founded in 2018 after a gunman killed seventeen people and wounded seventeen others at a high school in Parkland, Florida, uses machine learning models to better understand the causes of mass violence in hopes of preventing future instances. In 2021, Nallapati and her colleagues applied their deep learning models to data they procured from fringe communities online, which included QAnon discussion threads from 8kun and Parler posts before and during the US Capitol insurrection on January 6 of that year. "Our research discovered that the biggest, often overlooked appeal in joining the insurrection and related activities centered around a religious calling to destroy evil and bring light by usurping corrupt structures," Nallapati said. "Q, the author of QAnon, would often make religious references in the text—referring to the movement as an act dictated by Christ and an imperative for Samaritan participation."

The same strong sense of anger, frustration, and alienation permeates other extremist efforts around the globe, Nallapati said. The combination of lockdowns and loss of employment during the pandemic exacerbated social exclusion and marginalization for many, and extremist groups found it all the easier to rally disaffected people against others. Once again, tribalism began to shift from affinity for the in-group to antipathy for the out-group, as the balance of cognitive and emotional factors swung to an extreme. Ever-widening digital connectivity took that to scale. "The internet fostered the globalization of QAnon," Nallapati said. "What was once limited to the United States has now disseminated to Japan, India, New Zealand, and other countries, all with their own take on the conspiracy."

Yet the same connections work both ways. The digitally native generations are now much more interconnected, and they have ramped up the scale and reach of their activism. Young leaders hold a unique opportunity to bridge intergenerational and international tensions to connect not only with their peers but with, say, the unemployed coal miner or the Congolese farmer who just got their first smartphone. Whether these young design activists will launch a groundswell of new designs remains to be seen, but as the cyber merges with the physical, so also will identity merge with inequity. Young leaders who can better accommodate the cyber-physical integration have unique tools to address inequity and, through them, establish elements of common identity—bonds that could connect a wider array of people and perhaps establish more effective forms of governance.

6 Catching Mice: Governing in a Trustless World

When Bilahari Kausikan began his diplomatic career more than four decades ago, Singapore had not yet become the global economic powerhouse it is today. The concept of globalization extended no further than cheaper manufacturing in less affluent economies. Kausikan spent about twelve years as Singapore's second permanent and then permanent secretary at the Ministry of Foreign Affairs, helping spearhead the nation's international relations during its meteoric economic rise in the first decade of the twenty-first century. He'd come to that role with an array of appointments under his belt, including as Singapore's ambassador to Russia and, from 1995 to 1998, to the United Nations. He now chairs the Middle East Institute at the National University of Singapore, where he continues to observe the tides of Asian and global relations. Few people on the planet have deeper experience with the shifting winds of globalization and governance.

Today, Kausikan said, we face an especially urgent paradox, one that gives him cause for concern. Throughout the world, the political logic within nation-states runs counter to the international cooperation needed to preserve common goods, he said. Efforts to mitigate damage to the earth's climate threaten the drivers of individual national economies. Spreading vaccine doses across the global population would help limit the emergence of new COVID variants, but no national leader will ship doses at the expense of vaccinations or boosters at home. The cognitive economy would gain from tremendous breakthroughs in algorithms, computing power, and bioengineered medicines with greater pooling and sharing of data, but countries and companies default to tighter controls—whether for good reasons (security of personal data) or questionable ones (populism or a single-minded focus on profit). "It's a contradiction between what needs to be done to manage global problems, global commons, and the state structure," Kausikan said. "But the state structure, despite many predictions of it disappearing, isn't disappearing."

With that state-dominated global system-of-systems, the resilient roots of which go all the way back to the Peace of Westphalia of 1648, refusing to fade gently into the past, effective governance needs to begin at the national level. In many cases, that narrowing domestic interest has led to a leadership vacuum, where complex and significant problems fall into the hands of simple and small leaders, as Carnegie Endowment fellow Moisés Naím writes in *El País*.[1] But in many other countries, particularly in Asia, competence has taken precedence over ideology. As geopolitical adviser and author Parag Khanna told us, "Asia is not interested in democracy. They're interested in good governance." Effective governance relies on a complex mix of variables—a government that one citizen calls effective could feel woefully inadequate to another—but any good governance at least begins with a sense of safety and stability. This allows a thoughtful exchange between different stakeholders, an analysis of options, the weighing of costs and benefits to all stakeholders, a final time-sensitive decision, and a communication of the rationale for that decision. The complexity and volatility of today's interlocking systems make all these steps extremely difficult, especially when confined to narrow political interests that seek to criticize the "other" rather than finding common ground. In the uncertainty of complexity, everyone scrambles in a zero-sum battle for the sliver of certainty they can find—identity, income, security, or environment. It's no surprise, then, that the policy experts who want to bring relief to as many constituents as possible fall victim to the demagoguery of strongman politicians who exploit these wickedly difficult situations.

With safety and stability destroyed, good governance cannot grow into the web of frameworks that make government work for the broader populace, make public services easy to access, and facilitate shared prosperity. The specific mode of political decision-making—democracy versus autocracy, for example—begins to matter less and less to populations, especially in Asia, so long as the public sector attends to its citizens. Perhaps the famous quote by Deng Xiaoping sums it up best: "It doesn't matter whether a cat is black or white, as long as it catches mice." Yet, for governance to be effective, people have to believe that their governments and institutions will catch the mice they need. Doing so requires a level of empathy with the various constituencies within a population.

Some governments, arguably smaller and more homogeneous ones, such as New Zealand, lean toward this responsiveness; others, often autocratic regimes like China's, approach policy on a purely macro-statistical level that objectifies their constituencies. Either way, the forces of change at the dawning of the Cognitive Era—including the major global and technological forces discussed in previous chapters—have transformed governance at all levels. Rather than a traditional balance between representation, efficacy, and the preservation of power, the emerging operating logic and phenomena in today's societies, markets, and domains require different approaches to sensing and integrating the diverse needs of constituencies—as well as the governance that responds to those demands. Ideally, governments will not simply react to disruptions but will use smarter cognitive tools to sense arising points of fragility and to proactively shape responses for them. Calls for new measures of prosperity and effective governance have started to arise, seeking to replace mere GDP as the benchmark for national success. The notion of "beyond GDP" is already shaping up in more formal ways, with a field of research and symposia arising around the idea.

Measures of prosperity need not be economic, either. Canada, for example, has burnished its international reputation with years of international aid and support, including peacekeeping missions and leadership on data privacy and other global tech and trade agreements. In a 2021 Ipsos survey of people in twenty-eight countries, an average of 80 percent of respondents said they expected Canada to have a positive influence on world affairs over the next decade—the highest of any nation.[2] At its core, Canada's appeal emanates from how it manages a balanced approach to international affairs. Indeed, the same balance works on the macro, meso, and micro levels alike, because positive change in any group dynamic can occur only when leaders care for the cognitive and the emotional. Whether in interactions between individuals, across organizations, or throughout the entire global economy, leaders cannot spark meaningful change without considering both the human condition and the cold, hard data. This concept of cognitive-emotional balance has its roots in behavioral science, but using it as a lens for effective governance helps root our thinking in the perspectives of constituents—the people with whom governments need to build trust to maintain efficacy.

Trust, after all, is the currency upon which we build organizations, economies, and entire societies. It takes years to regain once lost. Diminishing trust in governments mirrors the diminishing trust among members of societies, but the loss of faith and trust in the citizenry at large pales in comparison with the general loss of trust in institutions. According to Gallup polling in the US, for example, confidence in several key institutions has dropped to its lowest levels since the company started tracking it in 1973.[3] Some 39 percent of respondents said they had "very little" confidence in newspapers, the lowest point ever. Nearly half of Americans, 47 percent, said the same about Congress, though that was slightly better than some years past. Americans even lost faith in the church, with less than four of every ten people saying they had a "great deal" or "quite a lot" of confidence in organized religion. Back in 1973, the first year of polling, two-thirds of Americans trusted in the church.

The profound erosion of trust in public-sector and global institutions leaves constituents with few alternatives. They can revolt or, in democracies, vote out the unsatisfactory party or lawmaker. Yet the bureaucratic institutions established to keep governance, public services, and economies in motion rarely bend to anything less than radical intervention. If Americans don't like the direction of monetary policy, they might tweak around the edges by voting for a different president. If they don't like the regime of the US dollar, well, they have even fewer options. You could argue, of course, that that's why we train, hire, and pay or elect experts—people who know better in any given area than we do. The dismantling and wholesale discrediting of experts is a problem when the "wisdom of the crowd" doesn't lead to better outcomes.

A Governance Perception Matrix

Looking at national governments from this viewpoint, we might create a framework that helps us analyze various aspects of their effectiveness. We could draw two perpendicular axes and create a metric of "governance perception" (see figure 6.1). The vertical axis might represent a sensing architecture—how well the institution picks up ground-truth signals of pain points and needs from its constituents. It would run from "decentralized and edge-inward" (obtaining signals from constituents firsthand, synthesized but not politically filtered) to "centralized and core-outward" (obtaining signals from central decision-makers and their close sources, such as political advisers and pollsters). The horizontal axis might represent

Governance Perception Matrix

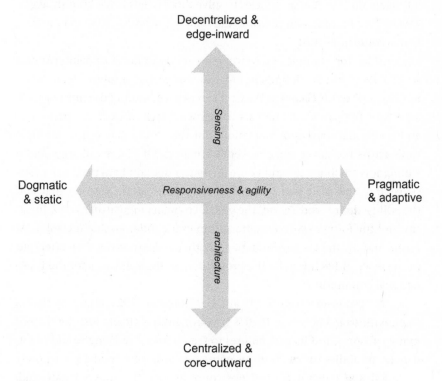

Figure 6.1

the solution responsiveness and agility of governance. It would extend from "dogmatic and static" to "pragmatic and adaptive." Clearly, no countries would fit neatly into any of these resulting quadrants. After all, what works well for some issues in some cultures would fail miserably in others. China's hard-line COVID-19 lockdowns would never fly in the United States. Rather than offering strict categorizations, this matrix provides a thought provocation for leaders who should concern themselves with redesigning institutions that are no longer, as Deng put it, "catching mice." It is a way to critically assess institutions, rather than a chart of empirical assessment of governance effectiveness. What this helps make clear, then, is that the *perception* of tangible, life-impacting governance plays a crucial role in building or eroding trust—the one absolutely indispensable element in the cognitive economy. Effectively designed systems that can assess and

measure the challenges of diverse niches of their populations and then flexibly adapt and synthesize policies to solve those issues while keeping aggregate welfare in mind will promote the stability, sustainability, and progress
that accompanies trust.

Consider, for example, a government's ability to prove or demonstrate a
set of facts to its constituents in order to create trust, a subject Juan Zarate
has explored in his classes at Harvard Law School. Among the most notable
aspects of the pandemic, he lists the growing lack of trust in institutions
and traditional sources of validation. But that could play out in multiple
ways across the governance perception matrix. "If you're talking about a
willingness to obfuscate and confuse, there's nobody better than the Rus-
sians, and that is in part because they have the strategy to do that and
the will to do it," said Zarate, the global co-managing partner at K2 Integrity and the former US "counterterrorism czar" under President George W.
Bush. "In fact, the US government and other Western venues are often put
in the place of having to be the prosecutors or the validators for the international community."

As the responses to COVID-19 and the January 6, 2021, attack on the US
Capitol illustrate, however, the US government has clearly lost the trust of
many citizens—and its past failures to "catch mice," as Deng would put it,
damage its ability to "catch mice" going forward. "Our model is purposely
fractured and balkanized and not controlled by the state," Zarate said.
"That's not the case in China and Russia, where the state can, at the end
of the day if not initially, control the means of power, influence, economy,
and information." The Chinese Communist Party has the power and ability to rein in Jack Ma and other powerful elements in the economy. Western systems don't allow for the same control, so Donald Trump can spew
vitriol at Jeff Bezos from whatever social media platform will welcome him,
but he can't do much to stop Amazon or the *Washington Post*.

Yet, each model of governance struggles in its own ways to establish
veracity, build trust, and deliver effective services. Governments that hope
to promote prosperity in a functioning economy and society need their
citizens to share a "ground truth" so leaders can make decisions about
what to invest in, which levers to pull, and how to govern for growth and
antifragility. That doesn't suggest governments should demand group-
think. There can and should be individual truths based on varied perspectives and perceptions. But they need a large, central overlap in the Venn

diagram of various truths—held together by empathy for each and a joint resolve to move forward with the whole—in order for governance to stand a chance. Misinformation campaigns actively shrink that shared middle space, while social media algorithms designed to get the next click narrow us into increasingly isolated corners. Too often, governments rely solely on the digital platforms and content providers themselves to fact-check. Yet the hyperscale platforms that form the information infrastructure of the cognitive economy are not incentivized to act in the larger public interest by business models that reward fragmentation.

Leaders cannot establish a "ground truth" through heavy-handed control of content, either. People will always find a way to disseminate a counternarrative, oftentimes especially under the tightest controls. But we might consider creative measures to counteract the *scaling* of misinformation, like professional surety bonds to assure accountability of algorithm owners, as proposed by Daniel Dennett, the renowned philosopher at the intersection of humans and AI.[4] And both corporations and governments should focus on growing that common ground through education and trust-building measures that authenticate identity and credibility.

"I do think the environment actually gravitates toward a paradigm of transparency—those that are trying to hide or obfuscate have to go to great lengths to do so in the current environment," Zarate said. "It doesn't mean they can't do it—you've got the Great Firewall in China—but the environment is conducive to transparency, and that is frightening to autocratic regimes that are trying to control information."

Rebuilding Trust, Healing Fractures

Despite these different government models and the eroding trust between and within countries and institutions, the affluent layers of global society remain largely unaffected. Global trade continues, wealth agglomerates, and those with privilege and resources can lead relatively unfettered lives. When increasingly severe storms, wildfires, and other climate emergencies arise, for example, those with affluence can shore up, ride it out, or just move. While the phenomena of fragmentation affect wealthy demographics, too, more affluent people have the means to access resources and support and retain greater control over the technological, economic, and governmental forces that break communities apart. Crises hit other, less-privileged fragments disproportionately harder. A system cannot heal, adapt, and evolve to become more antifragile if it pressurizes 99 percent of the people and keeps the other 1 percent stable and safe.

Yet global measures of destruction, discontent, disconnection, and disparity have all worsened considerably over the past decade. And while we've managed to keep our economies going, we have not improved their designs—in part because that fragmentation feels less acute to those who hold the power to make change, especially in countries experiencing significant growth. So we brace ourselves against waves of expansion and contraction, integration and disintegration, following one another in rapid succession, leading to systems that jump rather than moderately shift. As bestselling author Nassim Nicholas Taleb elegantly describes in his book *Antifragile* (2012), moderate shifts afford us time to lean in, adjust, and heal. Systems that make sudden and significant jumps will inflict structural damage and a breakdown of flows within economies—including any crucial flows of trust we failed to safeguard.

The sketch of the governance matrix provides one way to think about where we might find the leaks in the pipes where trust seeps out. Henry Mintzberg and Edward Freeman, two of the world's preeminent business and management scholars, have some ideas for how we might patch them. While the two academics don't always see eye to eye, both encourage a broader sense of inclusion to rebalance society. They differ on their diagnosis of the national and global tensions between government, business, and community. For businesses, Freeman's stakeholder theory suggests that companies derive value not just from shareholders but from the full universe of customers, suppliers, employees, and communities. "We need to understand business as a societal institution, and sometimes they need to cooperate together with other stakeholders," said Freeman, a philosopher and business administration professor at the University of Virginia's Darden School of Business. "But it comes from the ground up, not the top down." The problem with top-down systems theory, he said, is that someone has to manage the system, and that almost always leads to some sort of authoritarian or totalitarian regime—or people in power not attuned to the threats faced by those they lead. A heavy hand won't solve the major global crises and mend the fractures we face today. Rather, he argued, we need lots of experiments—people and companies—trying to figure out how to solve inequality, global warming, and gender discrimination. Some things will work, some won't, but those solutions have to emerge from the ground up. It is an unabashedly pro-private view.

Mintzberg, a professor of management studies at the Desautels Faculty of Management of McGill University in Montreal, argues that even stakeholder theory overemphasizes the role of capitalism in society, especially in the United States. That's not to suggest that the private sector can't drive innovation, he said. The smartphone is "the most innovative product that's ever been created, because it does everything," unlike many technologies that have only one primary purpose. "But to say only business is innovative shows a complete ignorance of the plural sector." The typical business-versus-government framing of these economic and societal arguments minimizes the crucial role that community and civic groups play in driving solutions for the most intractable problems.

The plural sector focuses on communities, rather than governments or businesses, and as such it should receive equal time with the public and private sectors in our conversations about how we rebuild and remobilize. "A healthy society combines respected governments in the public sector, responsible businesses in the private sector, and robust communities in the plural sector," Mintzberg wrote in his 2015 essay "Time for the Plural Sector." "Weaken any one of these and a society falls out of balance." When we talked to him in October 2021, he took issue with the prevailing conversations about where innovation and progress might emerge. Too many strategy, economics, and finance professors frame questions in the dominant vernacular of those narrow disciplines. While Mintzberg works in strategy, too, he is right to remind all of us that the stool balances on three legs, not two—with the plural sector exerting the force necessary to address major commons problems like inequality and climate change. Indeed, a great deal of frugal innovation in many of these areas flows from the ingenuity and improvisation of often underfunded private citizens in communities who are having to solve problems with very few resources, as our friend Navi Radjou, coauthor of the seminal book in this area, *Jugaad Innovation*, proves with myriad examples from around the world. Those solutions need to be promoted, capitalized, and scaled. It's when the solution for society is in the foreground and capital in the background that society gains in the most focused way. So "it's not about fixing capitalism," Mintzberg says, "it's about fixing society. And society gets fixed when capitalism gets put back in its place."

Regardless of where various nations in this global community come down on these arguments and the balance of private, public, and plural sectors, we surely can recognize the need to address the imbalance. Our current regimes and mindsets have stymied action on our response to COVID, our preparations for the Cognitive Era, our efforts to improve cybersecurity, our solutions to climate change, and our ability to forge much-needed collaboration between the US and China. We won't move past these stalemates unless we—as nations, businesses, and individuals—can overcome the affluent population's entitlement to power that puts a chokehold on our governments, boardrooms, and psyches. We might agree and disagree with different elements of Freeman's and Mintzberg's arguments. You might reject the analyses, frameworks, and designs we suggest throughout this book. But we should all agree that we need to design a new future, at whatever scale we feel is appropriate.

The Race to Remobilization

The efforts needed to reconstruct global systems in ways that enhance trust and promote sustainability and equity will require new actors, institutional overhauls, and a fresh set of rules. We can start by scrutinizing how systems that govern the flows of currency, people, intellectual property, goods and services, data, natural resources, and genetic material are evolving in the cognitive economy. We need to consider the growing tensions between contrasting interests. How, for example, can the essence of collaboration across regions and an even more fledgling aspiration toward digital trade and smart supply chains coexist with the needs of national governance protocols and privacy safeguards? How do we guarantee the functioning of distributed structures while not generating digital extractive rents with data manipulation and profiling? These questions need to be resolved to better understand and define the competition and cooperation spaces between China and the West.

We can start by reframing the "competition of values" that currently focuses on GDP, trade and investment, human rights, and geopolitical control. For too long, we held onto a somewhat naive idea that globalization and growing prosperity around the world would help align some of the major differences in values. Western leaders, for example, assumed that the rise of capitalism-driven affluence and economic prosperity would ease authoritarianism in China and entice more countries to embrace democratic values. It hasn't happened, and efforts to view this geopolitical relationship as a "my way or the highway" zero-sum game will take us nowhere. We cannot seek mere political stability or equilibrium. Rather, we need to reshape our international relations and global systems designs with a mindset of positive-sum games that reject the language of trade-offs, compromise, and balance that no longer applies in a multipolar, hyper-complex Cognitive Era.

For example, the quick and easy flow of money in a financialized economy still serves as the guiding principle for both the US and China, and both sides wobble when something disrupts it. Neither side will lose its hegemonic place in the world because of the other competing with it (short of a catastrophic war breaking out); rather, the countries will fail because they break down internally. Neither side can build a better world based on the metrics and labels currently employed; they will rise and fall on the quality of their values and whether those values can be translated into tangibly improved lives.

So, what will become the North Star for Global 2.0? We might look to integrate Ubuntu ethics in Africa, or instill some Shinto principles from Japan. The American Dream of upward mobility needs a recast, but it still entices hundreds of thousands of people to the US each year. A recast Chinese system of Confucianism can still bond and stabilize a country of more than 1.4 billion people. And European ideals of individual human rights, the Enlightenment, and dignity still serve as a guiding light for billions of people around the world. We might not know the right blend of North Star values that will inspire the global community, but they will emerge if we, as leaders, make a deliberate effort to shape our guiding principles in a way that fosters a more sustainable form of globalization. We need to do that now, at this time of transformation, so we don't settle for the same values that led us to this unsustainable present in the first place. But either way, economics and ethics will intertwine in the Cognitive Era, as more and more people demand global systems that work to their *felt* benefit, both psychologically and materially.

Tech "Big Think" for the Design Activist Leader

The advanced technologies that emerge in the years ahead might help us better understand our complex world and our complicated selves—and, by extension, provide new insights that help reinforce shared values around the world. But if we want people to trust these new sets of tools and technologies, then we'll need to prove that they benefit most if not all of humanity. Only then can we establish the much-needed depth and breadth of trust in both the technologies and the companies and governments that deploy them. That trust doesn't exist today, but not because we've lost our capacity to believe. The problem is that we've sprinted headlong into a cognitive economy that relies so heavily on digital tools, all the while building platforms that eat away at the societal and cultural structures on which trust is established. Leaders can help repair the damage, but only if they deploy their design activism toward weaving a new fabric of trust into technology.

Reestablishing trust will take careful consideration of the smallest details and interactions, but it also grows when we break out of digital smallness and aspire to the big, bold dreams that drive real technological innovation. Over the past decade or two, with few notable exceptions, the dreamers of global technology hubs, especially in Silicon Valley, have too often tied their dreams to IPOs, windfalls, and the strictures of modern startup funding. To break the pattern of tribalism, bolster our collective response to biological threats, heal our environment, and improve welfare for all of humanity, we need to reorient toward the big. We need to incentivize *meaningful* growth.

"Meaningful" used to refer to breakthroughs or discoveries that provided access to something previously unthinkable or even unimaginable. The idea of landing on the moon sounded absurd once, yet the dream to do so brought it to reality. No one could imagine then that we would carry devices with vastly more computing power than those Apollo spacecraft in our pockets. But then we had breakthroughs that started to build greater and greater meaningfulness for all of us. Jaan Tallinn and his colleagues created Skype, empowering people who previously couldn't afford long-distance calls to connect with family, friends, and business partners. As we wrote this in early 2022, *Nature* magazine reported that a man whose hand was paralyzed from a spinal cord injury "achieved typing speeds of 90 characters with 94.1 percent accuracy online, and greater than 99 percent offline with a general-purpose autocorrect."[5] The brain-computer interface that allowed him to "type" could identify lowercase letters and certain punctuation symbols from the neural signals his brain generated as he imagined handwriting notes. The technology has years to go before commercial availability, but ideas like this point us toward the types of life-changing, trust-enhancing possibilities that come from "pragmatically big" thinking. Despite our words of warning, we are deep-tech dreamers, and we are continually inspired by the thinking of brilliant scientists, solution developers, and entrepreneurs. We need technology to "hook in" and pull the proverbial climate cart out of the ditch.

We're especially eager to see the radical reconception of technologies across the Global South. As professors, advisers, and mentors, we get to interact with some of the most brilliant young minds from all over the planet, and they renew our excitement and hope for the world. In the online seminars we deliver in partnership with businesses and government economic development programs, we get to guide students as they develop the seeds of ingenious applications of AI and other digital technologies to tackle everything from typhoid in Cameroon to supply-and-demand mismatches in hospitals and health care facilities in Tunisia. Entrepreneurs across the developing world teach us new lessons about reverse innovation—not in our usual expectation of repurposing existing ideas for a different marketplace, but by focusing first on the most important human needs, rather than the lucrative financial exit or incremental next step.

Economic development needs to follow a more distributed pattern in order to meet people with diverse sets of qualifications wherever they reside. Large fabrication plants and headquarters relocations can only get us so far, and they mainly target and benefit highly skilled labor. Instead, we need to redesign our global systems to generate the kind of collective intelligence that emerges from "swarm economics," which connects like-minded people wherever they are and equips them in loosely structured, agile, cooperative models that readily lead to new behaviors, new patterns of production, and new ways of reducing transaction costs.[6] We need to encourage as many talented scientists, entrepreneurs, financiers, and governance leaders as possible to go back to Bryan Johnson's zeroth principles and radically reconceive how we improve our lives with an array of technologies. In our dawning Cognitive Era, meaningful growth will require more interoperability, more collaboration, and more compatibility. Our redesign of global technological systems will need to combine big ideas with painstaking attention to the trust-building details—and do both fast enough and at a scale large enough to improve our lives, safeguard our individuality, and celebrate our commonalities.

7 Crypto Goes Meta: Fleeing to a Parallel World

When Facebook announced it would rename itself Meta, it embarked on more than a rebranding exercise to salvage its embattled public image. The new name also heralded the company's vision of the digital future, a metaverse where the separation between the physical and digital dissolves. On October 28, 2021, Mark Zuckerberg offered a glimpse of that future in an hour-plus video announcing the name change. By the end of that day, though, the viral video clips that proliferated across social media made Meta's version of the metaverse look like a silly place, with Zuckerberg its resident clown. Memes ridiculed small pieces of the presentation and, especially, the starring role the Meta founder and CEO played in it. Unflattering comparisons to the Second Life virtual world abounded. A group called Inspired by Iceland even made a parody tourism video, complete with an Icelandic "chief visionary officer," whose name and outfit resembled Zuckerberg's and who invited viewers to enjoy "completely immersive experiences" in the "Icelandverse."

The chuckling at Meta's expense came and went, but the memes overshadowed something far more impressive, and perhaps troubling, within the fuller presentation. In the video, Zuckerberg and his colleagues laid out a far more intriguing vision of what the metaverse might become. This merger of the physical, cyber, and synthetic biology into a unified experience swept away what we recalled from previous virtual-world experiences. In this metaverse, haptic glove technology integrated artificial intelligence and electromyography, reading subtle neural signals from the wrist to let users send texts by simply thinking about hand movements. It included photorealistic avatars that incorporated real-time eye contact and facial expressions. It would develop a set of open standards, so you could port the items you buy or create on Meta's platform to a metaverse maintained by another company or group of users, and vice versa. It was more than just a second life for Second Life.

Humanity has moved from text, then photos, and then video to experience content, Zuckerberg said, but "the next platform and medium will be even more immersive, an embodied internet where you're in the experience, not just looking at it." While his introduction to the metaverse left plenty of openings for ribbing, his hints and examples later in the presentation offered a far more natural and immersive integration of the physical and the virtual than the memes suggested. Of course, Zuckerberg also noted that it will take billions of dollars and years of work before the metaverse reaches scale. He and his colleagues estimate that realizing the kind of next-generation metaverse described in the presentation will require about a dozen major technology breakthroughs in everything from haptics and displays to sensors that track hand, eye, and bodily movements. But even the early versions of the metaverse will reach a billion people, he predicted, growing a mostly crypto-based economy of hundreds of billions of dollars and creating millions of jobs over the next decade.

Indeed, that push had begun well before Meta's videos, especially in gaming. Online game companies such as Roblox and Epic Games have dabbled in increasingly immersive virtual worlds. "We don't see Fortnite as the metaverse," said Marc Petit, a vice president at Epic, "but as a beautiful corner of the metaverse."[1] Both companies have already built virtual worlds, in which participants socialize, play, and take part in a digital economy. Some users even make a living inside these metaverses by selling digital wares.

If these technologies continue to create an increasingly seamless and immersive physical-digital experience in realms beyond gaming, they could significantly alter the ways we interact and present ourselves, both personally and professionally. Indeed, if waning trust, deeper fragmentation, and the emergence of an immersive cognitive economy have led to the new operating logic of decentralization (in computing and governance alike), then the metaverse and Web3 might be the most important phenomena to emerge from the disruptions. It could change the way we move throughout the world to connect, learn, create, and re-create. It could lead to new incentives and structures for more inclusion, equity, and trust, but it could just as easily result in a race for the next dopamine-dollar and a drive even further toward digital smallness.

To be fair, Zuckerberg raised this point in his presentation, noting that Meta must keep responsible development and inclusion at the heart of its efforts to develop the metaverse tools. We've heard those comments from Silicon Valley before, of course, and the results haven't often matched the rhetoric. The buzz that surrounds Web3, crypto, and the metaverse might sound like so much "tech bro" hot air, but we need to be careful not to lump all the hard-won innovation together as mere hype. The confluence of built infrastructure with neurobiological and digital networks has the potential to generate opportunity (and complexity) beyond immersive stores and token payments toward virtual town squares, co-creation spaces, or travel and learning experiences. In this cognitive economy, any imbalance of equity or trust in one system will ripple through others, so the opportunities and risks of this new era call for a heightened vigilance for system fragility. In collision with social and political forces, the cognitive economy has the power to elevate or break societies, whether local or global. To what extent remains to be seen. Whether that elevation or destruction is creative or catastrophic depends on all of us as leaders and design activists.

In Crypto We Trust?

Perhaps more immediately relevant than the still-nascent metaverse is the phenomenon of Web3, the next iteration of the World Wide Web. Built upon blockchain technology and cryptocurrencies, it has grown out of the rising demand for greater decentralization, transparency, self-governance, and native built-in payments. Web 1.0 is often used to describe the beginning of the internet age, introducing static web pages, e-commerce, and email. Web 2.0 made possible decentralized collaboration and creativity using social networks and cloud computing, and it opened up opportunities for sharing economies. We have no singular definition for Web3, largely because it remains, at least at the time of this writing, in the early days of its evolution. However, some facets appear central to the concept. It will integrate many Semantic Web technologies, which allow machines to read and interact with content in a manner more akin to humans (e.g., AI and machine learning). Web3 concepts have integrated distributed ledger technologies, such as blockchain, focusing on their ability to authenticate and decentralize information. Together, these combinations of technologies chip away at the power that platform owners hold over individual users, and they enable machines to collaborate directly with one another through algorithms.

In the web's current incarnation, the big consumer platforms resemble a big-brained alien in a science fiction movie. Humans get tethered to it, get nourished by it, and have their thoughts and behaviors directed by it—sometimes aware of how deeply the alien controls them, but only in vague terms. The promise of Web3 is that it untethers us. It works more like a modern sushi restaurant, where we can pick what we like off the little sushi boats and pay with our mobile phones on the way out. Each color-coded boat is akin to a smart contract between you and the different sushi chefs in the kitchen, and the touchless digital payment like a seamless cryptocurrency transaction.

The cryptocurrency and the crypto ecosystem phenomena are indispensable elements of Web3, bringing about two important alternatives to existing institutions and systems. First, they offer a new form of exchange and value storage that operates outside the traditional financial systems and governments. Second, cryptos and blockchains, the fundamental platform cryptos run on, have made it possible to establish so-called decentralized autonomous organizations (DAOs), groups whose rules and processes are embedded in code on a blockchain. As technological innovation ushers in this shift toward a logic of decentralization, proponents of the crypto ecosystem saw an opportunity for radical institutional change without radical political action. Crypto offers an alternative not just to the consolidation of government and central bank power, but to the broader consolidation of market and technological power, as well. And it offers the prospect of freer and faster transactions guaranteed by a trustless system that no central authority could control.

"Trustless" is, of course, an unfortunate term of art, trying to signal that one doesn't have to place trust in any central authority or single person because no one single actor controls the blockchains on which these applications are based. But it is paradoxical, because one actually has to place trust in everyone involved in a decentralized chain or a DAO to not collude against them or to use the technologies for illicit purposes. Still, a rapidly growing share of digitally native generations—especially in underbanked and underserved populations—would rather place their faith in trustless systems than seemingly ineffective or corrupt governments. Indeed, as of late 2021, Nigeria and Vietnam were home to some of the fastest-growing cryptocurrency communities in the world, alongside Ukraine, Russia, and other countries in Africa and Latin America.[2]

Yet, at the same time, the crypto ecosystem has remained largely the domain of the technorati. The complexity of cryptocurrencies and decentralized finance (DeFi) systems—both in design and, for the technical layperson, in user experience—still inhibits adoption by the masses. The mere requirement of a digital wallet is enough to put off many potential adopters. The waves of cryptocurrency news, and the widening range of ideas about what cryptos and blockchains can do and how they can make money, are enough to leave anyone confused about its future. Just when one major announcement suggests a new threshold of credibility, another headline arrives to raise more questions. The spectacular collapse of FTX, the cryptocurrency exchange and hedge fund that filed for bankruptcy in November 2022, sparked a whole new wave of concern among the public and regulators alike, although its woes stemmed mainly from the fraud of its founder, Sam Bankman-Fried. Even as the underlying concepts of blockchains and decentralization gain broader acceptance, too many signs of a crypto bubble remain. The value of one Bitcoin, by far the most popular cryptocurrency, rose to nearly $69,000 in November 2021, but by the following November it had dropped as low as $15,460, according to historical trading data at Coinbase.[3] That volatility was far from unusual. At the time of this writing, Bitcoin had crashed more than a dozen times since 2011, by as much as 30 to 80 percent, the historical data show.

Lazy comparisons between crypto's boom-and-bust cycles and prior bubbles too often overlook a crucial point. The enduring lesson from those previous examples isn't just the way a bubble inflates, but how it deflates—and what's left behind when it does. Much like what occurred during the dot-com bubble, the frenzy of interest in crypto has launched a wave of technological and structural innovation—some of which will undoubtedly fail, but much of which will last. Young people are particularly drawn toward owning cryptos, often spurred by YouTube videos and social media posts by influencers. Many of them live in countries that don't have reliable or trusted banking systems. In the midst of chaos and uncertainty, when the current economic and social systems seem to be rigged against stability and progress, and homeownership and upward social mobility feel like privileges reserved for older generations, why not take a risk on building up wealth from something new and outside the control of the old guards?

Put your money in traditional company stocks, and the companies might turn out to be doing something illegal or unethical—and even if not, senior executives get disproportionately high compensation.

"It's so hard to prepare for the future now. It's never been more difficult," Shane Blake, a twenty-six-year-old digital marketing worker from Brighton, UK, told the *Guardian* in 2021. "The competition is out there. Everyone has a degree, so degrees are meaningless. It's so difficult to buy a house."[4] Shane is a millennial. But when you pair his generation's income frustration with the coming earnings power of Gen Z, the other crypto-embracing generation, the trajectory becomes clear. A November 2020 Bank of America (BofA) report called Gen Z "the most disruptive generation ever," noting that they are the first generation born into an online world.[5] Now that they're entering the workforce, the report said, they're "compelling other generations to adapt to them, not vice versa." The two major events that bookend the generation were the 9/11 terrorist attacks and COVID, but they remember only the last one, a BofA strategist told CNBC a week after the report's release. With Gen Z's income expected to increase fivefold to $33 trillion by 2030, the strategist said, their embrace of crypto, DeFi, and other decentralized digital opportunities will nudge us further toward a sustainable post-melt upgrade.

Buyer Beware

As use of crypto expands—whether driven by dissatisfaction, better functionality, or both—thoughtful and agile regulation will become increasingly necessary, and business strategists and policymakers would make a serious mistake if they ignore this paradigm-changing innovation or choke it off with draconian regulation. Crypto has already birthed new economic models, infrastructure, and actors. Alongside the slate of Altcoins (Bitcoin alternatives) and payment tokens, more than sixty countries have tested national digital currencies since the start of 2020, most notably China, which rolled out the electronic Chinese yuan (eCNY). Unlike pure cryptocurrencies and the decentralization that underlies most of the crypto ecosystem, these digital currencies remain under centralized control, offering a digital form of existing bank notes. Yet, updates by the US and the EU moved slowly, raising questions about whether any globally trusted regulation of digital currency and other crypto-related elements could evolve.

But forays like President Biden's executive order "addressing the risks and harnessing the potential benefits of digital assets" and the UK's Financial Conduct Authority's deliberations over regulatory approvals for cryptocurrencies indicated that the domain would continue to mature.[6]

The frothy pattern of Bitcoin's bubbles too often obscures what a higher-resolution lens reveals—that the crypto world has managed to erect a set of innovative pillars that will likely survive a potential cataclysm and establish new, credible, and robust ways of creating, holding, and exchanging value. The innovation born of distrust has reached a point at which its elements are too deeply entrenched—including within traditional financial structures—to be swept aside. Some of these new pillars have already emerged within the evolving frontier of blockchain infrastructure itself. Although Bitcoin remains somewhat overhyped, as it currently offers little more than a means for speculation, a growing number of sophisticated investors have explored the broader use of coins and tokens in designs that could radically change our future social and business landscapes. One important development is "stablecoins," which can act as a bridge between old and new forms of money. Tied to the real world of government-backed fiat currencies, and often pegged to the price of the US dollar, stablecoins allow anyone to easily enter and exit positions in different cryptos at low fees, without having to exchange back into fiat currency. This creates a simple medium of exchange that allows for a predictable and safe trading environment between banks and the crypto world, the final financial border between real and virtual currencies.

The broader ramifications of the expanding crypto ecosystem could reset the patterns for global flows of money. For example, crypto-powered systems could establish a frictionless and lower-cost channel for the $650 billion market for global remittances, not to mention hundreds of billions more in cross-border payments. That potential has piqued the interest of many people across the Global South who want to break out of the restrictive, costly, and bribery-ridden monetary systems currently in place. Adoption of cryptocurrencies in Africa, for example, jumped 1,200 percent from 2020 to 2021, easily outpacing growth rates across the rest of the world. Although African countries account for just 3 percent of global cryptocurrency activity, six countries entered the top 20 for global activity in 2021, and Togo eked into the top 20 for DeFi applications.[7] Furthermore, Africa leads globally with the use of peer-to-peer (P2P) crypto marketplaces, such as Paxful and Binance, which provide an onramp for cash-bearing unbanked and underbanked Africans to purchase cryptocurrencies directly from other people.

These platforms have opened financial and investment opportunities where few previously existed. To date, people have used these P2P market-places to protect savings from fiat currency devaluation, generate a better return on investments, and facilitate faster and cheaper cross-border remittances. Rather than consult with formal financial advisers, information is shared through community discourse in group chats in WhatsApp, mir-roring the decentralized nature of the crypto ecosystem. The caveat emp-tor remains: cryptocurrency investment scams have also proliferated, once again raising the call for appropriate controls and governance alongside the new underpinnings of the crypto-enabled decentralized digital economy.

DAO Shall Be Blessed

The biggest mistake we can make in the Web3 world is to conceive of DeFi as mainly a financial system, in which trust is mostly about money. That may be where it started, but at its core, Web3 and crypto are an attempted governance and socioeconomic organization revolution. Case in point: DAOs have become one of the more groundbreaking uses of the crypto ecosystem and blockchain. Put simply, a DAO is essentially a virtual collab-orative with a flat, democratized ownership structure. The people who own the tokens of a DAO, typically purchased, earned, or granted for member-ship in a community, vote to decide how their organization should operate, and specially designed voting mechanisms aim to avoid the type of power concentration typically found in corporations.

MakerDAO, one of the pioneers of the form, provides a useful illustra-tion of its potential and ramifications. MakerDAO allows a participant to deposit Ethereum in exchange for a stablecoins called DAIs. A participant can use the DAIs to buy other cryptocurrencies or exchange them for dollars or other fiat currencies. In essence, they receive a perpetual loan against the Ethereum they deposited. This is already novel—akin to taking out a loan in Euros against your own deposit of US dollars, something traditional banks would rarely offer without a huge fee. But what makes DAOs revolutionary is that all its future rules, operations, and processes are determined not by a central CEO or board of directors but by the token holders themselves.

People who use the MakerDAO platform receive a governance token called MKR. They can hold them or trade them, but whoever owns the MKR can vote on policy and protocol changes for the DAO itself. Once a vote is complete, the result of the token vote is executed and implemented via a smart contract—essentially, a computer program on a blockchain or similar crypto platform that automatically executes a predefined decision (e.g., release funds) when a predefined set of terms are met (e.g., a majority votes yes). Since no one has the special power to contravene or amend those smart contracts absent a vote of all the MKR holders, the organization is decentralized. In short, MKR tokens allow participants to vote on how the DAI stablecoins will operate.

MakerDAO has since inspired other organizations to further redefine the traditional lending and depositing model, as well as extend into insurance and derivatives. DAOs have even made inroads into exchanges, an economic mechanism our societies have been relying on for millennia. Unlike Coinbase or Binance, both of which are centralized exchanges based on existing Web 2.0 protocols, these new decentralized exchanges (DEX) aim to eliminate virtually any intermediary, with tokens trading directly in a peer-to-peer fashion, in a process controlled by code and recorded on a decentralized ledger. Uniswap, for example, uses algorithms and its governance token known as UNI to automate the entire operation of its exchange. Given that DEX are decentralized and dispersed among thousands of participants, there is no owner, company, or entity to hold responsible.

The fact that the DAO revolution started with financial services is no coincidence. Finance is made up of digits, and the authority and power of moving money always rests in the hands of financial institutions and the largest capital holders. DAOs have raised new possibilities to turn this model upside down. But, for a number of reasons, we believe that decentralization will open up opportunities across a range of fields. First, MakerDAO and its ilk sit atop existing blockchain platforms, so they do not consume as much energy as a separate blockchain would. Second, decentralization and automation represent a cheaper way of running a business. For instance, the DeFi insurance protocol Etherisc provides crop insurance to farmers in Kenya by automating the role of claims adjusters, allowing faster, cheaper, and more objective claim settlements. A growing number of decentralized lending platforms have developed as well, utilizing smart contracts to allow everyday people to lend their cryptocurrency and receive interest in exchange. While decentralized lending is collateral-based, unlike many traditional lending schemes, it allows users to take out loans without declaring their identity or providing a credit score—key for borrowers in developing countries.

A new layer ("Layer 2") of applications that run on top of an existing blockchain can make the chain more scalable and accessible to more users. This, in turn, makes it possible to expand the use of blockchain as an infrastructure and provide DAOs and the rest of the crypto economy fertile grounds for a variety of business model innovations across finance, logistics, law, transportation, and many other sectors. Ultimately, DAOs could give us more choices over where, when, and how we work, and they could foster greater opportunity for fulfillment by providing more alternatives for people to customize their workplaces, income, transactions, investments, and social impact.[8]

Non-fungible tokens (NFTs) don't bring to mind the same kinds of significant transformations, but the concept could have some meaningful applications, too. These cryptographically unique tokens, which are linked mostly to digital content or assets, such as pieces of art, photos, or documents, are akin to a serial number that establishes proof of ownership.[9] While NFTs drew plenty of scorn as we wrote this in 2022 (the fact that Twitter founder Jack Dorsey could sell an NFT of his first tweet for $2.9 million did not help matters), the underlying idea of creating digital scarcity, if truly possible and enforceable, hints at remarkable possibilities.[10] Even if people subsequently copy and paste their stuff ad infinitum, designers who previously had no sales outlet for their work might now use an NFT to reap value for what they create—starving artists putting a little more ramen on the table. With NFTs, a whole array of designers, artists, celebrities, and other creators can reach potential customers directly. But in a world where people have already paid a whopping $80,000 for an NFT avatar, will we merely create another inequitable world of haves and have-nots?[11]

Innovation in the Web3 space remains in its adolescence, and much of it will fail. But it doesn't require too much imagination to envision how crypto and blockchain innovations—and the faith they can foster if developed thoughtfully—could herald a more transparent model for economic, social, cultural, and political transactions. The pendulum of regulation will swing and, one hopes, reach an equilibrium at which innovation can flourish and investors can transact without fear. Perhaps the bubble will explode and a crypto cataclysm will ensue. Or perhaps smart regulation will slowly deflate it, and a more professionalized ecosystem will absorb the chaos and heal it.

Regardless, the foundations for a decentralized structure of global transactions, governance, and organizations is emerging, affording us an opportunity to shape a more resilient, equitable, and trusted paradigm. While the debates over the evolution, regulation, and benefits of the metaverse, Web3, and the crypto ecosystems will continue, efforts to carefully nurture the promising elements of these new platforms and integrate them into the right global systems can help us build toward the future we desire.

IV Impact and Triage

IV Impact and Hope

8 The Chaos Ahead: Practicing Pivots toward Opportunities

The hyphen in the FLP-IT acronym makes it work as a catchy phrase, but it also separates the framework into two phases. The first part guides leaders through the critical analyses of the existing or emerging forces, logics, and phenomena in times of upheaval or uncertainty. Whether around the globe, in your industry or within your neighborhood, understanding which way the winds are blowing and why is crucial to knowing how to set your sails. The second half of the framework builds that analysis toward a projection of future impacts, which leaders can use to triage their resources and priorities in ways that will move their organizations or communities forward. While no future projection comes with 100 percent certainty, thoughtful use of the FLP-IT framework provides both clarity for current action and an ongoing flexibility and antifragility that allows leaders to constantly reassess and recalibrate for unexpected turmoil.

None of the steps are easy, but impact might be the trickiest for many leaders, because it calls on the cognitive *and* the emotional, the objective *and* the imaginative. Furthermore, this phase of the framework does not fit easily into a one-size-fits-all process—while we can often generalize forces, logic, and phenomena across groups, industries, or populations, the impacts they have tend to remain specific to individual people or entities. Still, most leaders can rely on a similar set of high-level analytical processes when assessing different impacts for individual circumstances. When looking at meso-level impacts on their industry, for example, a leader can consider how the new operating logic and phenomena could play out against existing strategic models, such as Michael Porter's Five Forces industry analysis framework.[1] Using Porter's tried-and-tested model, a leader could assess how the operating logic might impact the competitive landscape and the structure of the industry itself, and then begin to contemplate ways to better position themselves within that evolving industry ecosystem. They could play the logic on the intersections of the different actors in Porter's framework and infer how the relationships with their customers or suppliers might change. They could see whether and how the logic could drive attractiveness of substitutes or enable new entrants in the industry. Similarly, a not-for-profit or government leader might project how a new operating logic in a constituency, geography, or stakeholder ecosystem would morph the interests of those stakeholders or partners, with some becoming more or less urgent or vocal.

On a more granular scale, a leader might also want to assess impacts on their product or service value chain. While they can base their impact assessment on a current, data-grounded analysis of their value chain as a departure point, it might require some imagination to figure out which value chain segments would experience more or less leverage and, thereby, more or less margin strength. Assessing who might gain and who might lose leverage could then yield openings for offensive or defensive moves in a value chain or ecosystem. In chapter 1, for example, we noted a fashion house that assessed the impact of the pandemic on its supply chain, noting that quarantines might limit supplies of raw materials and brick-and-mortar store closures would put more pressure on digital sales. Political leaders might note how climate emergencies forced new migration patterns, and then assess how the resulting movement of people will impact employment and production among their constituency. One might also use a strategic resources and capabilities framework, asking which of those become more or less strategic, which resources previously deemed strategic become mere table stakes for your business, and which become obsolete altogether.

Regardless of which approach one takes to impact assessment, it's crucial that leaders tailor this and the other FLP-IT steps to their unique domains and impact goals. We could write an entire book about a singular deep-dive example of FLP-IT. Instead, we sought to lay out a vision and the framework on a higher level, so design activist leaders *across* domains could begin to address the major tectonic shifts and tackle the *joint* redesigns necessary for a better world. After all, before we can drive toward the future we want, we have to imagine what it looks like and how we get there. And for that, it's often easier to imagine these steps, especially the impacts, through a scenario-planning exercise. For years, large companies have used combinations of scenario planning and strategic foresight to imagine the future in broad strokes, set a direction for their organization, and then watch for the red flags and disruptions that necessitate a review. We have run dozens of these exercises in our years of consulting work with business, government, and private-equity firms, and each reveals the power of narrative in this tricky phase of impact assessment and new portfolio configuration.

So, what follows are two staggered stories—one near term to 2028, and one longer term to 2035—that are rooted in the possible but purposefully provocative. Together, they construct a "future history" that contemplates some of the impacts that could arise in the years to come. We developed the first story to help readers get a better sense for how one hypothetical leader might recognize the *forces*, *logic*, and *phenomena* in turbulent times so she could assess the *impacts* they would have on her life, business, and world (and then make the necessary *triage* decisions as circumstances evolve). We wrote the second story to build off elements of the first one, but it is designed to spark leaders' thinking about what sort of future we might want and imagine some of the potential impacts we will face as we strive to design more sustainable global systems. If you could design a better future, how might we get from here to there? What would be a plausible path, spanning roughly one generation—enough time for concerted action today to bear fruit in complex systems? What investments might you redirect, possibly giving up near-term gain for a greater long-term payoff?

We use the device of a story because our brains are equipped to latch onto them. Stories are a highly effective mechanism for bringing emerging landscapes to life. And they make complexity visceral and accessible. They also illuminate the human element of the futures we seek, embodying the ethnographic and people-centric view we stress with clients. Societies and economies are made up of people first; the numbers follow. So, to see the people, not just their wallets, we start these two stories with the narrative of Fiona Foo, a business leader, wife, and mother who looks back from one possible future that, while not perfect, might embody more resilience, equity, and sustainability.

Fiona and Quan Li Foo lost everything in the storm of 2024. Fiona wept when they boarded the government-aid bus that transported them to shelters in the hills near Huế, the old seat of the French governor of Vietnam. The area had escaped the worst of the typhoon, which overwhelmed 80 percent of the Mekong Delta and coastal lowlands, including the Foos' small rental house near Qui Nhơn. Fiona had banished her tears by the time the buses arrived. In the weeks that followed, she refused to move back to Australia—despite pleas from her parents and, occasionally, from Quan. She wouldn't flee one climate disaster, only to move to one of the most combustible landscapes on the planet. She still vividly remembered the devastating firestorms that ravaged the country in 2021. Fiona and Quan had loved Vietnam, but with neither close ties nor income available there anymore, they had to leave. Fiona begrudgingly accepted her parents' "loan"—she knew they'd never let her pay it back—and they relocated to a small flat on the outskirts of Berlin.

She'd be damned if she let herself run out of options again, so Fiona buried herself in research about the forces that disrupted her life and livelihood. She might not be able to fully control them, she thought, but there was no way in hell she wouldn't be prepared for them the next time. An involuntary migrant herself, she started with migration and the raging climate's impact on where people lived. She then turned to white papers on blockchains and cryptocurrency after having trouble accessing their savings at a Vietnamese bank. It all took her down a rabbit hole as she studied more about finance and entrepreneurship. Her imagination had caught fire. She could now see an emerging new logic at play with trustworthy financial and governance systems that retained much-needed oversight, but also operated across borders and free of the most burdensome regulatory requirements that prevented migrants from easily transporting their financial resources and data. That model of blockchain-based decentralized finance, less political manipulation, and more inclusivity resonated after the hardships she had witnessed. She decided to launch her own platform to help migrants retain their savings and their identities and access them from anywhere. It was Quan, playing around on Google Translate, who suggested the Maltese word for "purchase." XiriCoin now had a name.

It started so simply, just Fiona and a contract coder, Abdur, whom she'd paid in equity, both tinkering with a small experiment while she settled into life in Germany. Abdur had been a computer science professor in Afghanistan before the US and its allies—Germany being one of them—pulled out in a hurry in 2021. His contacts at the American embassy couldn't get him on the last planes to the US, but they worked with their German peers to get him to Berlin, which had always been a place where misfits and migrants could find refuge in a proverbial cross-cultural salad bowl. In Germany, though, his credentials got him nowhere, so he spent his time doing online work at the library. When he saw Fiona reading a "biography" of Satoshi Nakamoto, he struck up a conversation with her. Intrigued by her ideas and eager for something fulfilling to work on, he agreed to help out—no pay, he said at the time, just a stake in the company if it goes anywhere.

Abdur came over for dinner with Fiona and Quan the night after the deal was struck, and they started to sketch out the details. Given the forces that had disrupted their lives and this new logic of trusted decentralization, Fiona said, they needed to create a way for refugees who lost all their physical resources to access virtual assets, currency, or credit so they could put their lives back together wherever they resettled. They could begin to address the phenomena of climate-forced displacement and migration with phenomena over which they had control—cryptocurrencies, peer-to-peer credit, and other blockchain-based services. With their financial snags still fresh in mind, they decided XiriCoin should start as a cryptocurrency, giving users a way to easily and cheaply save money, and then send and access it from anywhere around the world. They would try to build an initial customer base among those suffering the worst of the impacts they'd identified—migrants and other people threatened by political and climate disruptions—providing them secure access to their resources no matter where migration paths might lead them. Then, with the help of investors and philanthropists, they could open more services and maybe even branch out to mainstream commercial markets. They'd provide blockchain-based remittances services, a secure base for people to save, and virtual collateral that customers could use to get financial support in times of emergency.

The global recession hit right around the time XiriCoin launched. Growth in China had already started to slow significantly in the prior three years, and the debt-driven financial pressures only accumulated from there. After Russia stumbled in Ukraine and ramped up its support for secessionist groups in Kosovo, Moldova, and Lithuania, food and energy prices skyrocketed further, especially in Europe, and fifteen million Eastern Europeans joined the ranks of the twenty-two million climate refugees and an equal number of political refugees already moving across borders. China's economy creaked under the weight of international and domestic pressures. And given the quiet standoff between the West and India and China over Russia's invasion of its neighbors, Beijing kept pouring money into a revived version of Belt and Road Initiative (BRI) abroad while still investing heavily in everything from AI and quantum computing to aerospace and semiconductor manufacturing at home.

But trying to pull ahead of the US in advanced technologies took a much longer runway and consumed far more resources than the Chinese Communist Party (CCP) had imagined. Its innovation prowess grew in consumer-facing technology, but thanks to a decades-long head start, the American and Dutch stranglehold on global R&D ecosystems for deep-tech, such as semiconductor equipment, could not be replicated by simply throwing lots of money at development. China's efforts to narrow the gap in sub-5 nanometer chips, breakthrough AI methods, cognitive neuroscience, and quantum computing wobbled and couldn't find scale outside its borders. The grand story of a reemergent China started to feel stale. As growth slowed, notes of dissent rose, with the CCP playing whack-a-mole to keep the country contained. And then all hell broke loose. The typhoon that sent Fiona and Quan fleeing should have been a warning, but no one could have foreseen the Category 5 storm that rolled up and perched itself above Xiamen for six days. China eventually succumbed to global pressure and let UN aid workers enter, but the sprawling city and industrial base—home to nearly five million people—would take years to recover.

Xiamen was by no means alone. Cities along China's coastline were pounded by typhoons that year and the next, and the wildfires Fiona feared in Australia were barely a blip compared with the Richmond fire in California. People living in the Bay Area had grown accustomed to the smoky haze of seasonal wildfires, but this fire climbed both up the Berkeley hills and then down toward the bay, as well as northward toward the Chevron and Valero refineries in Benicia. Firefighters from across the US flew in to help, but two months in they could not protect the powder keg. Several months after the fire receded, the black scars on the hills visible across the bay in San Francisco were too much. The four Nobel Prize winners who had left UC Berkeley made all the headlines, but tens of thousands more people fled California.

The rain, wind, and fire left the infrastructures and workplaces on the coasts shells of themselves. The rush of people and their wealth into more temperate climates only heightened inequality within China and the US, just as it had globally. The number of people on the move swelled from 275 million in 2019 to 580 million by 2025.[2] With so many climate migrants, mostly from developing countries, fleeing their homes with little or nothing to their names, the global Gini index of financial inequality skyrocketed all over the place. No wonder XiriCoin got so popular, so fast.

While Abdur refined the underlying code for the company, Fiona started pitching the idea to the swelling communities of immigrant friends and neighbors. No one could put much capital or computing power into it, but nearly everyone wanted to have some piece of the idea: untethered, hypermobile currency for untethered and hypermobile lives. For those who could invest money or time, the digital tokens Fiona offered gave them a modest voice in shaping XiriCoin's services. They didn't have to be tied to some headquarters or remote subsidiary; all they needed was a phone, an app, and a secure ID code generated by TerraQuant—a quantum information processing startup out of Europe. The tokens also made them part of an on-the-ground organization that could work as franchisees of the XiriCoin platform. With their own small stake, they started signing up their friends. XiriCoin spread faster than wildfires or flash floods.

For years, investors had poured money into companies that embodied the logic of trusted decentralization, often getting burned as ideas rose and fell. But the phenomenon of XiriCoin's DAO, which gave disenfranchised migrants a voice in shaping the company's services, piqued the interest of especially deep pockets. The Gates Foundation put a modest investment but a big name behind the idea. The partnerships with Tala's and mPesa's vast networks instantly gave XiriCoin a massive presence in Africa and India. The UN and the World Bank never officially endorsed the initiative, but their people on the ground spread the word. Governments preoccupied by their frantic responses to climate disasters, cyberattacks, and the resulting domestic social strife didn't care enough to stop it. Soon, a young cohort of disadvantaged youth around the world found XiriCoin's easy access and ease of use the perfect opportunity to dabble in crypto as an investment possibility, with expat workers using it in lieu of traditional remittances to support their families back home—or, for many of them, in their new home countries. Within three years, XiriCoin had established itself as one of the more stable and easily exchangeable tokens available.

China remained a holdout domestically, but even it had come to endorse XiriCoin's use around the BRI projects it constructed across the globe, if for no other reason than to appease migrant workers. As partner countries struggled to repay loans, Beijing's liquidity crunch made it more difficult to structure ninety-nine-year leases for the underlying assets. Xi's powerbase had little choice but to embrace crypto abroad, with tens of thousands of small merchants and community leaders serving as XiriCoin conduits. After the initial backlash against the BRI, China had become far more comfortable with outside ideas, at least outside its own borders. President Xi had been forced to recalibrate his leadership, first easing back but then pushing forward again with equitable offers to BRI partners that burnished China's soft power, rather than its economic leverage over them. It was two steps forward after one step back.

The decoupling of the US and China had never gotten very far, except in public rhetoric by politicians and the industries critical to national security, such as semiconductors, AI, and the like. So when China's economy nosedived, Americans suffered, too. The recriminations that followed only heightened the tensions between the superpowers, both of which took pains to flex their military muscles as much as they could without starting an outright war. The shots fired at a US cruiser in the South China Sea drew the whole Pacific fleet within miles of Chinese waters, but cooler heads prevailed—in part because leaders on both sides felt the heat from their already struggling industries. With the economic red flags rising and the tensions still fresh in mind, Ford and Chinese battery powerhouse CATL started researching ways to cement their lucrative business partnership. They turned to blockchain technology as a way of establishing global transparency and auditability in their contracts. Ford had been slow to the EV market, but with the launch of the Verdant—a fully electric SUV with a thousand-mile range—its sales skyrocketed. Dependent on CATL for its battery supplies and knowing that Chinese EV technology had plateaued, Ford needed to secure its supply chain and its IP. The Sinoblock blockchain they launched could do that outside the manipulation of those in Beijing and Washington.

While Ford introduced it domestically to quantify the carbon content of its EV charging stations, it still caught nearly everyone by surprise when China tacitly approved Sinoblock's use within its borders, as well. With the global economy still reeling from the climate disasters of 2024 and Beijing needing to make the BRI loan tokens interchangeable, it had little choice but to accede to Sinoblock's use, or at least not get in the way. And when the founding companies soon opened it up to the auto industry worldwide, other Chinese manufacturers were the first outsiders to come knocking— with Amazon, Walmart, and other retailers more than happy to jump on to handle the Asian branches of their supply chain operations. When Apple and Foxconn moved onto Sinoblock, it felt inevitable.

Meanwhile, at XiriCoin's development office, Abdur had no idea that the cyberattack threatening to choke the company to death would become its luckiest break. Fiona called him one afternoon, saying she was having trouble getting a partnership token for a new country manager at a BRI project in Serbia. The manager wanted to tap into the migrant workforce streaming toward Europe from Asia, and he figured XiriCoin would provide a payment platform that most of the workers already knew and trusted. He had joined Fiona in XiriCoin's virtual office, and they bonded over the virtual shirts they'd worn to the meeting—limited edition NFT designs by Graf E Tee. Now, though, Fiona couldn't generate the token she needed.

Eventually, Fiona and Abdur learned that the attack rode on the same hack the US had used years prior to recover ransom money from the Colonial Pipeline hack in 2021. Somehow, though, it had gotten embedded in a zero-day exploit from Israel's NSO Group for the latest iPhone update, and then opened doors to hackers all over the world. The SolarWinds breach had exposed far more than anyone realized at the time, but enough hints of stolen cyberweaponry had leaked in recent months that the pathology of the attacks became obvious. After a couple calls to their cybersecurity partners in the US, Fiona and Abdur at least had an idea of what was happening. The forces of cyberattacks, the logic of how it spread and developed, and the phenomenal fact that the US and Chinese cyber-defense forces took interest but ultimately did nothing to stop the Russian hackers who infiltrated XiriCoin's network made clear the potential impact—and the triage decision they would need to make. Fiona pulled some strings across the BRI countries and got a meeting with the product managers at Sinoblock. CATL and Ford, seeking to scale their ledger services, launched a partnership program that brought on select startups, funded their transition to Sinoblock, and offered them access to its robust platform of ecosystem cybersecurity. Abdur figured it could help them scale and solve at least some of their security concerns, so Fiona agreed they should make the switch.

XiriCoin survived the threat because Sinoblock's primary backers included so many well-resourced and cash-rich companies, but also because Fiona had created her company to solve some of the most pressing problems now ripping through the world. By integrating identity management and transparent governance into the business model itself, she and her colleagues made XiriCoin far more stable and exchangeable, allowing them to build more services and enter new untapped markets. It was a natural fit, having already penetrated most of those markets through migrant flows, which allowed XiriCoin to gain more data insights and provide more services. Underserved migrant communities could receive support, resources, and targeted training to quickly establish themselves in new locations without relying on corrupt, cynical, or ineffective host country administrators. The United Nations High Commissioner for Refugees (UNHCR) and bilateral development agencies finally had the means to manage the measurable, allowing local agencies and potential employers to make more targeted interventions and conduct more fine-tuned talent searches. Identifying the forces, logic, and phenomena swirling around her—the climate change, the financial collapse, decentralization, cybersecurity hacks, and the persistent aggravation of the pandemic—allowed Fiona to recognize the impact those elements had on her customers, her company, and the organizations with which they partnered. It was enough to make XiriCoin more important than ever. Now, she could continue to triage her decisions and her resources to prepare the company for the future that might unfold.

One Vision for the Future

Sweeping predictions for the future of the globe are always going to be wrong. We might make one right call, perhaps even five, but none of us can chart an immutable path for the next five years. At some point, we will need to recalibrate and redirect even our best-laid plans. We imagined the fictional XiriCoin scenario path over a roughly five-year span, during which Fiona relies on FLP-IT to develop and then regularly adjust her strategies as new forces, logics, phenomena, and impacts emerge. We deliberately did not paint a static so-called end-state that often tops off scenarios and solidifies the final character of an archetypical future, because that approach suggests a steady-state situation. We don't believe that will exist again for quite some time, so painting one would not be helpful. Instead, we need to prepare for a path with all its twists and turns, setting up an eventful, productive, and healthy experience as we travel. It won't be anything like a smoothly paved road for the next ten to fifteen years, but maybe we can create a recognizable trail that weaves its way around jagged rock formations, across white water crossings, and through the thorny underbrush. It is more fruitful to navigate that path with readiness and resilience than to dream of utopia.

Yet if we, as leaders in a Great Remobilization, hope to redesign global systems in ways that address the major global tectonic shifts along this path, we need to think well beyond the next five years. So, we encourage you to look out further, a decade or two, continuing the practice of the first five years and staying attuned to the possible red flags and green lights that signal pivot points and decisions for collective action.

We believe we can't build toward a better future until we have the tools to build the path that could take us in that direction. So, what follows is an ongoing journey that launches from Fiona's narrative to a broader global lens and a longer time frame, running up to 2040. As humans, we tend to predict small degrees of change and undersell the major disruptions and tectonic shifts that truly shape our world. But as leaders, we must try to constantly push our thinking forward by imagining the provocative yet plausible futures that might lie ahead. Only then can we imagine the potential long-term impacts of the significant disruptions that might emerge and remain vigilant to the triage decisions we'll need to make on an ongoing basis.

The climate shocks, the on-again/off-again battles with global recession, and the persistence of the coronavirus—it all finally broke the dam between the West and China in 2029. With Chinese residents now sarcastically recalling the halcyon days of 3 percent GDP growth, the Communist Party needed something to bolster its credibility. The government still wanted the people to believe in Chinese greatness on the global stage, but they had overreached with the BRI. China teetered on the geotech competition front, and it lacked the means to deflate the persistent debt crisis at home. Despite intense investment by the government, domestic capacities couldn't prop up domestic growth. With public and private businesses swimming in debt at home, Chinese banks started to rein in lending. The government's massive public investments might have helped, but the climate disasters created too big a black hole for the economy to reach escape velocity. No advanced organism thrives in isolation, the drafts of the 16th Five-Year Plan said, so China needed to enhance its greatness through coexistence with the rest of the world. Government-funded researchers had already pushed the boundaries of China's capabilities in quantum computing, microelectronic technologies, AI, factory automation, and enterprise services far enough that Chinese companies now made attractive partners for the top tier of US innovators. Beijing realized Chinese innovation, economy, and geopolitical influence could not reach their full potential without closer collaboration among regional and global partners.

Americans had also felt the economic pain in the second half of the 2020s, with inflation rates climbing into the double digits and stagflation hamstringing labor markets. Chinese exporters had gone looking for alternative markets as US government interventions faltered, and the White House never found a coherent response to the major hack of the SwissKnox software in early 2028. Because the platform was developed upstream from the service layer of financial institutions and regulators, no safeguards existed to keep it from taking down the global SWIFT payments system. A moratorium on debt payments helped ease the fallout, but equity markets cratered and banks begged the White House for support. Liberal politicians blamed the financial elite. Conservatives wanted to retrench and pointed fingers at the concept of the global SWIFT platform itself. But in the end, the president had little choice but to agree to yet another unpopular Wall Street bailout—a decision that saved him and his friends a fortune but destroyed any hope he had for reelection.

No matter the political blame, the economy ground to a halt, with no one but the most cash-loaded companies transacting. Expensive food spoiled on shelves, energy bills shot up higher and higher, credit checks and loan applications crumbled, and millions of young professionals sank into anxiety and depression. The number of people suffering from mental health problems climbed from 51.2 million in 2019 to a whopping 108.5 million by the end of 2028, thanks to the economic woes compounding the ongoing waves of climate crises and COVID variants. Globally, the number of people with mental health issues neared one billion.

The Great Global Meltdown of 2028 would have finally tanked consumer sentiment in the US for years had it not been for the unexpected leaps in brain-computer interfaces (BCIs) and cognitive and behavioral neuroscience. In the early days of AI health applications, companies like Woebot and Mindstrong blazed the trail. By 2028, companies like Kernel and Neuralink in the US, Brainland and Neurogress in China, and BrainQ in Israel leveraged new research collaborations funded by the reemergence of the $1 billion BRAIN program, which had launched years earlier during the Obama administration. The BRAIN funding was temporarily halted a couple years earlier, after false rumors about malware in Parkinson's BCI implants had all but killed the concept, but it reemerged with the advent of transparent data markets that guaranteed personal control over private data. Now, privacy-assured data market mechanisms like the BouncerBot, DataVault DAOs, and Jaron Lanier's mediators of individual data (MIDs) had finally gained enough scale to push back on the data abuses of Meta, Google, Alibaba, and other digital oligopolies. Early experiments showed that people trusted digital cognitive interventions when they could own the output and keep control over what it was used for, including therapy choices. It didn't hurt that they could decide which parts of their data footprints to ring-fence, cloak in decoys, and keep private, and which to anonymize, sanitize, and sell for scientific studies to accredited institutions, using Coinbase and new XiriCoin services. Pundits had predicted a new Great Depression that would unleash a double whammy of economic and psychological regression, but by the end of the decade BCIs and cognitive neuroscience had combined with the ability to securely monetize data to open up at least a peak at new horizons for American consumers.

Fortunately, the threat of total upheaval finally brought the global superpowers into closer collaboration, too. The COP29 climate summit in 2030 offered a perfect venue to begin the denouement while saving face for all sides. After months of back-channel negotiating with envoys from the US, China, and the EU, the three powers surprised the conference with an agreement to slash their carbon emissions and support rapidly developing countries with aid that would help them accelerate industrial growth without reliance on fossil fuels. The allies that stood against Russia had been forced into an energy pivot away from Russian oil and gas and toward a more independent mix of carbon-based and renewable wind, solar, and nuclear power, which had experienced an uneasy renaissance. Europe's proposals of carbon import duties and a Global Carbon and Data Trading Trust took hold in 2031, instituting an AI- and quantum-powered carbon-trading platform that was audited and overseen by a council of a hundred rotating experts from every participating country—themselves vetted by more than a thousand civil society institutions from every nation on the planet.

Elon Musk blasted off for Mars a week before the announcement, yet even the stunning string of headlines updating his bold adventure couldn't entirely drown out the buzz of the unprecedented collaboration. The investments would seek to both decarbonize and capitalize on the economic acceleration across Africa. They would ride on the surge of digital and multiverse platforms that had started to capture both the diversity of Africa and the scale of its pan-African potential. Having learned from the US and Chinese platforms, the first pan-African metaverse platform, Andobo, forged connections with several unicorns and dragons. The globally distributed partnerships and increasingly rich digital-physical interactions on the metaverse began to remove location from the equation, creating new niche labor forces, subcultures, and collaborations—first across African countries, then the BRI, US, and European outposts on the continent, and then finally expanding its partnerships with India and other countries across the Global South. The Andobo global network grew to five billion members by 2032, subsuming Meta and making the region around its Ghanaian headquarters one of the world's new hotbeds of high-tech innovation.

Meanwhile, Africa's physical infrastructure had actually benefited from its delayed acceleration. After a string of typhoons in Asia and massive wildfires in California and Australia, Africa's coastal countries began to move critical infrastructure away from vulnerable coastal and desert locations. Aided by China's amplified sensitivity to climate-induced migration and displacement of its own coastal populations, the countries initiated BRI projects that connected their growing advanced manufacturing facilities—now built inland—to modified ports. And while the inequality between shrinking coastal and growing inland areas began to shift, the economy and service sector grew plenty fast enough to employ and pay the young population coming of age in both places.

Africa's growing industrial resilience also made it an increasingly crucial downstream supply chain hub by the end of 2032—a natural home for the newly formed Global Procurement Operations Center (GPOC). The GPOC started to scale its semiautonomous, multisided platform that coordinated smart contracting, switching, and carbon accounting for supply chains. With more and more global logistics systems controlled by cognitive technologies, industries around the world coalesced around the organization, which could aggregate the technological capacity needed to efficiently allocate and sustainably ship supplies across borders. Now, it sought to develop systems that would analyze massive data sets for market signals and then strike supply-demand balances for both profit and equity. The GPOC soon developed a program to help redirect resources, including CRISPR-modified seed stocks, to areas where climate change had decimated agriculture. Few governments possessed the capacity to regulate the flows of trade, people, and resources effectively, so regulators started flocking to GPOC, as well. By late 2033, GPOC launched an initiative to help development organizations design infrastructure networks with climate-stable hubs along migration paths, so refugees could find employment and resources in intermediate destinations.

Concerns about cybersecurity had eased with the emergence and growing reach of diffused community-network approaches to collective reconnaissance, with both public- and private-sector entities realizing after the SWIFT hack that the health of their individual organizations ultimately relied on the health of the entire ecosystem. And with their transparency of rules, regulations, and transactions, auditable blockchains emerged as the leading platform that could secure the trust of both the global powers and the rapidly growing Global South.

Collectively, in 2033, these crypto platforms were home to an astounding 40 percent of all money, up from an estimated 5 percent in 2021. The clash between fiat currency and cryptos had been predictable. Back in 2022, regulators had taken cryptos too lightly and thought they had ten years to sort it all out. But the huge flows of people pushed out of their homes in the crisis-ridden "Raging '20s" changed all that, driving a wedge between the new "crypto migrants" and fiat proponents who stayed local and transacted locally, too.[3]

Europe's heavier regulatory impulses in the cognitive economy and its concerns about the unfettered flow of sensitive digital and biological "code" had been critical during the Great Global Meltdown of 2028. Years of contentious revisions to EU rules had worn the European Project down to a mere trade union, with several countries launching digital versions of their pre-euro currencies. The D-Lira, the eFranc, and the DigiMark—all stablecoins that were pegged to the euro—sent a charge into digital and crypto innovation in the EU, aided by the overdue recalibration of overly restrictive regulations from Brussels. Europe as a whole struggled to rebound from the economic chill that followed the Russian War, climate disasters, the cyber-cataclysm, and the SWIFT crash. By the early 2030s, it had at least managed to stabilize its relationship with Russia, initially using its accelerated green energy investments to lessen its dependence on the oil and gas choke points that Moscow had loved to squeeze.

Europe also continued to set vital standards on the protection of individual privacy, security, and agency. And despite the political tensions that arose as the US took what European governments saw as an overly aggressive and then overly accommodating position toward Beijing, the Transatlantic Partnership never fully frayed. Digital and cognitive companies groused but quickly adjusted to the EU's new Privacy Shield II agreement with the US, as well as China's Personal Information Protection Law. But when China asked the signatories of the BRI contracts to follow its stricter rules, many of them pushed back. Beijing did not much care for their initial suggestion that the BRI use requirements similar to the new Transatlantic Free Data Trading Area, largely because its privacy and security conditions allowed only the private sector, not governments, to access the data streams unless in a global health or security emergency.

At a crossroads in 2034, it was a coalition of private- and civic-sector partners who finally drew up the concept paper for a Joint Data Arbitrage Court, which would adjudicate the appropriate interventions for the public sector. Although it retained the split between private and public access, the agreement to give two of the five seats on the court to justices from the emerging Asia bloc, one of which would permanently go to China, satisfied Beijing's concerns enough to move forward. After all, China still had its ways of exerting influence in corporate boardrooms at home and could press its leverage through them. No longer hostile to Western governments outright, it was still difficult to figure out who was paid by the Chinese government, and for what. The 2030s emerged as an era of uneasy compromises, but also of greater antifragility and new balances.

If the rise of the Asia bloc wasn't apparent beforehand, it clearly culminated with its majority on the data court. The countries didn't integrate as fully as Europe had in the EU, retaining a looser collaboration that helped the region avoid thorny issues related to taxation regimes and overly stringent standards. Westphalian state borders persisted, but they were permeated by a web of crypto and cyber reconnaissance channels that limited deception and escalation. Even India, Japan, and South Korea—still skeptical of the CCP—joined the court, although they rejected many of the diplomatic requirements. The opt-in/opt-out model left rifts on a lot of issues, but it allowed the countries to collaborate on a host of other significant areas, including climate change and migration. The landmark breakthrough on maritime conventions along the Pacific Rim nudged that collaboration further than anyone expected, though conflicts on jurisdiction remained.

Asia's agreements opened the door for even more decentralized finance (DeFi) services. With economic flows proliferating throughout the continent and the world, DeFi companies developed novel business models that could lift incomes and improve social welfare. They created more robust projects that make credits more widely available, using new quantum computing and generative AI algorithms to create more accurate assessments of credit history based on massive pools of personal and environmental data. GPT-3 and ChatGPT had laid the groundwork for that data analysis in 2021 and 2023, but their evolutions in the following years culminated in 2035 with GPT-6, when the advanced transformer technology made it possible to "write" a financial history by drawing on snippets of historical data. GPT-powered systems could now assess creditworthiness based on the crowd's interactions with a given applicant, data on where people lived, their migration routes, and the demographics of the communities in which they'd eventually settled.

The world had gone from war and climate cataclysm in 2024 to a balance of uneasy and tenuous compromises—or at least a positive trajectory that offered some draft blueprints for more antifragility. Regional and subregional clubs had permeable borders for migrants to flow through, add value, and get paid before moving on again, alleviating pinch points in overpressurized local political and social security systems. That helped modestly accelerate global GDP growth by 2035, running around an average of 6.5 percent. But that wasn't the big news anymore. Now, people put more stock in metrics like the social progress index (SPI), which had ticked just above 80 that year. In just over a decade, the global SPI had risen to the levels that Singapore and Costa Rica enjoyed back in 2021. And the addition of decarbonization blockchains and markets had boosted the Ecology sub-index from 55 to 74, the single largest driver of the global gains.

The world wasn't perfect in 2035, by any stretch. But the narrow rail it teetered upon between 2023 and 2028 had widened into something more inclusive, antifragile, and sustainable.

Impact and Triage

We might argue about levels of plausibility in this scenario, and domain experts in individual facets of the story undoubtedly have insights that would provide more nuance. But the general plausibility of these hypothetical future events can help us assess the long-term impacts in a manner that allows us to begin carving out a path to a better future. We have to start building that path now, because current global forces are driving us toward a cliff in the near distance. It is our responsibility as leaders to guide others to create better lives, organizations, communities, and societies. Money and power will follow. None of us can solve the whole picture, of course. No organization or individual holds enough power, and no cultural or economic tentacles reach far enough, to pervade every thread of the global fabric of society. But each of us can act in our own domains. And so long as we keep other domains in mind, we will create many more docking points between other leaders around the world—making it all the more probable, if not certain, that we discover much-needed synergies in our aims and means.

The final two steps of the FLP-IT framework are crucial for finding and acting on these points of common interest. By contemplating how the impact of disruptive forces, logic, and phenomena will ripple throughout the many systems that govern our domains, we can begin to figure out what they mean for the well-being of our regions, countries, communities, and families. Who will gain and who will suffer as we start down this path? How will we lead toward new economic and political realities? Or, in more practical terms, when climate change decimates the coastal lowlands critical to our food supplies, how will we calibrate our agricultural and migration systems to rebuild them?

The last question is hardly hypothetical. It's one that Singapore-based Olam Group, for instance, faces every day.[4] The company processes, packages, and sells agricultural commodities—everything from coffee and cotton to nuts and spices—to more than twenty thousand enterprise customers around the world. But without mitigation of and adaptation to climate change, Olam will face severe supply shortages and the loss of thousands of workers and suppliers as they migrate to the Global North. This shift raises all kinds of questions about potential impacts. How will Olam secure labor in light of migration away from its Global South markets? How will it adjust to new food preferences and pathways as its customers—increasingly migrants—assimilate and fuse their cooking with that of their new homes? How will it transform its supply chain to source, track, ship, and pay for harvests from new farms in new regions? How will it deal with competitors that develop new climate-resilient synthetic foods? What proactive stance will it take on regulations governing the use of supply chain data, carbon tracking, and cross-border GMO transparency? How will it deal with the consolidation of local and regional food companies into global powerhouses, as well as with diffused blockchain-based food DAO syndicates? Will activist shareholders exert pressure to change strategy and distribute dividends more quickly in light of emerging risks? And how will it secure all of those systems, crops, and people against digital or physical attack, whether by humans or viruses?

As we begin to assess just these few probable impacts of climate forces and phenomena on Olam, we can already get a sense for just how dense a jungle we face as we cut this path to the future. Imaginative leaders will also begin to see the possible trade-offs and decisions that governments, industries, communities, and even Olam itself could begin to make to move toward a healthier and more sustainable future. Seeing opportunity in these implications and then designing an action portfolio against that opportunity is what the last phase of FLP-IT, the triage process, is all about. With the right T, we can build smarter designs of antifragile systems that can calm the chaos along the path.

9 The DAL Manifesto: Designing a Smarter World

They called it the Black Summer. As the calendar turned over from 2019 to 2020, a conflagration spread through southern Australia. While the fire season remained relatively calm in the north, bush fires left a path of utter destruction across forty-six million acres of the southern half of the continent, killing at least thirty-four people, leaving about two thousand homes damaged or destroyed, and generating property damage estimated as high as US$7 billion. Australian economist John Quiggin suggested that the ultimate cost of that summer's wildfires could reach as high as US$70 billion.[1]

Like the millions of Australians forced from their homes or affected by the smoke from the wildfires, Genevieve Bell, who discussed rites of passage and liminality in the introduction of this book, felt a profound change with the Black Summer. What became clear to Bell, the director of the Australian National University School of Cybernetics, was that humanity could not quite articulate the interconnection points within and across systems. She had come to realize, she said, "that the system feels like the critical unit of analysis for the twenty-first century." If her intuition was correct, she asked, how do we build a theory around it? How do we train people to see it, regulate it, and build resistance when necessary?

Bell's search for answers led her back to the global reemergence from World War II. In 1946, a multidisciplinary group of brilliant minds gathered periodically in New York City to ponder the power and perils of technology and consider whether humanity could build a better world with thoughtful and deliberate interventions. The conversation included a contemplation of the future of computing that would enhance humanity and reject the divisions that led to major wars between world powers. They framed the conversation under the banner of cybernetics, which American mathematician Norbert Wiener defined as "the science of control and communications in the animal and machine." Cybernetics laid the foundation for a generation of technologists and thinkers who would help establish the internet—people like Stewart Brand, Douglas Engelbart, and Kevin Kelly, whom Bell dubbed the "cybernetic children." Yet, somewhere along the line, its evolution got sidetracked by a dot-com boom that saw the digital revolution and then AI as narrow tools to extract data and generate profit, rather than purposefully and more broadly improve the fragility of global systems. Too much power lies in siloes, as the inventor of the World Wide Web, Tim Berners-Lee, frames it.[2] The halcyon vision of Silicon Valley when it works well—telling a story about a future that is better than the present, and then cracking open the door to make that story possible—devolved into the search for convenience and gratification from Amazon deliveries, Instagram likes, and TikTok stunts.

Today, at the dawn of the Cognitive Era and the next great shift in the global order, we need to renew those lost conversations. We need to ask ourselves, as Bell did, "How do we tell a story about a future that is better than the present? How do we break open the world and train people for the future so they can build something different?" What's clear to Bell, and to us, is that "better" has to be more just, more fair, more equitable, more sustainable, and, most of all, more antifragile than the systems in place today. We need to reengage the cybernetics mindset and contemplate how humanity, ecology, and technology will intersect and interact. We need to become the design activist leaders (DALs) who can draw a blueprint for the decades to come.

As we contemplated some possible starting points for smarter global systems redesigns and a Great Remobilization, we began to realize just how ingrained traditional operating rules were. If we manage to transition from today's fragile and narrow perspective to a holistic system-of-systems analysis of the global tectonic forces, logics, and impacts buffeting our world, we'll immediately realize we have no choice but to undertake some significant triage of our resources, decisions, and investments. We might have to give up sacred cows—a company disinvesting in a core product category in favor of growth elsewhere, or a government sunsetting one of its most powerful agencies so it can restructure in ways that allow regulators to accommodate the broadening ripple effects of new cognitive forces.

Today, global economic agreements prioritize the flow of trade and commerce over the lives those flows are supposed to enhance. Easily measurable profit takes precedence over the harder and more subjective to assess the welfare of actual people. In many cases, our political, economic, and business principles have become so axiomatic that they have actually become de facto values—growth is always good; fast is better than slow; value requires scarcity; doing more with less yields efficiency. As we considered some of the proposals and the resulting triage decisions we discuss in this chapter, we had to stop and reevaluate exactly what each of these terms meant—GDP, growth, profit, resilience, risk, efficiency—and we needed to get far more precise in our assumptions. We found ourselves stuck on first principles and realized we needed to go back to Bryan Johnson's zeroth principles, to the new fundamental building blocks that question our assumptions and allow us to create new logics for our world. Collectively, we all will need to do the same to develop the new cybernetic governance structures and other systems for the cognitive economy. While climate change solutions call on the resources of nearly every government agency, for example, too few of them work in concert. Similarly, the World Trade Organization doesn't take labor decisions and labor trends fully into account, because so much of that falls under the domain of domestic labor ministries. We've kept our structures focused and bounded, which results in a narrow view of the world—a view that no longer reflects the world in which we live.

As natural and human-made systems (e.g., viruses and economies) intersect and grow increasingly interdependent in ways they weren't before, our incentives, monitoring, and governance methodologies need to cut across all those systems, as well. So, we need to find ways to see beyond the narrow and immediate, to envision the interconnected system and the second- and third-order effects of our decisions and products. We need to think about how the flows of everything from people to ideas to resources will shape and be shaped by systems, and then become far better at guiding those flows toward constructive ends via better pathways and incentives. We need to understand that failure is an everyday occurrence, whether immediately recognized or not, but if we adopt the entrepreneurial mindset of failing, learning, and rebuilding in shorter and smaller increments, we can flip failure into fortune. To that end, we need to calibrate systems so they fluctuate in more limber ways, instead of getting so pressurized that they jump wildly or swing out of balance.

In the following section, we present ideas that design activist leaders might consider as they navigate the present complexity toward a better future. We organized this "DAL manifesto" around our Five Cs—COVID and pandemic management, the cognitive economy, cybersecurity, climate change, and China—because we believe these tectonic forces pose the greatest threat to the foundations of our global systems, and because addressing the disruptions they've caused will have the greatest payoff for our economies, societies, and lives. However, rather than taking a step-by-step walk through the FLP-IT process for each one of these tectonic forces, we opted to present these as unabashedly entrepreneurial visions that ask: "What if . . . ?" As science and technology activists, we see the value of applied science to help transform the world, but also as a powerful tool to help build trust and empathy. These problems require courage and faith to drive a vision larger than the algorithmic value of a prediction—one that's grounded in pragmatic and balanced designs with human centricity, rather than utopian dreamworlds. And, as you'll find throughout, they often require that we make difficult near-term trade-offs for long-term prosperity and well-being.

The suggestions are first steps, but only first steps. Going forward, they will all require a constant reevaluation of the forces, logic, phenomena, and impacts, and we will constantly have to triage our cognitive economy "portfolios." But ultimately, like the cybernetics conversations decades ago, we hope these ideas spark the kinds of discussions that help us remobilize the human, ecological, and technical systems that surround us.

A Global Pandemic Radar Network

The rapid development of the initial COVID-19 vaccines might obscure the need for ongoing support of fundamental research and development, but the variants, the various levels of vaccine effectiveness, and the sporadic sputters of our economies and lives should bolster the point. We like to believe that new inventions and breakthroughs will happen fast if the need is great enough, but there's no guarantee that science can speed up the discovery of biological processes, which are inherently messy and unpredictable. The COVID vaccine emerged from science that had been more than a decade in the making, borne of long-standing collaborations between experts over the course of a decade or more, reaching back all the way to mRNA research at DARPA in 2011. The fundamental works of lithium batteries for electric vehicles date back to the 1970s. Neural networks, the core idea of modern AI, came of age in the 1960s. We can't let our recent scientific successes lull us into a false sense of security.

COVID should tell us that such fundamental research is vital to address-ing global health. So how can we create a better system to prepare for the next pandemic? As cycles between mutations accelerate, how do we accel-erate the cycle of detection, vaccine development, delivery, and care? How do we ensure that our systems-level view includes a more effective delivery of vaccines into arms?

We might start with an early warning system that detects new viruses and alerts the global health community to their emergence. This might build off the work that our UC Berkeley Haas and Hult colleague, Omar Romero-Hernandez, is conducting with One Health, a global initiative that views well-being through the lens of our entire ecosystem. One Health brings together veterinarians, botanists, biologists, and experts from other sciences on the premise that health in one field creates synergies with health in others. "When you try to focus too much on either the popula-tion, the plants, or the biota by itself, you might be creating an imbalance," he explained. Rather, you need to have a bird's-eye view of changes across populations and systems to identify threats or opportunities that could pop and spread. Such an approach could naturally accommodate the intelli-gent and programmable microorganisms that Bryan Johnson described in chapter 4, potentially creating a field of biological sensors in our planetary ecosystem that aligns with our goal of early virus detection.

Even before then, though, our current digital tools can alert us to the rise of new communicable strains and diseases that we have yet to fully understand—if we can establish a trusted and apolitical global institution to process the early warning signs, direct information and resources to the science needed to analyze them, and then help marshal an equitable global response to the threat. "This is our 'now or never' moment in public health," said Tom Frieden, the former director of the Centers for Disease Control. "We have to maintain the funding, the momentum, and the inter-est to protect ourselves against the next health threat, because the question is not whether there'll be another health threat; the question is just when it's going to come, and from where."

Frieden argues for a reconsideration of the global public health archi-tecture. The World Health Organization and other global institutions have improved, he said, and their response to COVID clearly exceeded their response to the 2014 and 2015 Ebola outbreaks. But as the imbalanced dis-tribution of vaccines and the subsequent pandemic variants demonstrated, that response wasn't adequate. Despite the alphabet soup of public and private health agencies that emerged over the past decades to combat different diseases and maladies around the world, politicization and the lack of coordination among these agencies allowed cracks to open throughout the critical reconnaissance-projection-mitigation pipeline. The Global Fund, an international partnership that mobilizes and invests more than $4 billion a year in support of local efforts to combat HIV, tuberculosis, and malaria, has a larger annual budget than the WHO. Its initiatives have saved more than thirty million lives. But that's not enough on its own. We need a new capacity, Frieden said, either part of an existing institution or embodied within a new one.

It starts with a smart sensing mechanism, like the early tsunami warning network in our oceans, but that kind of network in the microbiological realm needs to be able to assess threats and intervene to mitigate them— "Kind of an Interpol looking for rogue microbes to prevent a sneak attack from nature or from an errant laboratory," Frieden said. The most effective design for this system would include ways to integrate community-based expertise and institutions with national and global organizations. Local networks could cycle experts and information back and forth with national agencies, which themselves could tie into the WHO or similar institutions to share best practices and monitor compliance. Such a global system could facilitate brainstorming about diagnoses and solutions, while making national and global scientific policies more relevant to local communities.

The WHO remains essential, Frieden said, and a strengthened version of it will need to play a central role in any global health redesigns. The new global health framework should also integrate the ability of an organization like the Global Fund to provide quick, flexible funds to help countries build the surveillance, response, and management systems they need to address outbreaks. It will need resources to fill gaps in technical expertise, as well as the authority to impose sanctions if countries don't comply, including a mechanism that obligates companies and countries to license and distribute the most effective vaccines at rates that safeguard minimum profitability *and* equity for poorer populations.

These proposals won't magically solve the inequitable distribution of medical resources, nor will they eliminate the politicization of health insurance and vaccine acceptance. They are design principles that we would do well to heed in our overhaul of the virus surveillance, early warning, and mitigation systems. But as we experiment and chalk up successes with those new elements of systems-based approaches that better integrate the macro, meso, and micro levels of our societies and environments, we can start to sway hearts and minds, as well.

Spheres of Cognitive Convergence

The US, China, and the EU have experimented with their own versions of a digital economy for decades, but the world lacks an inclusive and empowering digital economic order for the Cognitive Era. If we hope to rebalance the economy toward an equitable expansion of improved services that can help solve global needs and make systems more antifragile, we need to take back control of the political and economic incentives that hijacked the last phase of globalization.

We might start in the issue areas where interests overlap, like a Venn diagram. The first of the overlapping circles encompasses the world's shared challenges and their digital and cognitive components. Examples might include climate-change-driven flooding of coastal areas that serve as primary entry points to an entire region's technological and economic infrastructure. Another shared interest might involve the unmasking of digitally cloaked terrorist groups that seek to disrupt critical socio-technical infrastructure, such as hospitals, schools, or voting systems. Short of war scenarios, destabilizing regions helps no one given our global interconnections, especially if we hope to collectively design more antifragile systems. Nothing about solving these challenges is easy, of course, but we have precedents to draw from, including the progress toward the UN's Sustainable Development Goals.

The other circles in the Venn diagram represent the different competing visions in countries that govern the development of technological solutions for these societal challenges. How countries develop their human and technological capacity and orient their solutions to societal challenges will become paramount in how they fit in a shared order for the cognitive economy. A top-down, government-controlled approach in autocratic nations would prove far more efficient in times of crisis, for example, but that must be balanced against human rights and long-term effectiveness of a democratic country's iterative private-sector approach to technology development.

Whatever that balance, increasing that overlap will take complex negotiations, but we might be able to "negotiate" these complex problems through collaborative solution hacking or digital twinning simulations to which both sides bring real-world inputs. A side-by-side hacking of a system, if monitored closely, could yield transparent progress one line of code at a time. This could prove especially effective if those hacking and monitoring the designs include more women and other underrepresented populations who bring broader experiences, complementary cognitive capabilities, and more reasons to expand the overlap in this Venn diagram.

In particular with women, we have a powerful boost in our capabilities awaiting us once we finally fully embrace the intellect, imagination, and innovation of more than half the global population. We cannot stride into the Cognitive Era on one leg. Global alignment toward solutions to gender disparities, the UN's Sustainable Development Goals, or any other public good should rank high on our list of priorities—certainly higher than the current struggle for geopolitical and economic dominance. The development, distribution, and deployment of powerful cognitive systems that help shape our societies and lives need to be co-created by all the impacted stakeholder groups.

The realists in us must acknowledge that the competition of models for data control, hardware design, surveillance, and other advanced technologies will always influence global engagement between the US, China, and the EU, no matter how noble the cause. Some "hacking negotiations" will fail. There are some domains and topics that governments, notably China and the US, will deem "no-go areas." We will hit those roadblocks in the area of surveillance, for instance, which is present in many countries, from China to the US, Russia to the UK, Nicaragua to Israel, and many others in between. But surveillance, at least in the sense of situational reconnaissance or awareness, can also yield shared progress in many areas of joint interest, such as tracking of carbon, pollutants, radioactive isotopes, viruses, terrorist or criminal activity, money laundering, food supply chains, accidents, and so on. Disagreement will and should persist when personal liberties and freedom of expression are touched. And while we believe that is a red line not to be crossed, it is also not present in each use case. Are the no-go areas worth forgoing all other areas of solution hacking and a joint push for the greatest overlap in the diagram?

It's just one more reason for the world's major powers to engage and define the policy and political agendas that are expressed through the designs for global problems and global markets. Without some guardrails for the competition between them, the countries caught in the middle will refuse to follow, which in turn will limit the integration of markets. No new global order will perfectly align the three models, but we can foster interoperability for the common good of the global system. That is the conversation and negotiation we need to begin immediately.

Given the inertia at the macro level, we might need to begin pushing in a more ground-up manner, creating new market and industry designs for the cognitive economy, and then using them to press for geopolitical change. The potential of blockchain, DAOs, and tokenized governance structures within the growing crypto ecosystem could provide one such force. Emerging Web3 platforms could decentralize access and distribute control to participants in a "cognitive cooperative" type of structure that shares inputs, governance of operations, and outputs alike. Thoughtful use of these technologies could decentralize and democratize governance of certain issues and priorities in ways that move the needle on macro governance decisions, too—for example, by allowing vast fields of members to contribute their resources to a marketplace created by and for individual actors. As we write this in early 2022, these concepts remain idealized and uncertain goals for the current state of the crypto ecosystem, but we can already see interest, action, and momentum building behind them.

Agency-Assured Data Markets

If access is one critical area to be improved in stakeholder-inclusive systems, agency is the other. Access without agency is a spear without a tip. Some of the most intriguing possibilities for the nexus of access and agency have emerged in data market designs that seek to set value for our personal or organizational data—and, in some iterations, do so in a way that helps ensure privacy. These centralized platforms and decentralized blockchain protocols—we will need both for different domains and geographies—could allow users to purchase data sets or gain access to real-time data streams, generating a potential data economy that experts expect to be worth more than $3 trillion.[3] Early attempts to effectively price data, including ideas promulgated by researchers at Microsoft and Amazon, proved largely ineffective, beleaguered by regulatory compliance risks, competitive concerns (e.g., the protection of trade secrets), and the tenuous balance between the loss of privacy and the potential economic benefits of sharing one's data. But new data market designs have emerged in attempts to establish privacy-assured auctions, create actor certifications (e.g., a Data Trading Commission), value data as a form of labor, or carve out anonymized data for use in public health and similar research. Further development of these markets—with an end goal of returning value and control of data to individuals and organizations—will provide for greater security and trust in a cognitive economy.

Of course, trust for this kind of intimate collaboration springs from within our productive selves. As we pair our natural intelligence with its artificial counterpart, our data becomes labor. And so, we also need to consider the radical changes that AI-based cognification will bring to the workplace. The cognitive economy allows us to redistribute the productive burden between humans and machines, potentially freeing people to ask what kind of productive lives they want. We have reams of studies about the types of jobs and tasks that cognitive technologies can automate and replace, but far too little understanding of how a symbiotic combination of human and machine intelligences can augment, rather than displace, workers. We reduce the role of machines to the execution of mundane and repetitive tasks we don't enjoy, and don't focus their capabilities on facilitating our individual growth as empaths, caregivers, idea creators, strategists, designers, and visionaries—in both cases, largely because current economic structures and regulatory incentives do not reward those types of roles.

We need to reform tax laws and policies so they incentivize companies to invest in technological augmentations for workers that recognize their innately human skills rather than displacing their jobs entirely. Properly calibrated tax incentives could encourage a new age of human-machine partnership that recognizes and amplifies the unique strengths of each for a more productive and fulfilling whole. For example, governments could reward companies that participate in public-private partnerships created to design and test the ways machines and humans might augment each other. (One such example is the FutureWork program at Karlsruhe Institute of Technology in Germany.[4]) They could set up more robust credits for digital and cognitive entrepreneurship training. Similarly, they could grant incentives for corporations that participate in global work redesign and reskilling platforms. And they could support startup programs that tear down antiquated models of work and establish new ones.

These sorts of policies would go a long way toward establishing an inclusive and empowering foundation for whatever form of metaverse might evolve. Beginning to build a more fulfilling and equitable work environment would take us a significant step toward financial stability, personal agency, and collective inclusion in the integrated cyber-physical environment.

Multilateral Organization for Genetic Data and Genomic Safety

As we create the digital nervous system for the Cognitive Era and metaverse, we need to ensure the safe and secure flow of more than just data across hundreds of trillions of nodes worldwide. Moving to a fully interoperable digital regime will take far more than flipping a switch, especially given the world's disparate technology-governance models and the competing political and cultural philosophies about the internet. But the growing integration of the digital with synthetic bioengineering and other sciences, as well as the ethical issues raised by those cognitive confluences, will put even more pressure on our differences at a time when those collisions of domains carry fantastic potential for the evolution of humankind.

To harness it, we will need at least two new multilateral institutions. The first would monitor international flows of data and set standards for confidentiality, privacy, classification, and packaging. This might eventually resemble the SWIFT network for money flows, but with a far less centralized form. Leveraging Web3-style token governance and federated AI algorithms would allow for audits by both national regulators and, when appropriate, civil society actors. Institutions like these could provide safe channels between different types of data markets that might evolve, providing industry standards and oversight for the gaps between transparent and trusted markets around the world.

The second, similar global institution would monitor and safeguard genetic mutations and their "travel." Human identities are an especially delicate matter, and one that can easily inflame fears, anxieties, and violent public backlash. A global surveillance and response mechanism for biological and genetic abnormalities could catch potential threats before they spread, preserving health and well-being while also curbing opportunities for national foes or extremists to point blame and incite animosity toward others. Again, these could prove critical in filling the gaps between different national and regional organizations, including the brain research and data hubs that we propose in the next two sections.

bCERN: A Globally Inclusive Research Hub for the Brain

The need to balance individual freedom and self-actualization with community and collective trust-building will become ever more apparent as we add brain-computer interfaces (BCIs) into the mix. As the hundred billion neurons in our heads collide with three hundred trillion trillion trillion

IP addresses on the internet, we need a cybernetic governance system to preserve individual identity, dignity, and agency so each person can decide for themselves how much they want to expose or put at risk for a certain trade-off or potential benefit. The potential is phenomenal, and we ought not stifle experimentation and innovation. But to safeguard experiments, we need to develop better governance of cognitive technologies so we can monitor for and mitigate against unintended consequences. We propose a four-pronged approach for this governance.

One, we propose a bCERN—a CERN-like collaboration for the brain. At the original CERN in Switzerland, scientists from around the world come together to study the essence of the universe. If the brain is the most sophisticated organ we're currently aware of, with as many neurons as there are stars in the universe, then we should give similar attention to that inner universe. Jointly, we can push the edge of the scientific frontiers with an obligation to 100 percent transparency on its findings, facilitating broad stakeholder discussions about the promise and perils of these discoveries.

Two, we need to dedicate significant funds, whether to bCERN or other credible research consortia, to study the automation of certain brain processes. For example, we might seek to align our neurological, ecological, and economic goals in ways that help communities strike a healthier balance of both. Efforts to optimize our individual health and longevity could flow into efforts to optimize our collective ecology and economy to ensure that we don't maximize one at the expense of another. We need a dedicated, well-funded, multibillion-dollar research program at the intersections of these fields to develop policy recommendations that assure antifragility and strive for geo-economic, geopolitical, and geo-ecological equilibria.

A Global Brain Data Bank

Three, we propose a global brain data bank located in Switzerland and governed by an independent, international body of science, ethics, and civil society leaders, as well as entrepreneurs, from both the Global North and Global South. Nationally approved trials involving brain science should flow data into the bank, and scientists the world over could gain access once they are accredited and approved. While we believe in the power of individual agency over individual data and the right of individuals to trade data in ways that assure privacy, we also recognize that data directly derived from neuronal interaction patterns, the insights gleaned from them, and the tools developed with them represent a step-change in the human condition. As such, they deserve special safeguards and oversight, at least until we know more about what's actually there.

Starting immediately and then continuously over time, the expert governors can make informed and agile recommendations about what kinds of data can be released—in an aggregated and anonymized form—to health care researchers, scientists, entrepreneurs, insurance companies, or government policymakers. The same deliberative process would allow an individual's data to be released for their own use, so they could trade or sell their data under local laws. This effort to allow fast-moving innovation and entrepreneurial development while also ensuring individual data privacy and security is similar to how medical data is regulated in many parts of the world today. But because data flows don't stop at borders, these rules would have to be globally accepted and enforced. The initial partners and data deposits would likely have to begin with the US and its allies, but collaboration with China could be negotiated to preserve data security.

Four, we believe it makes sense to put more cognitive tech observatories in place, akin to the OECD.AI Policy Observatory and similar institutions established by the EU, International Labour Organization, and other transnational organizations.[5] These current observatories study issues such as cognitive automation and its effects on labor markets and civil society, but new brain-focused observatories could layer in the specificity of neuroscience, sensor hardware and medical procedures, and regulations that existing organizations could not absorb. More important than the organizational design, though, are the key objectives of the institutions—primarily, keeping BCI advances in service of humans and their individuality, identity, dignity, and agency, rather than advertisement or political control. As we forge into the most inner sanctum of human existence, the brain, this new frontier deserves extra care and curation.

A Sonar for Autonomous Actor Mapping (SAAM)

The authenticity and dignity that's rooted in our unique identity is essential for trust, but establishing identity becomes exceedingly difficult in Web3 and the metaverse, where actors are often cloaked by design. To solve this, we have proposed a Sonar for Autonomous Actor Mapping (SAAM)—a tool that could map actors, characterize or name them, authenticate their individual or institutional identities, summarize their agendas, and chart their activity vectors in virtual arenas.[6] Importantly, it could also map affiliations and interactions, helping companies and other organizations understand the trajectories and inclinations of parties with which they might transact or collaborate. The SAAM would provide a dynamically evolving sonar that goes below the surface of virtual activity to create a fact base for executive decision-making and strategic responses. This would provide a more informed view of both threats and opportunities in virtual, cognitive spaces. While this kind of tool will initially emerge as a business or national intelligence application first, a subsequent version could create shared awareness between governments, as well.

Law of the Metaverse
Whatever the solution, if we fail to strike the right balance between the freedom of individual expression and the responsibility of authentic identity, we risk the re-creation of today's anonymized divisions on social media—only this time, bringing even greater negative impacts directly into our real lives. To avoid this outcome, we propose a law of the metaverse, akin to the International Maritime Convention but with regionalized forums. These forums, perhaps modeled on the World Economic Forum's Center for the Fourth Industrial Revolution, should provide sandboxes in which companies and developers can test policies and algorithm designs, and then oversee their deployment with a careful eye toward second- and third-order effects. The groups might resemble the US Food and Drug Administration's processes for testing and oversight of pharmaceutical development and distribution, only in this case it would track algorithms and the creation, collection, and curation of data to ensure transparency and security. Even better, tracking these sandbox tests within a blockchain would provide an opportunity for anyone and everyone to audit compliance, rather than relying solely on industry standards or government oversight. Such a framework would represent an important step forward from the complete lack of guardrails on digital platforms that mutilates trust today.

All of this will require far more than tweaks to tax or technology policy. The transition to cognitive systems and infrastructures will be very expensive and disruptive, and powerful interests will try to bend the rules to their benefit. Stopping to first remind ourselves of the grand possibilities will help inspire the grindstone work needed to deconstruct current systems and build better ones. If the sticks are government policy and shifts in market demand, perhaps the carrots become the remarkable, life-enhancing advances that new cognitive technologies can deliver—cures for disease and trauma, deeper respect for the wondrous complexity of the natural world, and heightened happiness and fulfillment for people worldwide. As the Cognitive Era advances, scientists, technologists, and policymakers will need to work hand in hand with the ethicists, sociologists, historians, and philosophers who can help make sense of what matters most at the intersection of cognitive economy domains.

Agency for Digital Infrastructure Integrity Monitoring

Many expert voices have called for a "Bretton Woods 2.0" to overhaul and redesign global institutions for the cognitive economy. Our existing intergovernmental organizations worked well, if not perfectly, as we recovered from World War II, moved through the Cold War, and emerged into the Digital Era. But as the world's interconnected system of systems grows ever more complex and moves faster and faster, we need to cognify the institutions that govern the cross-border flows of people, capital, data, trade, and other resources (natural and otherwise). A cognification of existing intergovernmental organizations will likely take decades—if it could even succeed at all. The world still needs physical infrastructure, utilities, food, education, and health care—after all, unsafe water kills more people each year than wars.[7] But the power to control and govern the flow of critical physical resources is held by those who design and own the software-enabled cognitive tools that regulate them. Furthermore, the economic and political empowerment of underprivileged voices around the globe increasingly happens through digital, rather than physical, means.

A new start with greenfield designs for "AI-native" institutions will likely scare politically powerful established interests, especially in northern and Western postindustrial economies. What might instead stand up a few cognitive economy governance institutions, and then equip and empower them to create a handful of high-profile lighthouse successes with inter-regional accords and pilots. As they gain traction, we can fuse them to existing institutions or inject their best practices into these existing organizations. For instance, branches of a new agency for Global Digital Infrastructure Integrity monitoring could eventually attach itself to the World Bank, African Development Bank, and Asia Infrastructure Development Bank.

Engagement with Beijing will be crucial to developing these new models. China's intended application for DEPA membership might offer an interesting foothold for this effort, because that partnership already consists of a mix of democratic and "not-so-democratic" countries. As inefficient as the world's fragmented digital governance is, the endless flavors of regulations can yield endless opportunities for meshing and distilling new innovative approaches for agile global institutions that work in the cognitive economy.

Cybersecurity Collaboratives

For all the mission- and life-critical functions we delegate to our digital and cognitive technologies, the fact that we do not already have a comprehensive global accord to define the rules for cyberspace is shocking. When UN member countries started developing the rules of the cyber road around 2015, it took nearly two years before they could agree that, yes, international law should apply in cyberspace. "As an international lawyer, I'm still stunned that it took them multiple years to agree to that statement," said Duncan Hollis, a professor and expert in international cybersecurity law at the Temple Law School. "And who knows how much wine and how many dinners went into it?"

By 2022, Hollis said, two competing groups at the UN had somewhat surprisingly aligned behind a pair of consensus reports, reiterating that international law applies to cyberspace and emphasizing the need for peaceful dispute settlement. In fact, prompted by the rise of ransomware attacks by non-state actors, the reports even shifted from things nations should avoid to things nations should actively do to ensure cybersecurity, Hollis explained.

It's still too early to tell how these consensus reports will play out. "The real challenge is: how do we move from having these words on paper . . . to seeing them implemented and operated in and among nation-states?" he said. For example, neither the accords nor the negotiators have a solid grasp on how to handle second- and third-order effects of cyberattacks. The computer worm Stuxnet targeted a specific nuclear facility but spread around the world. Companies that could provide little to no gain for attackers still got caught up in the SolarWinds hack. "You're going to spend millions of dollars, victim by victim," Hollis said, "and you're not going to trust the underlying processes as much anymore."

On the plus side, though, the consensus report at least marked a clear and constructive step toward a much-needed multilateral solution. We might supplement those emerging agreements with a reconsideration of the blacklists, bans, and tariffs that competing global powers have erected against technologies developed by the others. Yes, the US and China have legitimate concerns about foreign technologies, but indiscriminate blacklisting of certain technologies or companies destroys the potential of researchers and developers on both sides to benefit from the innovation of the other. Subsequent iterations of the accords should build toward clear ground rules for discrete, ring-fenced spaces for collaboration on climate change, decarbonization, migration, food and nutrition, clean energy, health, and education.

Drilling down a level, we also need to define the rules of the road for zero-day exploits, the cyberattacks on vulnerabilities that software vendors or antivirus companies don't yet know about. Entire industries and marketplaces have been built around the search for such exploits, as Nicole Perlroth notes in her book *This Is How They Tell Me the World Ends* (2021).[8] Countries will need to establish clear rules for the identification, prosecution, and punishment of non-state and commercial actors—whether they're motivated by money or support for national goals. Arms dealers in cyberspace should receive the same scrutiny as those in the analog world. Fortunately, we have precedent for these steps, as states have always needed clear rules to cooperate with each other. As far back as 1846, countries enacted rules against privateers on open seas. And we already have the tools to protect weaker states, municipalities, small businesses, and other organizations in our systems, even without the resources deployed to combat sophisticated or concerted attacks. In the game of cyber superiority, we need rules that define which types of pawns are legitimate and which are not.

Surveilling the Surveillants

No matter how we resolve a global construct for cybersecurity, hackers will still hack. Cybersecurity is a constant process, so we need to remain vigilant internally while pushing our defenses further and further out from our soft middle. To create that buffer, we should shift cybersecurity discussions away from worries about cost and damage to focus instead on opportunities to capture value. The tech-market research firm Gartner estimates that by 2030, 30 percent of a chief information security officer's effectiveness won't be measured by the ability to prevent breaches but by the ability to create business value.[9]

Organizations can begin to capture the value of data by adopting a more active, bodyguard-type approach that shifts the focus from unified entities to individual users. This bouncer approach, which establishes cyberdefenses outside the organizations, will "surveil the surveillants," tracking data leakage and turning it into trust, insights, and value. For example, consider how much proprietary data employees inadvertently leak or signal in the data exhaust of their everyday online activities. A patent analyst uses Google Patents to research citations. A software engineer uses Stack Overflow for coding questions and to check their salary against outside job offers. And a marketing director searches for news reports on products similar to an upcoming release. A nefarious competitor with a relatively simple AI system could easily access all that data exhaust and draw out patterns that expose your company's plans. It's already happening in our individual lives with a startling lack of transparency, privacy, and agency as we move and transact online. Outside parties triangulate our identities and life patterns everywhere on the internet. In business settings, competitors can use this information to ascertain product road maps, worker morale, and other internal patterns they could use to preempt your next move.

The same system designed to track data and allow employees to control their own preferences, in line with company standards, would do more than avoid lost opportunities to rivals. It could help capture the value that data exhaust could have within the value chain of suppliers, distributors, R&D partners, and other stakeholders. And if adopted across a broader ecosystem of collaborators and customers, it could assure trust and agency for anyone who regularly interacts with the firm.

Ultimately, we will need overlapping protection regimes with early detection and warning systems that cover different arenas and attack vectors. As such, we should approach cybersecurity with an "ecosystem security" perspective that looks across our complete value chain—from supplier intelligence to customer intimacy—because the trust we build through holistic cybersecurity will be the foundation on which we build value. This approach will become especially crucial for individual businesses that need to ensure security across numerous nodes and potential hack points—from their own brick-and-mortar stores to the new blockchain-based systems that process payments and track goods. As with the SolarWinds hack, one vulnerability in one supplier can put thousands of customers across a whole partner network at risk, including sensitive government accounts.

The increasingly interconnected nature of our governments, businesses, and lives makes us increasingly interdependent on one another to keep our data and systems secure. Layering in a bodyguard approach to cybersecurity—one that allows companies to track their data and how it is used—could ensure the critical privacy and security elements needed to make a local and collective approach work.

Hacking Climate Economics

Estimates of how much a major climate disaster would cost look truly ominous. As we wrote this in late September 2022, Hurricane Ian was pummeling southwestern Florida with destructive winds and flooding coastal cities with massive storm surges. More than 2.5 million power outages were reported within twenty-four hours of the storm's landfall, on top of the 1.5 million who lost power when Ian hammered Puerto Rico eleven days earlier. Two major bridges were rendered impassable and would require "structural rebuilds," Florida governor Ron DeSantis said the morning after the storm hit, calling its impact "historic."[10]

Florida knows the impact of hurricanes all too well, but climate scientists are growing increasingly concerned about the warming planet intensifying these storms. One model estimated that a potential "megaflood" in the Central Valley of California—where fields and farms grow roughly a quarter of US food supplies—would cause $1 trillion in damage.[11] That would be five times the cost of Hurricane Katrina's destruction in New Orleans, and that's just one catastrophe. Imagine three or four of these types of disasters around the globe.

If we hope to mitigate the massive disruptions that climate change will generate in our societies and economies, we'll need more concrete ways to assess the value of human health and welfare—and the cost of carbon— and then turn that knowledge into tough-minded economic incentives that offer a carrot for businesses and individuals to lower their emissions. As the 2022 US Inflation Reduction Act proved, tying climate-related incentives to investment, jobs, and health benefits is the most promising way to overcome political opposition. But we can't be naive, either. We also need a stick: regulations that assess the damage of climate change on the economy and society at large and then impose a tax to cover those costs, as posited by Nobel Prize winner William Nordhaus and his proponents. We need to dis-incentivize the release of greenhouse gasses (GHGs), especially carbon, into the atmosphere, where they damage the ozone layer and human health. However, we need to be careful with the sticks we use, and be prepared to amend them as our knowledge of climate change continues to evolve. Current models likely underestimate the cost of emissions, because their ripple effects through societies and economies are extremely difficult to trace. And the taxation of carbon fuels typically punishes underprivileged communities who have longer commutes to work.[12] We need to concede that traditional methods of "top-down" economics have not yielded the results we desire, whether due to political futility or too narrow a focus on the financial and economic at the expense of the social.

One way we could deploy both carrots and sticks is to incentivize scal-able innovation of new technology-driven solutions that assess, monitor, value, and repurpose carbon. By incentivizing and requiring the develop-ment of a circular economy for carbon, we can create and then capture value from it. "There are essentially two ways to prevent the increase of carbon content in the atmosphere," said Boris Schubert, chief development officer at Silicon Ranch, a leading solar energy developer, as well as chairman of its carbon solutions arm, Clearloop. "We can keep it from being pumped there in the first place—carbon avoidance. Or we can find ways to absorb what's already there—carbon reduction." For carbon avoidance, Schubert explained, we need to lower energy demand or meet it with sources that emit less or no carbon, such as replacing fossil-fuel generation with wind, solar, and other renewables. Energy-efficiency measures reduce demand on a per-person level, but humanity's quest for new tools, discovery, and expansion will continue to push our aggregate demand ever higher. So, the switch to clean sources is critical, and existing carbon markets help incentivize this transition—generating revenue for those who are "clean" and creating a cost for those who are not. At Silicon Ranch, Schubert said, "we're avoiding carbon by deploying solar farms in high-emission regions of the US power grid."

The carbon-reduction approach—absorbing carbon from the atmosphere and sequestering it, for example—remains less developed. Fortunately, though, the demand for these types of carbon credits and the nascent promise of the advanced technologies in development are enticing more and more investors. Plus, Schubert said, an array of effective "low-tech" options already exists today. For instance, Silicon Ranch reduces carbon with flocks of sheep it manages at its solar projects. As the animals wander and graze, they fertilize the ground with their manure and promote the growth of native grasses. "We're reducing carbon by applying regenerative agriculture practices on our land," Schubert said. "This increases the carbon in the soil, but it also improves air quality, water quality, and biodiversity."

Whether avoiding carbon or reducing it, neither approach will reach the efficacy and scale we need until we establish a transparent, multiparty system to track carbon emissions across borders and a set of widely accepted measuring, reporting, and verification standards based on blockchain ledgers and trusted markets. "In five to ten years, we might have a blockchain-based system in place" to do that, Schubert said. "But it is mission critical to drive deployment-led innovation that can make a difference today—like solar energy and sheep."

So while we absolutely need governmental edicts and global accords to save our environment, we also need to develop policies and agreements that align climate-mitigation objectives with the interests of industry—whether getting energy companies in the West to abandon coal-burning power plants, or getting newly industrialized factories in developing economies to prioritize carbon mitigation alongside profits, new jobs, and global competitiveness.

Blockchain-Based Carbon-Smart Supply Chains

Industrial policies also need to foster technological solutions that allow us to measure, account for, and centrally verify carbon emissions, so we can more effectively set a price on offset credits and more easily trade them across borders. Currently, offset mechanisms are mostly local or regional in nature, but that doesn't work for a global problem. Carbon emissions, much like viruses, don't stop at national boundaries. If carbon-capture, sequestration, and packaging technologies advance as well, we could go beyond offset credits and add the trading and recycling of the carbon itself. Technologies already exist to condense carbon into pellets, which can be shipped and repurposed elsewhere.

Climate-sensitive blockchain applications could prove remarkably useful in providing the transparency needed to attract investors and hold recipients accountable to environmental terms included in the contracts.

A clear record of carbon content, productive activity, and decarbonization targets on a blockchain, as well as the results of efforts to close gaps, could provide a transparent and auditable record for rewarding successes and exposing shortcomings. DAOs could establish detailed carbon-mitigation efforts among industry partners, with tokenized governance allowing the individual partners in that agreement to amend, update, and enhance specific actions and requirements in a more democratic fashion. Add to that a financial backer's requirement that a company participate in such a framework and a mechanism for governments to audit the crowd's verification of the chain, and we could begin to see a growing financial incentive to collaborate on and transparently record discrete climate change actions.

The same technologies and models might also help strengthen some of the existing mechanisms to decarbonize the economy. While by no means a set of end-all, be-all solutions, enhanced carbon-trading markets and carbon taxes can put specific price tags on carbon emissions, said Severin Borenstein, a business administration and public policy professor at UC Berkeley and faculty director of the Energy Institute at the Haas School of Business. Given his druthers, Borenstein would enact a straight carbon tax, because the floor and cap in a carbon-trading market is never truly a floor or a cap. Whatever the mechanism, he said, it's vital to make redistribution of the tax or market proceeds explicit—developing countries keep tax proceeds, richer countries transfer some of theirs, and all the transfers focus on the research, development, and distribution of decarbonization technologies. Those funded projects should and likely will include a mixed portfolio of clean energies and carbon-capture technologies, he said, including biofuels, hydrogen, solar, and wind.

As we wrote this in September 2022, the United Arab Emirates was considering a plan to develop a central, blockchain-based carbon accounting system that would help establish more accurate pricing of offset credits on an open marketplace. The idea behind it is simple: We can only avoid, reduce, or offset emissions if we know how much carbon we're emitting in the first place. However, execution of the accounting system will be anything but simple. For one, accurately measuring and tracking carbon emissions across a company's entire value chain, much less an entire economy, is an extremely complicated task. So having a central, auditable blockchain on which to record emissions can help avoid double-counting or missed sources. Second, these applications need to work on blockchains that don't

consume massive quantities of electricity, as many versions of the technologies do. The UAE's idea would consider such a national carbon accounting
system for its entire economy, supplemented not only by a market for trading but also by active carbon-reduction projects, such as tree planting and
solar power projects, that generate tradable certificates. Eventually, bilateral or multilateral agreements could be struck to integrate carbon markets
between countries. The motivation for those agreements could accelerate
once Europe forges ahead with its controversial carbon import duties.

Meanwhile, measurements of carbon emissions in supply chains themselves should become more practicable with the proliferation of networked
sensors, sophisticated cognitive technologies, and deeper human insight
into nature, thanks to quantum computing. As we gain more clarity on all
of these, we can integrate those harder numbers into other key metrics—
such as a calculation of gross domestic product that includes the cost of
greenhouse gas emissions (ghgGDP) for nation-states, or a greenhouse gas
social progress index (ghgSPI) for companies. In the meantime, though,
offsetting growth measures with even an estimate of the environmental
damage that emissions generate can provide a more realistic picture of
economic vitality and give investors and financiers an empirical basis for
their funding decisions. Increasing or decreasing a country's GDP to reflect
its climate impact could affect everything from geopolitical alliances to
credit ratings and foreign direct investments. If a country can't manage
the environmental crisis by converting its captured carbon emissions into
tradable assets, how investment-worthy is it? If a rapidly growing business
pursues profitability to the detriment of the environment and public welfare, should countries levy a tax to mitigate the cost and impact of its ecological damage?

One could imagine these evolving metrics as a foundation for an integrated transatlantic carbon-free trade zone that eventually expands into a
global or at least multiregional regime. We've already seen investor concerns about climate change spur companies to adopt environmental and
social governance (ESG) practices, which have gone from a corporate buzz-
word to table stakes for a groundswell of shareholders. Firms that don't
comply might find fewer willing investors, raising their cost of capital and
operations. One international bank with which we work has developed a
service to help capital providers find, monitor, and lend to businesses that
maintain higher levels of ESG compliance.

National Climate Defense Strategies

A creative proposal developed in 2022 by Shawn Ewbank and his peers in the UC Berkeley public policy master's program offers one possible way to break through the policy logjams and the bureaucracy. In their working paper, Ewbank and his colleagues recommended the creation of a partnership that would merge the technical expertise of the Department of Energy with the coordinated national security initiatives of the Department of Homeland Security. The National Climate Defense Strategy they conceived would, among other things, oversee the deployment of direct air capture technologies to remove existing carbon, create a priority queue for decarbonized energy generation projects, and coordinate AI and other advanced technology R&D efforts for decarbonization. The regulatory and industry infrastructures of the US energy sector "were not designed to confront an eminent national security emergency," the group writes, "and [they] will make the necessarily rapid, nationally coordinated planning and deployment of renewable energy resources practically impossible."

The ideas we heard from Ewbank and his peers will likely get at least a hearing at the Energy Department. They should get hearings globally. If every country had an explicit Climate Defense Strategy, regional Climate Defense Organizations could form around shared risks and exposures. However, none of these concepts or partnerships come to fruition without major financial commitments. The amounts of money pledged by national security agencies—potentially rivaling many countries' entire defense budgets—will eventually have to get matched by financial institutions, whether multilateral development banks or private investors spurred by policy schemes. We might create special conditions on decarbonization of certain industries or product categories, and then incentivize those goals through a global collection of partners, such as the Asia Infrastructure Development Bank, the World Bank, and bilateral organizations such as the United States Agency for International Development (USAID) or the German Agency for International Cooperation (GIZ). Sovereign wealth funds and blockchain-based investment fund DAOs could also play a role in mobilizing capital that takes a long-term view.

We need to make peace with the fact that most of these investments won't fund a shiny new object or a magic wand solution, despite recent breakthroughs in fusion energy. As much as we need to welcome and fund those innovations, developing them to the point of mass deployment will likely happen too late to save us if we do not take more immediate action. We will still need to invest heavily in the removal of and transition from legacy infrastructure and deeply entrenched interests in every corner of the world. The costs associated with decommissioning an infrastructure based for decades on fossil fuels will be enormous, said Cho Khong, an associate fellow at the University of Oxford's Saïd Business School and former chief political analyst at Shell. "Going around the world and seeing this immense amount of stuff that's been created to produce energy from fossil fuels, from hydrocarbons, it's very sobering," he said. There is a huge economic adjustment cost to move from a hydrocarbon-based economy to an economy based on renewables and sustainable energy, he said, and getting governments to realize and accept that cost will require "some sticks as well as carrots in order to ensure that we're all moving in the right direction."

Whatever mechanism we use to tackle emissions—whether carbon trading, carbon taxes, or carbon regulation—we must recognize that dealing with climate change requires a collective effort by every country and every person. Emissions know no borders, nor will the millions of climate refugees or the financial flows away from stricken societies and economies. To ensure no one gets left behind, wealthier countries need to help finance the efforts of developing countries and disadvantaged parts of their own societies via efforts like the so-called Marshall Plan for Climate, using the funds from carbon trading or the revenues from carbon taxes to shield those who are most vulnerable to the ripple effects of climate disaster.[13]

The G2+X World: Collaboration with China

Expanding antifragility in this increasingly plurilateral world will demand the inclusion—or at least the accommodation—of multiple models of governance. Western democracies will need to find points of engagement with the array of government models in China, India, Brazil, and across the Global South. A global hero-versus-villain battle with occasional flashpoints and sprints is evolving into a marathon between global powers and ideals, with all sides trying to maintain their influence on systems that have become too pressurized and complex to be managed with narrow-minded, point-to-point policies and strategies. Alliances change from one domain to the next, and what's collaborative from an economic or business standpoint might spark friction in the geopolitical arena. We are not looking at a static G0 (no dominant superpower) or G2 (US and China) world. We are looking at a G2+X world, with the X-factor alliances varying from one issue to the next (but most often involving the EU and/or India). The US and China cannot single-handedly decide the fate of the global economy; they cannot even govern the fate of a specific region. There will always need to be more partners at the table, and the alliances they form will constantly shift. No country will make significant progress on COVID-like pandemics, the cognitive and crypto economies, cybersecurity, or climate change without embracing collaboration with a set of major "functional" powers in a given system or domain. It will be impossible to discuss the shape of global digital markets without Europe, given its five hundred million people and the significant influence it has on regulatory development competence beyond its borders. Similarly, South Asian and African crypto innovators will not roll over and bow to the demands of once-colonialist nations without having a formative role in global regulation.

Of course, the US and China and their respective geopolitical allies will still clash over safeguards and political objectives in all these fields. And in many cases, the rest of the global community will need to negotiate the trade-offs—accept the terms of one or the other, or collectively develop an alternative that might alienate them from large markets and pools of resources. No one will rest easy in static camps, though, and we won't have a clear endgame we can pursue, however much we might long for the clarity that would provide. Indeed, pursuit of that mirage will lead to futility at best—and, at worst, an unwinnable war that directly fractures two billion lives and causes severe ripple effects for the remaining six billion people on the periphery. If a "regional" Russian invasion of Ukraine unleashed pain and trauma that will take years to heal, overcome, and normalize, it is hard to fathom the suffering and recovery process that would result from a military conflict between the US and China.

Fortunately, despite the chill between the hegemons, we can minimize the probability of military action. A world with an array of interoperable systems, infrastructures, and goals makes a cataclysmic conflict less likely, even as humanity faces unprecedented challenges. But we can't take that for granted, either. We need to find ways to negotiate and patch fragilities and misunderstandings. We can't argue for harmonization, but we can at least seek accords of long-term convenience, because no country will be big enough to be independent, nor small enough to be unimportant.

That's not to say we abandon our values. The West should strongly oppose the annexation of Taiwan, human rights violations against minority communities, or other power grabs. We need to meet those aggressions with resolve and force aggressors to process a painful calculus of trade-offs. A realist has to acknowledge that China and its political system will remain the chief rival for the US and European systems for the coming decades. But outright war between the two remains highly undesirable. "We're in this very tense relationship with China," said Janet Napolitano, the former head of the US Department of Homeland Security. "But on the other hand, economically, we're so entangled. We can't just move all of the economic relationships we have in China—supply chains and all the rest—back to the United States when we have multinational corporations that have huge markets there."

Relations between the West and China will chill and thaw, and fragile systems and agreements will break along the way. How we manage the ups and downs of that relationship will dominate the coming decade, Napolitano said. But the costs of a complete breakdown would be immense, and President Xi and the CCP are very attuned to cost-benefit analysis. "We have to make sure that the benefits are in the correct axis and the costs are in the correct axis," Napolitano said. The ability of both sides to recognize and, eventually, align those benefits and costs gives us a sense of the possibilities that might emerge. Do we truly believe that China could not possibly become a formidable *collaborator* on scalable solutions for global problems? As we aim for less fragility in our global systems, shouldn't we be equally prepared for more alignment with Beijing as we are for less? Would that not make sense especially if—as we believe—the Middle Kingdom is bound to go through its own nonlinear changes in the not-too-distant future, beginning with its rapidly aging population?

Experimentation Sandboxes with China

The US and China will need to reconcile their mentalities and mindsets with each other and with the rest of the world, but we don't have to wait to take pragmatic steps on areas of overlapping interest. A new competition model between the West and China could help both sides leverage their complementary strengths as they develop their cognitive economies. China, for example, generates vastly more data on the consumer side, driven by its sheer population size and technological integration. The transatlantic allies excel on enterprise data. Both sides have much to gain by sharing anony-mized data and best practices in precompetitive activities, such as basic and foundational research in climate change, migration, public health, educa-tion, deep space exploration, and beyond.

What might an Apollo-type moonshot program look like if it were framed not as an us-versus-them space race, but as a collaborative effort to advance our humanity and global welfare? We might begin to imagine a joint US-China mission to Mars; a Pandemic Early Warning System jointly headquartered in Hangzhou and Atlanta; a globally open Tsinghua Univer-sity/UC Berkeley joint campus for climate and ocean sciences at the North Pole; or a Baidu Apollo–orchestrated fleet of autonomous and electrified Volkswagen or GM microbuses in metropolitan areas throughout the devel-oping world. And because both sides would have an interest in safeguard-ing these types of collaborative projects and programs, they would provide a focal point for cybersecurity agreements that protect what was jointly created—perhaps planting seeds that grow into a broader accord.

Similarly, we might work together to create a more secure and open regu-latory platform for cryptocurrencies and DeFi applications. China prohibits cryptocurrencies outside its central bank digital currency (CBDC), the digi-tal yuan, and that's unlikely to change in the near future. But simply work-ing to ensure that CBDCs can interoperate with one another—or, through markets and exchanges, with Altcoin or Stablecoins—could help preserve the beneficial elements and stability of the emerging crypto ecosystem without sacrificing security and regulation against illicit use. It serves no one's interest to sit idly by while the two universes of digital and fiat curren-cies collide and ignite chaos in global markets over the next fifteen years.

A Road Map of Small but Rapid Steps with China
None of these potential design ideas will work on a larger scale without identifying the shared values that overlap from all sides, especially as a new generation begins to take on the mantle of global leadership. The world's demographics point toward a transformed construct of globalization that prioritizes sustainability, equity, and technological innovation over extrac-tion, emissions, and automation for profit's sake alone. The up-and-coming generations will push us into a Globalization 2.0 that moves beyond Brexit and birthright isolationism, fossil fuel dominance, and traditional career pathways into a more fluid, environmentally friendly, and adaptable world.

But all these influences will bend and move in vastly different ways from one country to the next, especially between China and the US, and we can debate ourselves into the ground on ethics, rules, and guidelines if we don't solve discrete problems to make systems more antifragile.

"The history of humanity, some people would say, evolves toward happier approaches to life and ethics and so forth," said Philip Verveer, a senior research fellow at the Harvard Kennedy School and former ambassador and deputy assistant secretary of state for international communications and information policy at the US State Department. "But we don't have time for that, at least I don't think we do in these realms. What we need to do is try to see if we can't come to understandings that people will sign—some kind of a big, appropriate ceremony in Geneva or someplace—that we know won't be adhered to 100 percent but will provide at least some better sense of security." The past decade of US-China relations looked more like a clash of strong personalities than true geopolitics, he said, and bilateral discourse rarely moved beyond trade agreements with any success. The interactions between the powers need to move from talk to action on more fields, particularly when it comes to technology. "We probably need more trade agreements than we have, but we have to get beyond that," he said. "We've got these technologies that are proceeding very, very rapidly, with capabilities that are almost unimaginable in terms of quantum computing and AI and so forth, and we don't have anything like adequate agreement about what ought to happen."

To focus on collaborative solutions to discrete problems, leaders should first create models of joint governance that actively encourage experimentation with vigilance and seek yet-unknown opportunities in a zeroth-principle manner, rather than deterministically protecting the status quo or predicting worst outcomes. Beginning with a joint "Road Map of Small but Rapid Steps," leaders in China and the US could begin to identify experiments and frame them within surgically focused "think-and-do-tanks," created and supervised by a standing G2 Global Compact Commission. These agile organizations could bring together experts from both sides to focus on topically and geographically bounded problems, collaborating to develop workable solutions and resolve tensions between values as a second-order phenomenon. They could focus on precompetitive, medium-term issues that untie important knots for global society—fusion energy, water extraction and purification, deep water fisheries, or radiation hardening for

humans traveling to Mars. Working things out on a compact and opera-
tional level sidesteps the furor and populism of less tangible debates on
principles.

Two Undersecretaries for Collaboration

This is not idealism run amok. Real precedents exist on both macro and
micro levels. Even during the height of the Cold War, the US and Russia
experimented and collaborated in many areas, such as the space station,
nonproliferation, and arctic management. In each area, the sandboxes that
contained the collaborative experiments had walls, compartmentalizing
what was inside the shared realm. Even in hotly disputed areas of military
action, there were collaborative communication protocols to avoid misun-
derstanding. We can do the same with China, so long as we retain the same
vigilance and verification.

As a first step, we recommend that the US and China each appoint an
undersecretary-level envoy, directly reporting to their respective country's
president. Given a charter to design shared experimentation spaces, goals,
and "vigilance protocols," each envoy would work with their defense and
cyber agencies to define carve-outs and targets for surveillance and monitoring, as well as protocols for investigation and resolution of disputes. The
US undersecretary would have a seat on the National Security Council, and
they would lead a China Collaboration Council with their counterparts in
the EPA, NASA, and the State, Commerce, Energy, Agriculture, and Defense
Departments. The Chinese official would have a similar charter and likewise
hold posts across critical agencies there. Some of the first responsibilities for
both undersecretaries would focus on joint training about administrative-
political guidelines and processes, the demarcation of no-go areas, and
communication protocols for each sandbox.

This effort, if executed with productive vigilance, might generate more
shared innovation experience, more empathy, and, perhaps eventually,
more trust. And that productive "trust but verify" partnership would create
a gravitational pull for other partners to come help remobilize the world
toward a more cognitive, smarter, and less fragile Global 2.0 future.

Conclusion: The Road to Remobilization

By most accounts, the last major shift in the world order followed the destruction of World War II. The fall of the Soviet Union some forty-five years later marked a sharp turning point in global power, as the rise of China is doing now, but the general divides between the alliances of the major Western democracies and power-centralized countries, primarily Russia and then China, have persisted since the fall of Nazi Germany and Imperial Japan. Subsequent efforts to rebuild the ruins of that war into better designs resulted in the United Nations and Bretton Woods institutions. The European Project took hold, eventually leading to a political union of twenty-eight (now twenty-seven) countries, and a monetary union of nineteen disparate and previously competing economies on the continent. Those institutions laid the foundation for the first wave of what we now call globalization. As flawed as it was, Globalization 1.0 helped lift hundreds of millions of people out of poverty, largely eradicated polio and smallpox, generated a global pipeline for goods and services, and gave it all the backbone of a global internet—an imperfect but critical infrastructure for modern human activity.

Yet that same global world order also opened up avenues for new types of financial, digital, and military colonization. It magnified the radical inequality between affluent and disadvantaged populations. And it ushered in an era of online misinformation, digital smallness, identity theft, autonomous weapons systems, and climate destruction. Now, with all of those troubles laid bare and/or accelerated, we find ourselves confronted with another set of global crises that differ from but rival the aftermath of World War II. The questions have grown louder and louder. What new infrastructure, institutions, processes, and designs can we build for a Globalization

2.0 that promotes renewed relations and a greater antifragility based on equity, sustainability, peace, and prosperity? What will be our defining moment?

We wrote this book to stimulate discussions about a new architecture for a more resilient globalization with a smarter operating system—that is, the cognitive economy—with cybernetics equalizing the wild swings that cascade across domains and break us. We don't yet have a final view of what infrastructure and designs will guide the coming decade, let alone the next half century, but we can take heart knowing some of the key forces—the Five Cs—that we can harness to help shape that future. COVID revealed the power of science and discovery we can capture from genomics and related structural changes in the organization of life, but it also showed that we have a lot of space to improve on coordination between global actors. The cognification of our economies, societies, and lives through AI and other advanced digital technologies will reshape the future of work and data trading, while the blockchain and decentralization have opened new avenues for everything from global finance to organizational structures. We are in the middle of a trust revolution—both in politics, where we see a recasting of truth and veracity, and in civic and economic life, where DAOs, Web3, and the multiverse could offer provocative alternative models to replace traditional top-down frameworks.

A new, more expansive view of trusted computing for entire ecosystems and value chains, rather than singular organizations, is also ushering in a new era of cybersecurity for cognitive systems, which are quickly becoming integral to our economies, businesses, and lives. These and other new technologies could help mitigate or exacerbate climate change, but we will need to come to terms with climate instability as the status quo while we overcome a lack of geopolitical will, which continues to inhibit progress toward a decarbonized economy. And we cannot harness the best of our potential in any of these, nor in virtually any other field, without collaboration between the West and China.

Each of these Five C forces causes uncertainty, risk, and ambiguity, but also the potential to shape the world in a way that facilitates far greater human growth. To be sure, the Cognitive Era will not usher in the full agreement and cooperation of two hundred countries, nor even just the G20 or G7. The confluence of these tectonic forces will instead lead us into a hybrid G2+X world, shaped by the tensions that arise from the constant interplay of technologies, economies, nations, and societies that form clubs that overlap like a Venn diagram. The concept of globalization no longer represents the merely physical phenomenon of people, goods, and money moving around the world. It now encompasses an entire set of unwieldy, nonlinear, and overlapping circulatory systems for the flows of currency, people, ideas, goods and services, data, natural resources (including carbon), and even genetic material. But power architectures have always organized around resources. So, as new flows get added during this liminal phase of our global rite of passage, we need to be ready for the reincorporation of the future global architecture. The resulting complexity exceeds our human capacities to understand it, and our uncertainty leads to tensions that create extreme polarization—the physical versus the virtual, the East versus the West, the near versus the far, the vaccinated versus the anti-vaxxers, the centralized versus the decentralized, the elite versus the crowd, and misinformation versus truth.

The systems we create to govern the clash of these forces and flows will require constant updates because the complexity and speed of these global phenomena will make it impossible to break them down to individual, easy-to-predict elements. Although we humans have always been mystified by our evolving world, we have never before had to process the simultaneous and interrelated impact of these forces on both the *internal* and the *external* in such a compressed time frame. At the moment, as technologies continue to merge the biological "inside" and the digital "outside" of our existence, we can only confidently predict one thing—that we will struggle to understand how the forces and flows of our planet will impact our bodies, brains, and identities even as they reshape our industries, politics, and neighborhoods.

But this is also where new frontier technologies will bring relief, as the cognitive innovation that creates complexity also helps relieve it. Pandora's box is also a panacea. If we want to harness the positive side of that duality, we need to design our technology to understand and protect the less tangible sides of humanity—our values, aspirations, and identities. Only then can cognitive technologies process the myriad variables and generate the options that allow us to mass-customize our governance of such complex issues.

The results might require the most sophisticated quantum computer running the most advanced AI algorithms to forecast with anything approaching accuracy. But whatever answer a magical machine might generate, we would still have to go through the process of shaping that design and remobilizing the world toward it. So why not seek to shape those designs and remobilize now, when we have a unique opportunity to take our fractured systems and rebuild them in antifragile ways that allow us to update and improve them as we learn and grow? Machines can compute new pathways and outcomes, inform our goals, create design options, and optimize outcomes, but they can't and shouldn't be the ones imagining and choosing the desirable paths. That is the role of the leader in the Cognitive Era.

Don't Let a Good Crisis Go to Waste

We set out the concepts and ideas in this book to provide the tools, the strategy, and, hopefully, the inspiration for more leaders to join the pioneers who will carve out the new pathways of the Cognitive Era. The FLP-IT model provides a framework for the strategic decisions and leadership mindsets we can use to flip our gaze forward—analyzing the forces, logic, and phenomena at play in this turbulent world; understanding the impacts they have for economies, societies, and lives; and then making the difficult triage decisions about what to keep, what to discard, and what to build from scratch. The beauty of our model comes from its flexibility—it is not hardwired to arrive at one firm outcome that conveys a false sense of certainty. It focuses instead on the paths that can lead to antifragile activity portfolios and human-centric global systems. As such, leaders can use it to create shared goals, whether for your family's future, your company's investments, or your national policy choices. On whichever level we lead, it's critical that we always infuse our strategic tools with empathy.

We all can envision the kind of world we want to build, but we need to recognize the urgency. In this rite of passage into the dawning Cognitive Era, we need a sweeping movement of global, national, business, and community leaders, young and old, to take the liminal uncertainty of today and reincorporate it into a more equitable, sustainable, and prosperous tomorrow. Yes, we have significant differences from one nation and one culture to another, but we have so many shared values and interests that we can transform many of those differences into a rich diversity that expands our perspectives and flavors our lives.

None of the proposals outlined in chapter 9 is fully formed, and all of them will need insight and debate from an array of global experts in fields well beyond our purview. We wrote this book in hopes of instigating those dialogues, and it's precisely why we're calling on everyone reading these words—as leaders in their own fields, in all walks of life, at all experience levels, in every country and community—to seize this moment. We can't let this crisis go to waste. If we do, we'll jeopardize this crucial opportunity to shape a Great Remobilization toward a better global future.

Acknowledgments

Without hesitation and with a great amount of joy, the authors of this book want to acknowledge the most important contributor to our work—our friend, colleague, award-winning economics journalist, and editor-in-chief at Cambrian Futures Dan Zehr. We owe Dan a tremendous debt of gratitude for the hundreds of hours it has taken to conduct interviews alongside us and then help us put our thinking into appealing and readily accessible prose. Thrust in the middle of three expansive thinkers, he helped harness our drive to be creative and to think outside of the box, pushing us to new frontiers and then also helping us maintain a high standard of accessibility. It's a Sisyphean task, but his ability to frame and streamline our thinking about complex interlocking forces, concepts, and systems was matched only by his unflappable patience as he captured the essence of our thinking while we riffed, hypothesized, and drafted. Moreover, his ability to match our excitement and energy while also gently and humorously but firmly nudging us made him a pure joy to work with—a chief ingredient needed for this book to materialize. *The Great Remobilization* is Olaf's second book with Dan after publishing *Solomon's Code: Humanity in a World of Thinking Machines* in 2018, and his first alongside Mark and Terence. The three of us will be privileged if it isn't the last.

The magnitude and sweep of ideas we tried to formulate for this book could not come from our minds alone. Hundreds of people contributed to the research, framework, and designs we discussed in these pages. Among them, our colleagues at Cambrian Futures continue to inspire our thinking and our creativity. A special thanks to Tobias Straube, whose work on many of the issues contained in this book helped shape our insights. In addition, Mark Nitzberg, Oliver Michaelis, Manu Kalia, Ander Dobo, Ryan Liu, and

Leea Craig constantly challenge and inspire our perspectives, while Ella Suh provided crucial support on the nuts and bolts of what we compiled.

Of course, finding an outlet to communicate all these ideas—and to do so in what we hope is a clear and readable manner—also requires an incredibly talented team. Our heartfelt thanks again to our agent at Aevitas Creative, Esmond Harmsworth, whose encouragement and calm counsel guided us through a turbulent process. Similarly, to our editors at the MIT Press—Emily Taber and Laura Keeler—our deep gratitude for reading, shaping, and refining the multiple drafts of this manuscript and pulling us to the finish line.

We conducted interviews with nearly a hundred people for this book. Many of them do not appear in the final version, most often because a topic that felt critical in 2020, when we begin this project, was displaced by a different reality in the two years it took us to complete the manuscript. We remain deeply indebted to *all* these brilliant people for their generosity in terms of time and insights. We're optimists by nature, and these conversations only amplified our excitement for the decades ahead. Thanks to Aaron Frank, Alec Ross, Adair Morse, Alexia Latortue, Alison Darcy, Amy Celico, Andrew Isaacs, Anja Manuel, Aura Salla, Ayesha Khalid, Ben Page, Bilahari Kausikan, Boris Schubert, Bryan Johnson, Cecilia Marinier, Chandran Nair, Chip Poncy, Cho Khong, Chris White, Christophe Le Caillec, Chuck Whitten, Cyrille Vigneron, David Gross, David Holtz, Deborah Taylor Moore, Denis Simon, Dmitri Alperovitch, Donn Treese, Ed Freeman, Eleni Kitra, Erik Peterson, Erin Conaton, Evelyn Farkas, Tom Frieden, Duncan Hollis, Edward Freeman, Elissa Prichep, Erik Peterson, Ernie Bower, Fergus Hanson, Gen. George Casey, Gen. Keith Alexander, Genevieve Bell, Gosia Loj, Helena Storckenfeldt, Henry Mintzberg, Ian Goldin, Jaan Tallinn, James Lewis, Jan Baránek, Janet Napolitano, Jeffrey Sachs, John Fargis, Josh Lincoln, Juan Zarate, Katherine Gehl, Kathryn White, Kelly Sims Gallagher, Ken Ford, Kriffy Perez, Larry Louie, Liz Pellegrini, Lloyd Williams, Marion Fourcade, Martin Fleming, Matt Johnson, Michael Schwarz, Michèle Flournoy, Monica Kerretts-Makau, Nicholas Davis, Nicolas Petrovic, Nina Xiang, Omar Romero-Hernandez, Parag Khanna, Paras Anand, Pat Cottrell, Peter Schwartz, Philip Sabes, Philip Verveer, Rachel Haurwitz, Rehan Khan, Rémy Baume, Renee Wegrzyn, Richard Lyons, Richard Roston, Richard Wilding, Sabra Horne, Scott Kennedy, Sean Gourley, Severin Borenstein, Shawn Ewbank, Sheila Olmstead, Shreya Nallapati, Susan Landau, Susan

Schneider, Sven Egyedy, Sven Smit, Thomas Pickering, Tom Sanderson, Wayne Visser, Wilson Wong, Yun Sen, and Ziyang Fan.

We also wish to thank H. E. Ohood bint Khalfan Al Roumi, Majid Abdulghaffar, Tarek Abu Fakhr, and Afif Ghalayini at the prime minister's office of the UAE for allowing us to share some of our jointly developed concepts.

Our students also rekindle our optimism for the future, and many of these design activist leaders pitched in on the background research and context for so much of what appears in this book. In particular, we want to acknowledge Abigail Newell, Chayanka Mohan, Harrison Winikoff, Sanjana Anil, and Claire Harmon, each of whom contributed significant time from their lives and studies to supplement our understanding of key issues. In addition, we'd like to thank the many students at the Hult International Business School who pitched in with additional research: Adama Varsey Sirleaf, Azita Hajihassani, Kiran Kittur, Leo Etscheit, Marina Eing Barbosa, Mark Smits, William Van Herzele, Yang Cui, Adrien Cailleau, Juan Trujillo, Juliana C. Teixeira da Silva, Sarthak Jena, Jack Fellows, and Tom Wardle. We also wish to thank Olaf's students at UC Berkeley Haas School of Business and Berkeley Executive Education for their contributions to the evolution of his thinking on matters in this book through their countless high-powered dialogues in his courses "Disruption Futures" and "Future of Technology." And we want to thank Joshua Entsminger for the constant intellectual engagement throughout the journey of this book.

Finally, we could not have completed a project this wide-ranging and complex without the patience and support of our families: thank you to Olaf's wife, Ann Reidy, for her tireless nudging and tweaking of his ideas and headlines and her own tireless, not-for-profit work dedicated to overcoming fragmentation and divides. Thanks also to Olaf's daughters, Fiona and Hannah Groth-Reidy, for their patience with the process and countless hours of weekend writing time, as well as their inspiration for his books' fictitious characters. Thanks to Terence's wife, Celine, who, without a single murmur, tolerated his many early wake-up calls to work on the book. And thanks to Mark's family, having supported his journey with constant smiles and a relentless sense of encouragement—you are the cornerstone of his life.

Notes

Introduction

1. "The First 90 Days: US Biopharmaceutical Finished Goods Supply Chain Response to COVID-19," Healthcare Distribution Alliance, accessed August 5, 2022, https://www.hda.org/resources/the-first-90-days.

2. Colby Smith, "Global Economy Faces Greatest Challenge in Decades, Policymakers Warn," *Financial Times*, August 28, 2022, https://www.ft.com/content/b71e259f-f2f0-4e25-bd22-0dbd0f344643.

3. Patricia Cohen, "Shock Waves Hit the Global Economy, Posing Grave Risk to Europe," *New York Times*, September 8, 2022, https://www.nytimes.com/2022/09/08/business/economy/russia-ukraine-global-economy.html.

4. "Ending Poverty and Hunger Once and for All—Is It Possible?," United Nations Department of Economic and Social Affairs, accessed January 30, 2023, https://www.un.org/en/desa/ending-poverty-and-hunger.

5. "Frequently Asked Questions (FAQ) on IPv6 Adoption and IPv4 Exhaustion," Internet Society, accessed February 15, 2023, https://www.internetsociety.org/deploy360/ipv6/faq/.

6. Matthew A. Winkler, "California Poised to Overtake Germany as World's no. 4 Economy," Bloomberg, October 24, 2022, https://www.bloomberg.com/opinion/articles/2022-10-24/california-poised-to-overtake-germany-as-world-s-no-4-economy.

Chapter 1

1. Oliver O'Connell, "How Much Does Jeff Bezos Make per Minute?," *The Independent*, October 13, 2021, https://www.independent.co.uk/news/world/americas/jeff-bezos-make-per-minute-net-worth-b1887310.html; Jodi Kantor, Karen Weise, and Grace Ashford, "Inside Amazon's Worst Human Resources Problem," *New York*

Times, October 24, 2021, https://www.nytimes.com/2021/10/24/technology/amazon
-employee-leave-errors.html.

2. Sergey Knyazev, Karishma Chhugani, Varuni Sarwal, Ram Ayyala, Harman Singh, Smruthi Karthikeyan, Dhrithi Deshpande, et al. "Unlocking Capacities of Genomics for the COVID-19 Response and Future Pandemics," *Nature Methods* 19 (2022): 374–380, https://www.nature.com/articles/s41592-022-01444-z.

3. Olaf Groth and Mark Nitzberg, *Solomon's Code: Humanity in a World of Thinking Machines* (New York: Pegasus Books, 2018); Terence C. M. Tse, Mark Esposito, and Danny Goh, *The AI Republic: Building the Nexus Between Humans and Intelligent Automation* (self-pub., Lioncrest Publishing, 2019).

4. "Recommendation on the Ethics of Artificial Intelligence," UNESCO, accessed August 31, 2022, https://en.unesco.org/artificial-intelligence/ethics.

5. Shawn Engbrecht, *Invisible Leadership: Transforming Risk into Opportunity* (Wichita, KS: Prime Concepts Group Press, 2018), 195–196.

6. "Why Skippers Aren't Scuppered," *The Economist*, September 18, 2021, https://www.economist.com/leaders/2021/09/18/why-skippers-arent-scuppered.

7. "The Diamond Model," The Diamond Model—Institute for Strategy and Competitiveness—Harvard Business School, accessed August 31, 2022, https://www.isc.hbs.edu/competitiveness-economic-development/frameworks-and-key-concepts/Pages/the-diamond-model.aspx.

8. Piyush Kumar, Mayukh Dass, and Shivina Kumar, "From Competitive Advantage to Nodal Advantage: Ecosystem Structure and the New Five Forces That Affect Prosperity," *Business Horizons* 58, no. 4 (2015): 469–481, https://doi.org/10.1016/j.bushor.2015.04.001.

9. "Resource-Based View," Wikipedia, last modified November 27, 2022, https://en.wikipedia.org/wiki/Resource-based_view; David J. Teece, "Technological Innovation and the Theory of the Firm: The Role of Enterprise-Level Knowledge, Complementarities, and (Dynamic) Capabilities," in *Handbook of the Economics of Innovation*, vol. 1, ed. Bronwyn H. Hall and Nathan Rosenberg (Amsterdam: Elsevier, 2010), 679–730.

Chapter 2

1. David Kirton, "Huawei Smartphone Revenue to Fall at Least $30–40 BLN in 2021—Chairman," Reuters, Thomson Reuters, September 24, 2021, https://www.reuters.com/technology/huawei-2021-smartphone-revenue-drop-by-least-30-40-bln-rotating-chairman-2021-09-24/; Arjun Kharpal, "Huawei Posts First-Ever Yearly Revenue Decline as U.S. Sanctions Continue to Bite, but Profit Surges," CNBC, March 28, 2022, https://www.cnbc.com/2022/03/28/huawei-annual-results-2021-revenue-declines-but-profit-surges.html.

2. IEA, "Energy Fact Sheet: Why Does Russian Oil and Gas Matter?—Analysis," 2022, https://www.iea.org/articles/energy-fact-sheet-why-does-russian-oil-and-gas-matter.

3. "The Coming Food Catastrophe," *The Economist*, May 19, 2022, https://www.economist.com/leaders/2022/05/19/the-coming-food-catastrophe.

4. Hua Xin, "Greece's Piraeus Port Refilled with Vitality under Bri Cooperation," *China Daily*, September 8, 2021, https://www.chinadaily.com.cn/a/202109/08/WS61381b5da310efa1bd66e1a6.html.

5. CB Insights, "AI 100: The Most Promising Artificial Intelligence Startups of 2022," May 17, 2022, https://www.cbinsights.com/research/report/artificial-intelligence-top-startups-2022/.

6. U.S. Chamber of Commerce and Rhodium Group, "Understanding U.S.-China Decoupling: Macro Trends and Industry Impacts," accessed August 22, 2022, https://www.uschamber.com/assets/archived/images/024001_us_china_decoupling_report_fin.pdf.

7. Stanford Center on China's Economy and Institutions, "How Does 'Decoupling' Affect Firm Performance and Innovation in China and the U.S.?," May 15, 2022, https://sccei.fsi.stanford.edu/china-briefs/technology-decoupling-firm-performance.

8. US Department of Defense, Office of the Secretary of Defense, "2020 China Military Power Report—U.S. Department of Defense," accessed August 22, 2022, https://media.defense.gov/2020/Sep/01/2002488689/-1/-1/1/2020-DOD-CHINA-MILITARY-POWER-REPORT-FINAL.PDF.

9. Spencer Bokat-Lindell, "Putin's Getting Sanctioned, but Russia's Getting Canceled," *New York Times*, March 9, 2022, https://www.nytimes.com/2022/03/09/opinion/ukraine-russia-cancel-culture-putin.html.

10. Duncan Hollis, "A Brief Primer on International Law and Cyberspace," Carnegie Endowment for International Peace, accessed August 31, 2022, https://carnegieendowment.org/2021/06/14/brief-primer-on-international-law-and-cyberspace-pub-84763.

11. Scott W. Harold, "The U.S.-China Cyber Agreement: A Good First Step," RAND Corporation, August 1, 2016, https://www.rand.org/blog/2016/08/the-us-china-cyber-agreement-a-good-first-step.html.

12. Eleonore Pauwels, "Hybrid Coe Strategic Analysis 26: Cyber-Biosecurity: How to Protect Biotechnology from Adversarial AI Attacks," Hybrid CoE—the European Centre of Excellence for Countering Hybrid Threats, May 3, 2021, https://www.hybridcoe.fi/publications/cyber-biosecurity-how-to-protect-biotechnology-from-adversarial-ai-attacks/.

13. Parag Khanna, *Move: The Forces Uprooting Us* (New York: Scribner, 2021).

14. Oceana, *Exposed: Amazon's Enormous and Rapidly Growing Plastic Pollution Problem*, December 2021, https://oceana.org/reports/amazon-report-2021/.

Chapter 3

1. Kevin Schaul, Chris Alcantara, Gerrit De Vynck, and Reed Albergotti, "How Big Tech Got So Big: Hundreds of Acquisitions," *Washington Post*, April 21, 2021, https://www.washingtonpost.com/technology/interactive/2021/amazon-apple-facebook-google-acquisitions/.

2. Canalys, "Global Cloud Services Spend Exceeds US$50 Billion in Q4 2021," February 3, 2022, https://www.canalys.com/newsroom/global-cloud-services-Q4-2021.

3. Shoshana Zuboff, *The Age of Surveillance Capitalism: The Fight for a Human Future at the New Frontier of Power* (New York: PublicAffairs, 2015).

4. IDC, "Data Creation and Replication Will Grow at a Faster Rate than Installed Storage Capacity, According to the IDC Global Datasphere and StorageSphere Forecasts," March 24, 2021, https://www.idc.com/getdoc.jsp?containerId=prUS47560321.

5. David Reinsel, John Gantz, and John Rydning, "The Digitization of the World From Edge to Core," Seagate, November 2018, https://www.seagate.com/files/www-content/our-story/trends/files/idc-seagate-dataage-whitepaper.pdf.

6. Olaf Groth, Tobias Straube, and Dan Zehr, "Data Marketplace," Cambrian Group, December 2019, https://www.cambrian.ai/data-marketplace.

7. Jason Lanier and E. Glen Weyl, "A Blueprint for a Better Digital Society," *Harvard Business Review*, September 26, 2018, https://hbr.org/2018/09/a-blueprint-for-a-better-digital-society.

8. Juan Pablo Carrascal, Christopher Riederer, Vijay Erramilli, Mauro Cherubini, and Rodrigo de Oliveira, "Your Browsing Behavior for a Big Mac: Economics of Personal Information Online," *Proceedings of the 22nd International Conference on World Wide Web—WWW '13*, May 2013, 189–200, https://doi.org/10.1145/2488388.2488406.

9. Sam Sabin, "In Data-Driven World, Consumers Likely to Overestimate Their Information's Value," Morning Consult, June 3, 2019, https://morningconsult.com/2019/06/03/data-driven-world-consumers-likely-overestimate-their-informations-value.

10. Michael Segal, "We Need an FDA for Algorithms," Nautilus, October 29, 2018, https://nautil.us/we-need-an-fda-for-algorithms-7765; "AI Algorithms Need FDA-Style Drug Trials," Wired, August 15, 2019, https://www.wired.com/story/ai-algorithms-need-drug-trials.

11. "China to Apply for Digital Economy Partnership Agreement Membership," Bloomberg, October 30, 2021, https://www.bloomberg.com/news/articles/2021-10-31/china-to-apply-to-join-digital-economy-partnership-agreement.

12. "A Bretton Woods for Data," ICO, September 9, 2021, https://ico.org.uk/about-the-ico/media-centre/news-and-blogs/2021/09/a-bretton-woods-for-data.

13. "Improved Connectivity, Not Urban Migration, Is the Best Way to Help People in World's Rural Areas Develop," United Nations, May 20, 2021, https://www.un.org/development/desa/dspd/2021/05/wsr2021-2.

14. Brent Hyder, "Introducing Trailblazer Ranch: Igniting the Next Chapter of Salesforce's Culture," Salesforce (blog post), accessed September 26, 2022, https://www.salesforce.com/news/stories/introducing-trailblazer-ranch.

15. Nicholas Carr, *The Shallows: How the Internet Is Changing the Way We Read, Think and Remember* (London: Atlantic Books, 2011).

16. Pankaj C. Patel, Srikant Devaraj, Michael J. Hicks, and Emily J. Wornell, "County-Level Job Automation Risk and Health: Evidence from the United States," *Social Science & Medicine* 202 (April 2018): 54–60, https://doi.org/10.1016/j.socscimed.2018.02.025.

17. Michael A. Freeman, Sheri L. Johnson, Paige J. Staudenmaier, and Mackenzie R. Zisser, "Are Entrepreneurs 'Touched with Fire'? (Pre-Publication Manuscript)," Michael A. Freeman, MD, April 17, 2015, https://michaelafreemanmd.com/Research_files/; "2021 Empathy Study Executive Summary," Businessolver, accessed August 23, 2022, https://resources.businessolver.com/c/2021-empathy-exec-summ?x=OE03jO.

18. Freeman et al., "Are Entrepreneurs 'Touched with Fire'?"

19. "Li Jin on the Future of the Creator Economy," *The Economist*, accessed August 31, 2022, https://www.economist.com/the-world-ahead/2021/11/08/li-jin-on-the-future-of-the-creator-economy.

20. Eleanor A. Maguire, David G. Gadian, Ingrid S. Johnsrude, Catriona D. Good, John Ashburner, Richard S. Frackowiak, and Christopher D. Frith, "Navigation-Related Structural Change in the Hippocampi of Taxi Drivers," *Proceedings of the National Academy of Sciences* 97, no. 8 (2000): 4398–4403. https://doi.org/10.1073/pnas.070039597.

21. Nicolas Carr, *The Glass Cage: Who Needs Humans Anyway?* (New York: Penguin Random House, 2016).

22. Larry Louie, accounting and finance professor at Hult, noted that salaries are expensed immediately, so they actually provide full tax deductibility in the year incurred rather than waiting three-plus years to fully expense a depreciable asset under US GAAP rules. Weighed with other factors, this can change the tax benefit of expenses versus investments.

23. Louie noted that some companies are predominantly valued on tangible assets. At real estate investment trusts, for example, the creativity and productivity of the humans working there are valued as part of the assets they developed.

24. As Louie noted, financial value from human ideas and innovation is only created when those efforts or the intellectual property generates incremental profits in the future. This is often difficult to measure, but the idea of value is central to investment analysis using discounted cash flows. We spend money now (e.g., on people in R&D) and we estimate what cash flows those efforts will generate in the future. Many people correlate spending on R&D with future value, but that's not always the case. There is plenty of wasted money in R&D. So, companies often state it as a percentage of sales to measure the level of investment in creating new proprietary products and services.

25. Terence C. M. Tse and Mark Esposito, *Understanding How the Future Unfolds: Using Drive to Harness the Power of Today's Megatrends* (Austin: Lioncrest Publishing, 2017).

26. Paul Daugherty, Marc Carrel-Billiard, and Michael Biltz, "Technology Trends 2021: Tech Vision," Accenture, accessed August 23, 2022, https://www.accenture.com/us-en/insights/technology/technology-trends-2021.

27. Nicolas Petrovic, *La société post-digitale: Retour vers le futur de l'industrie* (Paris: Nouveaux débats publics, 2021).

Chapter 4

1. The concept comes from Charles Seife, *Zero: The Biography of a Dangerous Idea* (New York: Viking Adult, 2000).

2. Carlos Outeiral, Martin Strahm, Jiye Shi, Garrett M. Morris, Simon C. Benjamin, and Charlotte M. Deane, "The Prospects of Quantum Computing in Computational Molecular Biology," *WIREs Computational Molecular Science* 11, no. 1 (2020), https://doi.org/10.1002/wcms.1481; "Quantum Computing Use Cases for Financial Services," IBM, accessed August 31, 2022, https://www.ibm.com/thought-leadership/institute-business-value/report/exploring-quantum-financial; Florian Neukart, Gabriele Compostella, Christian Seidel, David von Dollen, Sheir Yarkoni, and Bob Parney, "Traffic Flow Optimization Using a Quantum Annealer," *Frontiers in ICT*, December 20, 2017, https://doi.org/10.3389/fict.2017.00029.

3. Ja-Young Sung, Lan Guo, Rebecca E. Grinter, and Henrik I. Christensen, "'My Roomba Is Rambo': Intimate Home Appliances," *UbiComp 2007: Ubiquitous Computing* (2007): 145–162, https://doi.org/10.1007/978-3-540-74853-3_9.

4. Johnson notes that much of the research on social cognition and its role in business was developed by University of Chicago Booth School of Business professor Nicholas Epley. In particular, he recommends Nicholas Epley, Adam Waytz, Scott Akalis, and John T. Cacioppo, "When We Need a Human: Motivational Determinants of Anthropomorphism," *Social Cognition* 26, no. 2 (2008): 143–155.

5. Noreena Hertz, *The Lonely Century: How to Restore Human Connection in a World That's Pulling Apart* (New York: Currency, 2021).

6. Stripe Sahar Mor, "Brain-Computer Interfaces Are Making Big Progress This Year," VentureBeat, August 14, 2021, https://venturebeat.com/business/brain-computer -interfaces-are-making-big-progress-this-year/.

7. Rachita Rake and Shreyas Wadodkar, "Brain Computer Interface Market by Component (Hardware, Software), Type (Invasive, Non Invasive, Partially Invasive), and Application (Healthcare, Communication & Control, Entertainment & Gaming, Smart Home Control, and Others): Global Opportunity Analysis and Industry Forecast, 2021–2030," Allied Market Research, July 2021, https://www.alliedmarket research.com/brain-computer-interfaces-market.

8. "Societal Resilience," Microsoft, accessed August 31, 2022, https://www.microsoft .com/en-us/research/group/societal-resilience.

9. Olaf Groth, Mark Nitzberg, and Stuart Russell, "AI Algorithms Need FDA-Style Drug Trials," Wired, August 15, 2019, https://www.wired.com/story/ai-algorithms -need-drug-trials.

Chapter 5

1. "Trade in Goods with China," United States Census Bureau, accessed August 31, 2022, https://www.census.gov/foreign-trade/balance/c5700.html.

2. Parag Khanna, *Move: The Forces Uprooting Us* (New York: Scribner, 2021).

3. Peter Baker and Zolan Kanno-Youngs, "Biden to Begin New Asia-Pacific Economic Bloc with a Dozen Allies," *New York Times*, May 23, 2022, https://www.nytimes.com /2022/05/23/world/asia/biden-asian-pacific-bloc.html.

4. John Gramlich, "Fast Facts about Nigeria and Its Immigrants as U.S. Travel Ban Expands," Pew Research Center, February 3, 2020, https://www.pewresearch.org /fact-tank/2020/02/03/fast-facts-about-nigeria-and-its-immigrants-as-u-s-travel-ban -expands.

5. "Internet IP Address 2019 Report," IP2Location, accessed August 23, 2022, https://www.ip2location.com/reports/internet-ip-address-2019-report.

6. Kai-Fu Lee, *AI Superpowers: China, Silicon Valley, and the New World Order* (New York: Harper Business, 2018).

7. "Social Mobility Rankings," Social Mobility Report 2020, accessed August 23, 2022, https://reports.weforum.org/social-mobility-report-2020/social-mobility-rankings.

8. Ashley Kirk, Finnbarr Sheehy, and Cath Levett, "Canada and UK among Countries with Most Vaccine Doses Ordered per Person," *Guardian*, January 29, 2021, https://www.theguardian.com/world/2021/jan/29/canada-and-uk-among-countries -with-most-vaccine-doses-ordered-per-person.

9. Catherine E. de Vries and Isabell Hoffmann, "Globalization and European Integration: Threat or Opportunity?," eupinions, accessed September 1, 2022, https://eupinions.eu/fileadmin/files/BSt/Publikationen/GrauePublikationen/EZ_eupinions_04_2017_englisch.pdf.

10. Jeffrey D. Sachs, *The Ages of Globalization: Geography, Technology, and Institutions* (New York: Columbia University Press, 2020).

11. "It's Learning. Just Not as We Know It," Accenture, accessed August 24, 2022, https://www.accenture.com/_acnmedia/thought-leadership-assets/pdf/accenture-education-and-technology-skills-research.pdf.

12. Stephen Ezell, "Assessing the State of Digital Skills in the U.S. Economy," Information Technology & Innovation Foundation, November 29, 2021, https://itif.org/publications/2021/11/29/assessing-state-digital-skills-us-economy/.

13. David Autor, "Work of the Past, Work of the Future (Working Paper)," National Bureau of Economic Research, accessed September 1, 2022, https://www.nber.org/system/files/working_papers/w25588/w25588.pdf.

14. Bojan Evkoski, Andraz Pelicon, Igor Mozetic, Nikola Ljubesic, and Petra Kralj Novak, "Retweet Communities Reveal the Main Sources of Hate Speech," arXiv.org, March 17, 2022, https://arxiv.org/abs/2105.14898; Nicola Woolcock, "Pupils Humiliate Their Teachers for TikTok Challenge," *The Times*, November 11, 2021, https://www.thetimes.co.uk/article/teachers-humiliated-in-videos-posted-by-children-on-tiktok-zfbjqnwrq.

15. Justin Cheng, Michael Bernstein, Cristian Danescu-Niculescu-Mizil, and Jure Leskovec, "Anyone Can Become a Troll: Causes of Trolling Behavior in Online Discussions," *CSCW '17: Proceedings of the 2017 ACM Conference on Computer Supported Cooperative Work and Social Computing*, February 2017, 1217–1230, https://doi.org/10.1145/2998181.2998213.

16. "World Telecommunication/ICT Indicators Database," International Telecommunication Union (ITU), accessed August 23, 2022, https://www.itu.int/en/ITU-D/Statistics/Pages/publications/wtid.aspx.

17. Esmé Berkhout, Nick Galasso, Max Lawson, Pablo Andrés Rivero Morales, Anjela Taneja, and Diego Alejo Vázquez Pimentel, *The Inequality Virus*, Oxfam International briefing paper, January 25, 2021.

Chapter 6

1. Moisés Naím, "Big Problems, Small Leaders," *El País* (English edition), April 21, 2020, https://english.elpais.com/opinion/2020-04-21/big-problems-small-leaders.html.

2. Sanyam Sethi, "Canada's Reputation Shines Internationally and at Home," Ipsos, December 3, 2021, https://www.ipsos.com/en-ca/news-polls/canada-reputation-shines -internationally-and-at-home.

3. "Confidence in Institutions," Gallup, accessed August 31, 2022, https://news .gallup.com/poll/1597/confidence-institutions.aspx.

4. Daniel Dennett, "Counterfeiting Humans," with Daniel Dennett and Susan Schneider, Web-Conference, FAU Center for the Future of the Mind, September 22, 2022, fau.edu/future-mind.

5. Francis R. Willett, Donald T. Avansino, Leigh R. Hochberg, Jaimie M. Henderson, and Krishna V. Shenoy, "High-Performance Brain-to-Text Communication via Handwriting," *Nature* 593 (May 12, 2021): 249–254, https://doi.org/10.1038 /s41586-021-03506-2.

6. Olaf Groth, Mark Esposito, and Terence Tse, "Swarm Economics: How 3D Manufacturing Will Change the Shape of the Global Economy," European Business Review, September 19, 2014, https://www.europeanbusinessreview.com/swarm-eco nomics-how-3d-manufacturing-will-change-the-shape-of-the-global-economy.

Chapter 7

1. "The Video-Game Industry Has Metaverse Ambitions, Too," *The Economist*, accessed August 31, 2022, https://www.economist.com/business/the-video-game -industry-has-metaverse-ambitions-too/21806341.

2. "Share of Respondents Who Indicated They Either Owned or Used Cryptocurrencies in 56 Countries and Territories Worldwide from 2019 to 2021," Statista, October 2021, https://www.statista.com/statistics/1202468/global-cryptocurrency -ownership.

3. Historical prices and other market data for Bitcoin is available at https://www .coinbase.com/price/bitcoin. The data given here were accessed January 30, 2023.

4. Sirin Kale, "'I Put My Life Savings in Crypto': How a Generation of Amateurs Got Hooked on High-Risk Trading," *Guardian*, June 19, 2021, https://www.the guardian.com/lifeandstyle/2021/jun/19/life-savings-in-crypto-generation-of-amateurs -hooked-on-high-risk-trading.

5. Vicky McKeever, "Gen Z Incomes Predicted to Beat Millennials' in 10 Years and Be 'Most Disruptive Generation Ever,'" CNBC, November 20, 2020, https://www .cnbc.com/2020/11/20/gen-z-incomes-predicted-to-beat-millennials-in-10-years .html.

6. "Fact Sheet: President Biden to Sign Executive Order on Ensuring Responsible Development of Digital Assets," The White House, The United States Government,

March 9, 2022, https://www.whitehouse.gov/briefing-room/statements-releases/2022
/03/09/fact-sheet-president-biden-to-sign-executive-order-on-ensuring-responsible
-innovation-in-digital-assets; Emily Nicolle and Tanzeel Akhtar, "Britain's Crypto
List: Here's Who to Watch," Bloomberg, May 22, 2022, https://www.bloomberg
.com/news/features/2022-05-23/uk-crypto-s-key-players-here-are-the-people-to
-watch.

7. "The Chainalysis 2021 Geography of Cryptocurrency Report," Chainalysis, accessed
August 31, 2022, https://go.chainalysis.com/2021-geography-of-crypto.html.

8. Steve Glaveski, "How Daos Could Change the Way We Work," *Harvard Business
Review*, April 7, 2022, https://hbr.org/2022/04/how-daos-could-change-the-way-we
-work.

9. "Fungible" means that an item can be easily replaced by another without losing
value. Cash notes are fungible: a ten-dollar note is the same as another ten-dollar
note. "Non-fungible" is therefore something that cannot be replaced or replicated
with something else.

10. Daniel Van Boom, "NFT Bubble: The Craziest Nonfungible Token Sales so Far,"
CNET, March 22, 2021, https://www.cnet.com/culture/nft-bubble-the-craziest-non
fungible-token-sales-so-far.

11. Misyrlena Egkolfopoulou and Akayla Gardner, "Even in the Metaverse, Not All
Identities Are Created Equal," Bloomberg, December 6, 2021, https://www.bloomberg
.com/news/features/2021-12-06/cryptopunk-nft-prices-suggest-a-diversity-problem
-in-the-metaverse.

Chapter 8

1. "The Five Forces," Harvard Business School Institute for Strategy & Competitiveness, https://www.isc.hbs.edu/strategy/business-strategy/Pages/the-five-forces.aspx.

2. Parag Khanna, *Move: The Forces Uprooting Us* (New York: Scribner, 2021).

3. Alec Ross, *The Raging 2020s: Companies, Countries, People—and the Fight for Our
Future* (New York: Henry Holt and Company, 2021).

4. With gratitude to Tobias Straube for his research leadership for elements and
examples, such as this one, for our forthcoming course "Strategies for Global 2.0."

Chapter 9

1. "Calculating the Losses This Fire Season," Bushfire & Natural Hazards CRC,
accessed August 31, 2022, https://www.bnhcrc.com.au/news/2020/calculating-losses
-fire-season.

2. Steve Lohr, "He Created the Web. Now He's Out to Remake the Digital World," *New York Times*, January 10, 2021, https://www.nytimes.com/2021/01/10/technology /tim-berners-lee-privacy-internet.html.

3. Vasudha Thirani and Arvind Gupta, "The Value of Data," World Economic Forum, September 22, 2017, https://www.weforum.org/agenda/2017/09/the-value-of-data.

4. "The Project," FutureWork, accessed August 31, 2022, https://arbeit2100.de/en /the-project.

5. For more on the OECD.AI Policy Observatory, see https://oecd.ai/en/.

6. First conceptualized by Olaf Groth and Cambrian, LLC, with inputs by Thomas Sanderson and Donn Treese.

7. "Unsafe Water Kills More People than War, Ban Says on World Day," United Nations | UN News, March 22, 2010, https://news.un.org/en/story/2010/03/333182 -unsafe-water-kills-more-people-war-ban-says-world-day.

8. Nicole Perlroth, *This Is How They Tell Me the World Ends: The Cyberweapons Arms Race* (New York: Bloomsbury Publishing, 2021).

9. Beth Wasko, "How Security and Risk Leaders Can Prepare for Reduced Budgets," Gartner, July 7, 2020, https://www.gartner.com/smarterwithgartner/how -security-and-risk-leaders-can-prepare-for-reduced-budgets.

10. Rachel Treisman, "Damage from Hurricane Ian Cuts Sanibel Island Off from Florida's Mainland," National Public Radio, September 30, 2022, https://www.npr .org/2022/09/30/1126204141/sanibel-causeway-hurricane-ian.

11. Judson Jones and Brandon Miller, "A Disastrous Megaflood Is Coming to California, Experts Say, and It Could Be the Most Expensive Natural Disaster in History," CNN, August 14, 2022, https://www.cnn.com/2022/08/12/weather/california-mega flood-study/index.html; Raymond Zhong, "The Coming California Megastorm," *New York Times*, August 12, 2022, https://www.nytimes.com/interactive/2022/08/12 /climate/california-rain-storm.html (interactive story: graphics by Mira Rojanasakul; photographs by Erin Schaff); Matthew Cappucci, "A 'Megaflood' in California Could Drop 100 Inches of Rain, Scientists Warn," *Washington Post*, August 12, 2022, https://www.washingtonpost.com/climate-environment/2022/08/12/megaflood -california-flood-rain-climate.

12. Lydia Depillis, "Pace of Climate Change Sends Economists Back to Drawing Board," *New York Times*, August 25, 2022, https://www.nytimes.com/2022/08/25 /business/economy/economy-climate-change.html.

13. Ian Bremmer, *The Power of Crisis: How Three Threats—and Our Response—Will Change the World* (New York: Simon & Schuster, 2022).

Index